BOUND FOR AMERICA

MUSIC IN AMERICAN LIFE

A list of books in the series appears at the end of this book.

BOUND FOR AMERICA

Three British Composers

Nicholas Temperley

UNIVERSITY OF ILLINOIS PRESS
URBANA AND CHICAGO

Library of Congress Cataloging-in-Publication Data

Temperley, Nicholas.
Bound for America : three British composers / Nicholas Temperley.
p.   cm. — (Music in American life)
Includes bibliographical references (p.   ) and index.
ISBN 0-252-02847-3 (cloth : alk. paper)
1. Selby, William, 1738–1798.
2. Taylor, R. (Raynor), 1747–1825.
3. Jackson, G. K. (George Knowil), 1757?–1822.
4. Composers—United States—Biography.
5. Composers—Great Britain—Biography.
I. Title.
II. Series.
ML390.T278   2003
780'.92'273—dc21   2002152314

Contents

Preface

In this book I tell the stories of three British-born composers who, although well established in their native country, decided in middle life to change their domicile and to begin a second composing career in the United States. They are William Selby (1738–98), who arrived in Newport, Rhode Island, in 1773 and made his career in Boston; Rayner Taylor (1747–1825), who settled in Philadelphia in 1793; and George Knowil Jackson (1757–1822), who emigrated in 1796, reached New York in 1801, and moved to Boston in 1812.

There were other British composers who played an equally important role in American music at this time. The ones I considered most seriously for inclusion, but finally rejected, are Alexander Reinagle (1756–1809) and Benjamin Carr (1768–1831), indisputably two of the best American composers of their age.

Reinagle was a highly gifted musician of Austrian descent, born in England, who passed his early years in Glasgow and Edinburgh, visited Lisbon and Hamburg (where he met with Carl Philipp Emanuel Bach), and settled in Philadelphia in 1786. There he established himself as director of the New Theater company and dominated the theater music scene for the rest of his life. He also wrote four outstanding piano sonatas that are credited with being the first sonatas composed in North America. However, his theater music is almost entirely lost, while the sonatas were never published and seem to have been unknown to contemporary Americans. The music by Reinagle that actually represents his interaction with the American public is so sparse, and on the whole so trivial, that it cannot fairly be said to represent him as an American composer.[1]

Carr's case is quite different. There is no disputing his importance and influence in America, as a leading publisher, performer, and impresario, as well as composer, which very possibly exceed that of any other musician of the time.[2] But in his case the problem is with the British portion of his career. Though he did compose one opera for the London stage, it is lost, and the only surviving compositions from his London period are two songs and possibly one hymn tune. The position is similar with James Hewitt (1770–

1827), by general agreement a lesser composer than Carr. Since my main object was to compare the British and American halves of a composer's career, I reluctantly decided to exclude all these from my principal study, though they play important secondary roles in this book.

The three men finally selected were already well established in Britain when they decided to emigrate, though none had reached the highest level of achievement and reputation there. They then completed their careers in America. They left behind, largely in published form, a sufficient volume of compositions to permit a reasonable comparison of the two sections of their composing careers. That was the essential condition that led me to choose them over Reinagle and Carr.

A certain parallel with my own career stimulated my interest in these men. Educated in Britain as a musician, and then as a musicologist, I moved permanently to the United States at the age of thirty-four, for a mixture of reasons, economic, professional, and personal. There I continued my career and found that I had to modify my ideas and practices in various ways to suit my new surroundings. It is this sort of adaptation that I wished to investigate in Selby, Taylor, and Jackson.

For all three of my chosen musicians, there has been a vast difference in their reputations in Britain and the United States. They barely exist in modern accounts of British musical history. American scholars have given them respectful or grudging attention, according to their own historiographical stance (this question will be tackled in the last section of the introduction), but have concentrated their interest on the American segment of their careers.

The main reason for the difference is obvious. In the context of British musical history they were relatively insignificant, dwarfed by their contemporaries; and they disappeared over the horizon. In American musical history they loomed large as early leaders and pioneers. A second reason is nationalism. I cannot fault American scholars for favoring, claiming as their own, and sometimes overrating music composed in the United States, for I have done exactly the same with music composed in Britain. But the circumstances of my career have aroused in me an equal interest in both parts of these musicians' lives, and induced me to consider and compare them at a level of detail that might not have attracted a scholar specializing in either British or American music alone.

Fortunately for me, however, at least one American scholar has already conducted a close study of the life of each composer, giving proper consideration to the British half of his life: Barbara Owen for Selby, John Cuthbert for Taylor, Charles Kaufman for Jackson. I feel bound to acknowledge my great debt to each of these writers, both generally here and specifically in the course of the book. Their work has been the foundation for mine.

~

Much of the music discussed in this book is difficult to find. I have therefore provided substantial excerpts as music examples in the text. In these examples, the notation has been modernized where there is no doubt of the composer's meaning; manifest errors have been silently corrected; spelling, capitalization, and punctuation have been modernized in the texts of vocal music. In a few cases, facsimiles are offered instead of edited examples. When a reliable modern edition is available, this has generally been cited, to release more space for less accessible compositions.

I am deeply indebted to Ruth Mack Wilson, who generously sent me her notes and research materials on indefinite loan. I also acknowledge gratefully the direct help I have received from many other scholars, especially Simon Bailey, of Oxford University Archives; J. Mark Baker; David Baldwin, Sergeant of the Vestry, Chapel Royal; Richard Boursy, of Yale University Music Library; Richard Chesser and James Clements, both of the British Library Music Collections; J. Bunker Clark, of the University of Kansas; Allison Derrett, of the Royal Archives, Windsor; Joseph Ditta, of the New-York Historical Society; Christopher Field; Stephen Freeth, Keeper of Manuscripts at the Guildhall Library, London; David Johnson; Charles Kaufman, of the Mannes School of Music; Anne McClenny Krauss; Donald W. Krummel; Catherine Massip, of the Bibliothèque nationale de France; Anne Dhu McLucas, dean of the School of Music, University of Oregon; Simon McVeigh, of Goldsmiths College, London; Barbara Owen; Wayne Shirley, formerly of the Library of Congress Music Division; Winton Solberg, of the Department of History, University of Illinois; E. A. Smith, archivist of Westminster School; and Susan Wollenberg, of the Faculty of Music, Oxford University.

I am also grateful to the staffs of the many libraries consulted, particularly those of the William L. Clements Library, University of Michigan; Harvard Musical Association, Boston; Rowe Music Library, King's College, Cambridge; University Library, Cambridge; Newberry Library, Chicago; British Library, London; Guildhall Library, London; Illinois State University Library, Normal, Illinois; Bibliothèque nationale de France, Paris; Annenberg Rare Book and Manuscript Library, University of Pennsylvania, Philadelphia;

University Library, St. Andrews, Scotland; Music Library, University of Illinois, Urbana; Library of Congress (Music Division), Washington; and American Antiquarian Society, Worcester, Massachusetts.

Special thanks are due to my research assistant, James Randall, for resourceful work, and to the University of Illinois Research Board for financial support. I am also indebted to Judith McCulloh and Carol Betts, of the University of Illinois Press, for their sympathetic assistance at each stage of the publishing process.

Abbreviations

LIBRARY SIGLA

Australia

AUS-CAnl   Canberra, National Library

Great Britain

GB-Cu	Cambridge, University Library
GB-Ge	Glasgow, University of Glasgow, Ewing Library
GB-Gu	Glasgow, University Library
GB-Lbl	London, British Library
GB-Lcm	London, Royal College of Music
GB-LVu	Liverpool, University Library
GB-Ob	Oxford, Bodleian Library
GB-P	Perth, Sandeman Public Library
GB-SA	St. Andrews, University Library

Italy

I-Rsc   Rome, Conservatorio di Santa Cecilia

United States

US-AA	Ann Arbor, University of Michigan
US-ATet	Atlanta, Emory University, Pitts Theology Library
US-Bh	Boston, Harvard Musical Association
US-Cn	Chicago, Newberry Library
US-NH	New Haven, Yale University
US-NL	Normal (Ill.), Illinois State University
US-NYp	New York, Public Library
US-PROu	Providence, Brown University
US-R	Rochester (N.Y.), Eastman School of Music, Sibley Library
US-Wc	Washington, Library of Congress

SOURCES

BUC	*British Union-Catalogue of Early Music*
C	Britton et al., *American Sacred Music Imprints*
CLC	*Calendar of London Concerts 1750–1800* (database)
CPM	*The Catalogue of Printed Music in the British Library to 1980*
Evans	Evans, *American Bibliography*
IGI	*International Genealogical Index* (database)
K	Kaufman, "Jackson"
RISM	*Répertoire international des sources musicales*
Shaw-Shoemaker	Shaw and Shoemaker, *American Bibliography*
Wolfe	Wolfe, *Secular Music in America*

(Full citations of these sources are in the bibliography)

MUSICAL FORCES

a	alto solo
A	chorus alto
b	bass solo
B	chorus bass
chor	chorus
fl	flute
hn	horn
kbd	keyboard
pf	piano
org	organ
s	soprano/treble solo
S	chorus soprano/treble
t	tenor solo
T	chorus tenor
v	voice
vn	violin

GENERAL

ed.	edited (by), edition
perf.	performed (by)
pub.	published (by)
repr.	reprinted (by)
rev.	revised (by)

PITCHES

The Helmholtz system is used to identify pitches: CC–BB, C–B, c–b, c'–b',
c''–b'', c'''–b''', with c' representing middle C.

OLD BRITISH MONETARY SYSTEM

One guinea = 21 shillings (21s.) = approximately $5.25 at the time
One pound (£1) = 20 shillings (20s.) = approximately $5
One shilling (1s.) = 12 pence (12d.) = approximately 25¢
One penny (1d.) = approximately 2¢

ONE   *Emigrants and Immigrants*

American musical life in the early federal period was active and varied, but it harbored few professional musicians. The term "professional" can be used either to indicate a certain level of training and proficiency or to denote a musician who expects payment and attempts to make a living by his art. In either sense, few were to be found. They could exist only in a situation where a sufficient segment of the population was able and willing to devote financial resources to music provided by others.

We are dealing, of course, with Americans of European extraction. Native Americans and African Americans at this stage were making music for themselves and were not in a position to pay for their musical entertainment. But even in the white colonial settlements, music making had depended to a great extent on whatever skill, knowledge, and instruments the colonists brought with them, and it was only occasionally brought into contact with the latest developments in Europe. In some venues, such as the Spanish missions in Florida or the churches and singing schools of New England, amateur musicians built on what they could recall of a European tradition to create a new and distinctive body of music that satisfied the needs of the time and place.

THE DEMAND

When the English colonies joined to form a nation, a new force came to maturity: nationalism. First in war, then in all fields of human endeavor, leading Americans were determined to assert the claims and standing of the United States in the world. The only available standard to measure their progress was that of the European countries, most obviously Great Britain. Paradoxically, therefore, Americans had to become more European in their music in order to assert their national prowess. The style of the New England psalmodists, led by William Billings, has seemed to modern scholars and musicians to be genuinely and characteristically American. But to American musical leaders of the early 1800s, that same style was increasingly unwel-

come, because it seemed to stigmatize American music as inferior, its composers as primitive and ignorant. They wanted to move in the direction of
European art music.

A similar phase can be found in other nationalistic movements. At the
court of Catherine the Great in St. Petersburg, Italian opera, composed and
sung by Italians, monopolized available resources and prestige. When a Russian composer, Dmitry Bortnyansky (1752–1825), wished to compete, it would
have been useless to write operas on Russian stories, in the Russian language,
using Russian folksong; they would have been quickly dismissed as primitive and unacceptable. To prove his standing as a Russian-born composer,
Bortnyansky had to write Italian operas in the closest possible imitation of
Italian style; the next stage was to write Italianate operas with Russian texts.
Another two generations passed before composers could successfully explore
a distinctively Russian style for opera.[1]

Similarly, after France was defeated by Prussia in the war of 1870–71, the
Société nationale de musique arose to assert and promote the value of French
music. But it has been observed that the model that came to prevail among
the avant-garde composers who were members of the society was that of
Richard Wagner. Michael Strasser writes, "Like [Ernest] Renan, who insist-
ed that the road to national recovery lay in emulating the most admirable
characteristics of France's conqueror, the founders of the Société Nationale
looked to German masters from Beethoven to Wagner to light their way,
convinced that the 'pure' music emanating from across the Rhine was that
of a strong and vital society."[2]

In each case, the chief concern of this early phase of nationalism was not
to establish an independent national idiom, but to confer prestige on the
music of indigenous musicians; and that prestige was measured by the dominant foreign idiom of the time. The musical language that Billings worked
out was itself founded on a kind of English psalmody chiefly practiced by
rural enthusiasts.[3] But in England it was scorned or ignored both by the rul-
ing classes and by professional musicians.[4] Their contempt had not concerned
New Englanders, so long as they were unaware of it. But as they came to experience something of the grandeur of Handel's music, under a director such
as William Selby who was personally familiar with the proper style, they also
learned the standards of taste that prevailed in Great Britain and wished to
adopt those standards for themselves.

The reaction against indigenous American music began to predominate
after 1800. In that year the musical entrepreneur Andrew Law (1748–1821),
addressing "the Ministers of the Gospel, and the Singing-Masters, Clerks and

Choristers throughout the United States," deplored the frivolity of American psalmodists: "the dignity and the ever-varying vigor of Handel, of [Martin] Madan, and of others, alike meritorious, are, in a great measure, supplanted by the pitiful productions of numerous composuists, whom it would be doing too much honor to name."[5] Many compilers of church collections began to reduce, rewrite, or even exclude American compositions, as well as British pieces in the country style.

The most detailed exposition of the new philosophy was delivered by John Hubbard (1759–1810), a professor of mathematics and natural philosophy at Dartmouth College, in a lecture to the Middlesex Musical Society in 1807, and published as a pamphlet the following year. Hubbard suggested that "genius is needed to make harmony acceptable," and that those who did not know how to write it would do better to leave melodies unharmonized. "While the noble expressions of those great masters [such as Handel] excite our admiration, the counterfeit efforts of the unskilful excite our disgust."[6] He praised not only Handel, Felice Giardini, Giovanni Battista Pergolesi, Henry Purcell, and Samuel Arnold, but even the English country psalmodist Aaron Williams, for "instances of the *sublime*."[7] The style he called, in contrast, "the *bombastic*" was one in which "our unfortunate country has been particularly fruitful. Almost every pedant, after learning his eight notes, has commenced author. On the leaden wings of dullness, he has attempted to soar into those regions of science, never penetrated but by real genius. . . . Among the most common faults of this style, we may reckon the common fuge." For "correct" fugues he pointed to the work of Purcell, William Croft, Arnold, Jeremiah Clarke, and Maurice Greene, leading composers of Anglican church and theater music.[8]

These caustic views did not go unchallenged, but they were echoed in many other prefaces and writings. Especially the word "science" (or "scientific") became a catchword suggesting the technical competence displayed by "European" composers, and the ones held up as models are nearly always English by birth, or, like Handel and Giardini, had made their home in England. One writer, taking a more positive approach, saw an opportunity for Americans to inherit the greatest European traditions:

> The mighty oak is truly a grander object than the tiny acorn; but unless this had been planted, that had never adorned the mountain's side. The celebrated Handel is said to be indebted to Corelli for the elements, by which he breathes such energy and sensibility, and which give to his performances [i.e., compositions] such inimitable expression. If then there had been no Corelli, there possibly had been no Handel; and if no Handel, the melodies of Haydn,

Madan, and Arnold, never probably would have charmed the lovers of holy song. Instead therefore of ridiculing the productions of our age and country, and indiscriminately condemning to oblivion the incipient efforts of the American composer, let us, while we reject his worst, commend his best; and, by using them alternately with the labours of able masters, form him to a riper and a purer taste.[9]

Even Daniel Read, one of the leading exponents of country psalmody, toward the end of his life admitted that in his early publications he had not been a "scientific musician." He claimed, however, that through a study of learned writings and of such scores as Handel's *Messiah* and Haydn's *Creation*, "my ideas on the subject of music have been considerably altered; I will not say improved."[10]

The views quoted above are concerned largely with the idioms and standards of sacred music in New England. It was in that medium alone that anything identifiable as an indigenous American style had developed before 1800. Consequently, it was there alone that conflict between "provincial" and "cosmopolitan" schools of thought had arisen.[11] In music making, the British heritage had never yet been seriously challenged.

The inevitable result was that properly trained musicians from Britain were sought out and looked up to in America, not only to direct performances and offer their own compositions, but to teach, train, and guide American musicians and music lovers so that they in turn could become truly scientific. Any professionally trained musician from Britain was likely to be treated with respect as an "able master," and his services would be in some demand, particularly as a teacher. Indeed one British composer, George Jackson, made his status official by arranging to receive a musical doctorate before he set out for American shores.

In retrospect, the eventual triumph in America of the art-music idiom and its canons of taste seems inevitable, given the desire to compete in all fields with European nations, the steady growth of an affluent middle class, and the continuous influx of new immigrants from Europe. The process was slowed for a time by the movement for independence, which invested the native style with a certain patriotism, reduced direct communication with British leaders of opinion, and at the same time tainted anything British with suspicion; and indeed, for a time Paris rather than London was looked to as a source of musical sophistication.

Once political independence was assured, Americans began to assess their position in the family of Western nations and to strive to equal or surpass them. In music, this could only be done in a musical language that enjoyed high standing in Europe. For, after all, white Americans were nothing but transplanted Europeans; if they sought a higher level of their own culture, the only place to look for it was Europe. Among the European capitals, London enjoyed many advantages as a source of musical expertise: the huge network of familial and social ties, the quantitative level of emigration, the dominance of trading and shipping links. Above all, the common language made English songs, theater pieces, and church music instantly usable in America, and facilitated the passing on of musical knowledge and experience from teacher to pupil, and from author to reader.

Concert and theater music required trained professionals if it was to reach a standard that was remotely comparable to that of London. The theater was perhaps the arena where there was the least distinction between British and American aesthetic standards, because it was a place where the audience could directly impose its will. Composers writing for the English-language theater at this time, whether in London, Dublin, New York, or Philadelphia, were forced to bring their style down to the lowest common denominator. Broad humor, easy tunes, obvious harmonies, predictable dance and march rhythms, and a little flashy virtuosity were the qualities expected of theater music. Amateurism would not be tolerated for long.

Domestic music, on the other hand, was a field where the latest publications from London—or from Paris, Leipzig, or Vienna—could easily make their way to American parlors. But the young people, especially young women, who wished to master this music needed knowledgeable teachers, and there was little doubt that these were likely to come from Europe, where long-established institutions and richly varied practical opportunities existed for training professional musicians. In the colonial and early federal periods, Britain was still the main supplier, though not the only one.

In religious music, the European style was particularly associated with Anglicans (the Moravians of Pennsylvania being a remarkable but isolated exception). They, unlike the Congregationalists who were in the majority in New England, had encouraged the use of organs and the musical practices that came with them. Anglicanism in New England was in crisis during the revolutionary period, and its music temporarily lost its appeal. But in the decades that followed, leaders of the daughter Protestant Episcopal Church showed a strong desire to introduce chanting and other types of choir music; and to do so, they needed musicians trained in the mother Church of England.

British music at this period was dominated, in its turn, by foreign imports, above all from Italy. Colonies of musicians from Italy, Germany, Bohemia, and other parts of Europe were well established in London, Edinburgh, and some provincial cities, generally enjoying a status superior to that of native British musicians. As the Italian predominance gradually gave way to the German in every field except opera, British composers moved from an Italianate to a Teutonic style, with occasional glimmers of an indigenous idiom. Thus in imitating British models Americans were, almost unconsciously, adopting Continental influences. But the essential point was that the standards of taste that prevailed in London were sought and accepted in Boston, New York, and Philadelphia. No doubt this was chiefly due to the fact that most Americans, especially the leaders of opinion, were British by ethnic background. It was only after the huge migration of Germans and Italians to America later in the nineteenth century that the direct influence of these countries, bypassing London, began to prevail. For the time being, middle- and upper-class Americans on the East Coast looked to Britain for their cultural leadership.

THE SUPPLY

The situation I have just outlined was in many ways a favorable one for British musicians; and, as we might expect, a growing number of them traveled to America in order to take advantage of it. Before making such a life-changing decision, they must have weighed the pros and cons very carefully. At best, it was a big gamble. What sort of future could they look forward to if they stayed in their native country? What would they lose by leaving for an unknown land? Would they gain enhanced prestige in the United States, leading to economic security? Or could they expect to meet with antagonism, at a time of uncertain political relations between the two countries?

Such questions, of course, were also weighed by performing musicians who considered crossing the ocean. But the music of these singers and players has gone forever, while that of composers is still available, if only in the half-dead form of music notation. One can therefore form a judgment, not only of the change in their careers resulting from their transatlantic migration, but also of changes in the practices and styles of their compositions and in their reception by the public.

The three composers treated in this book had similar careers in many ways. All began their work in London, one of the greatest musical centers in Europe and probably the most lucrative of all at this time. They gained varying amounts of performing experience, but all had published a substantial body of their own music in Britain, and all in differing degrees had shown some interest in developing their art as serious composers.

But only one of the three (Taylor) rates so much as a mention in the standard modern text on British music in the eighteenth century.[12] Their stature as composers cannot compare with that of their best English contemporaries. Even in a period of modest accomplishment in English music, the theater music of Arnold, William Shield, Stephen Storace, and Henry Bishop; the oratorios of William Crotch; the symphonies of the Earl of Kelly and Samuel Wesley; the piano concertos of John Field; the songs of William Jackson, Charles Dibdin, and John Clarke-Whitfeld; the anthems of Jonathan Battishill and Thomas Attwood; the voluntaries of John Stanley and Samuel Wesley; the sonatas of John Burton and George Frederick Pinto—these works show a mastery and a sense of purpose that throw the efforts of Selby, Taylor, and Jackson into deep shade. And even this list excludes such foreign-born composers resident in Britain as Johann Christian Bach, Giardini, Muzio Clementi, Jan Ladislav Dussek, and John Baptist Cramer.

Our three composers, in middle age, fled from this competition, to start again under what must surely have been less favorable conditions, where they had to build their reputations anew, where there was less patronage, fewer salaried posts, and a much smaller though rapidly growing economy. They had mixed success in America, but all left enough of their music behind to justify a fair assessment and comparison. In retrospect, writers on American musical history have seen them as leaders, giving them full treatment and acknowledging their importance in American musical life.[13]

The first, most obvious question is why they moved. In none of the three cases can it be answered definitively, but one can profitably speculate, on the basis of circumstantial evidence. Was the decision a purely economic one? Did they embrace American nationalism and other attitudes in order to ingratiate themselves with the leaders of American opinion? Or, on the contrary, did a genuine sympathy with American ideals play a part in the decision to change their abode? Did family or personal considerations come into play?

A further question is how their lives and careers changed in the new environment. For most musicians everywhere, teaching was the bread-and-butter of livelihood; but a teaching practice had to be built, and probably depended as much on influential connections as on the teacher's reputation as a performer or composer. The three had to give up their carefully nurtured British connections. They had to construct a new, American network almost from scratch. How did they do it? Were they forced to adapt their compositional styles to already-formed American tastes? Or did their prestige as European professionals allow them to lead and form American musical opinion? Did they continue or give up their efforts to compose music of intrinsic worth?

Before considering the stories of these three men, it is worthwhile to look at the more general question of British immigration to the United States. Rowland T. Berthoff pointed out that "of course there have been nearly as many personal motives for emigration as there have been emigrants. Throughout three centuries, however, humdrum economic forces have probably moved most of the venturers."[14]

While this applies most obviously to those who came in the hope of acquiring cheap land to farm, or better wages for manual or skilled labor in industry, there is no reason to think that musicians were an exception to the general rule. Indeed, all three of our subjects migrated during periods when favorable conditions produced a wave of British immigrants. One such period was 1770–73, when lands were being opened up in the west and when "the political difficulties with the mother country slumbered."[15] Selby migrated in 1773, just before these difficulties flared up again.

Political troubles and the War of Independence dried up the flow, but once peace was formally declared, "a wave of enthusiasm for the new republic spread throughout England, causing many a yeoman family to migrate to Kentucky, Vermont, New York or Pennsylvania, and in 1784–86 a movement, comparable in size to that of 1770–73, was under way."[16] At this time several American theater managers were actively recruiting personnel from the London theater, including musicians, and it was then that Alexander Reinagle among others made the move across the Atlantic.

The next general wave occurred between 1790 and 1796. A clear case of "economic" migration in the musical field was that of Benjamin Carr, who belonged to a prominent family of music publishers.[17] He came to Philadelphia in 1793 and promptly founded a publishing business; within a few months his father and brother had followed him and set up a firm in Baltimore, evidently convinced that at this time they would do better in the burgeoning New World economy than in the affluent but overcrowded music publishing world of London. At this time, also, there was another large recruitment of actors and musicians, which brought to Philadelphia, among others, the soprano singer Georgina Oldmixon in 1792.[18] Taylor came in that same year, Jackson in 1796.

However, neither Taylor nor Jackson was recruited in this way, nor did they have any reason to expect to make easy money in America. We must look for other motives in their cases. This "wave" in the 1790s included many well-educated persons, notably liberals, who left England because they were stigmatized as Jacobins (that is, promoters of French-style revolution on English soil).[19] This serves as a reminder that the wish to leave Britain may have been quite as powerful a motivating factor as the desire to come to America. It will be worthwhile to consider possible political, as well as personal, motives underlying our subjects' decisions to migrate.

It is no coincidence that all three of our subjects were trained in the Church of England—by early experience as parish organists, and in two cases (Taylor and Jackson) as choristers of the Chapel Royal. In the English-speaking world at that time, the Anglican Church was the only institution that offered children and young people an intense and regular exposure to the disciplines of art music. It was also the only denomination that devoted financial resources, however meager, to the performance of rehearsed music in its services. In the mid-eighteenth century, when our subjects were growing up, most other Protestant denominations in Britain and its colonies banned organs and rehearsed choirs from worship (the Moravians were again an exception), while the Roman Catholic Church was legally restricted in its activities and lacked endowments to finance professional music. Though all three composers branched out into other areas, their training as Anglican church musicians was the solid core of their professional standing, giving them an incontestable technical advantage over most American musicians. Even Carr, who lacked this training himself, acknowledged the superiority of both Taylor and Jackson in certain branches of musical knowledge.

Of the three, only Taylor had built a reputation in the world of British theater. This did not give him as great an advantage in America as might have been expected, because other British and European musicians already occupied the key positions in the American theater world. All three were accomplished in the area of domestic music, especially songs, both before and after their move, but Taylor had a distinct edge over the others here, probably because of his mastery of theater music. All were persistent and successful teachers of music.

Before reaching more detailed conclusions, I will examine the background, life story, and music of each of the three musicians. In doing so I will attempt to give equal attention to the British and American halves of their careers.

HISTORICAL PERSPECTIVES

Richard Crawford, in a masterly survey of American musical historiography, has shown that the assumption that American music should be guided by European models continued to underlie most histories until the mid-twentieth century.[20] John Tasker Howard, in 1931, did question the assumption in a tentative way: "Would our Billingses, our Hopkinsons, and Lyons have sowed the seeds of a truly national school of music, which would have gained in background and in craftsmanship, if its growth had been uninterrupted by the coming of skilled, thoroughly trained musicians whose knowledge and talents paled the glories of our native composers? Or would the crude yet native spark of creative genius have become sterile on virgin soil, where there was not the opportunity for exchange of ideas in a cultured environment?"[21] Such hypothetical questions are not susceptible to definitive answers, but Howard did point the way to reevaluation.

The next generation of historians accepted the challenge. They tended to deplore the historical demotion of what Allen Britton called "our first original art music."[22] Irving Lowens reported that "the crude but eloquent American product had been supplanted by second-rate English importations and insipid 'arrangements' from the classic masters. It was fashionable to sneer at American music, and Read succumbed to the overwhelming social pressures inherent in the situation. In today's historical perspective, the newer music appears to have marked a deterioration rather than an advance in popular taste."[23] A wholesale reevaluation of what H. Wiley Hitchcock called the "vernacular" forms of American music has followed, spawning several monumental collected editions. Crawford himself has played a leading role in the rehabilitation process by his extensive writings, by the work of his numerous doctoral students, and by his direction of the American Musicological Society's series Music of the United States of America. He has also completed Britton and Lowens's bibliographical work on early American psalmody,[24] thus providing the first comprehensive foundation for serious musicological study of this particular area of American "vernacular" music.

The writer who most thoroughly turned the tables on earlier values was Gilbert Chase. In the introduction to his epoch-making study America's Music, Chase claimed that "the most important phase" of American music was that which was "most different from European music."[25] He declared war on the "genteel tradition" and accused Law of "snobbism" for his praise of European sacred music.[26] These attitudes remain very much alive in much scholarly work of recent times, though they are rarely expressed in such uncompromising terms. They may well have been a necessary precondition for the notable resurgence of confidence in the value of American music, but they have incidentally caused some damage to those who had earned their bread and butter as purveyors of the "genteel tradition." Many leading American composers of the nineteenth century, of course, from Lowell Mason and William Henry Fry to Horatio Parker and Edward Alexander MacDowell, built on the

European art-music tradition. Their reputations have benefited from the general upward reevaluation of American music. But the British immigrants who led the way in that direction, though recognized as leaders in musical life, have not enjoyed the same rebound as their American-born colleagues in the appraisal of their music. As composers they are in danger of being left behind.

This book seeks to rescue them from such a fate. I take no direct position on the nationalistic question, or on the "what-if" issue raised by Howard, for like Hitchcock I consider the "vernacular" and "cultivated" styles equally worthy of attention. Instead, I concentrate on the composers themselves. I ask how they reacted to their situation in a country where the leaders of opinion sought musical equality with Europe, while the majority of the public wanted only to be entertained in a familiar style.

TWO

William Selby

William Selby (1738–1798) gave up a moderately successful career as a London organist and composer, and emigrated to New England in 1773, where, after Independence, he achieved a position of musical leadership. He represented the styles and aesthetics of British, and hence European, art music, as opposed to the country or "native" school, founded on country psalmody, that was led by his American contemporary William Billings (1746–1800). His time in Boston was the very period in which the two styles were beginning to compete, and controversy between their respective supporters was warming up. Selby, to a great extent, embodied the newer ideal. But, as we shall see, he could not afford to antagonize those who cherished the country style.

It was Oscar Sonneck who first elevated Selby's importance in American musical history, conferring on him "the glory . . . of having indirectly laid the foundations for the Handel and Haydn Society."[1] This view was seconded and amplified by David McKay, who published an important article on Selby in 1971,[2] and it has been accepted in general histories and reference works.[3] It is based on a Boston career of twenty-seven years (1771–98), and to that extent it is misinformed. Sonneck's view that Selby arrived in Boston in 1771 was first questioned by Donovan Dawe, who found that he did not leave London until October 1773.[4] Barbara Owen was able to show that the earlier accounts conflated the careers of John Selby and William Selby.[5] But the fact remains that in the later 1780s William Selby attained leadership in Boston musical life as a recognized master of British, and hence European, music.

THE SELBY FAMILY

Four children of Joseph and Mary Selby were baptized at assorted London churches:

John	1735, January 12, at St. Luke, Old Street, Finsbury
Joseph	1738, October 15, at St. Giles, Cripplegate
William	1739, January 1, at St. Giles, Cripplegate
Philip	1745, December 31, at St. Sepulchre, Holborn

This William Selby, then, was probably born in late December 1738. William Selby, musician of Boston, died in early December 1798 at age fifty-nine, as announced in the *Columbian Centinel* on December 12. That concordance seems sufficient to identify William Selby, musician of Boston, with the one listed above and to establish that he was born between December 12 and 31, 1738.

His father, Joseph Selby, was a freeman of the Company of Fishmongers and may have been (though was not necessarily) an actual fishmonger. Joseph's marriage has not been traced, and the maiden surname of his wife Mary is unknown.

Owen has established that the Selby who arrived at Boston in 1771 was named John, not William, and that William traveled from London directly to Newport, Rhode Island, arriving in 1773. Was this John Selby William's elder brother, baptized at Finsbury in 1735?

An advertisement in the *Boston Evening Post* establishes that William and John were closely connected: "*Newport, October* 31, 1774. Ran away from the Subscriber [i.e., the undersigned] on the 16th Inst. an Apprentice Girl, named *Jane Fontena*, about 19 Years of Age: . . . Whoever shall take up said *Jane Fontena* and convey her to the Subscriber at Newport, shall have One Dollar Reward, and all necessary Charges paid by WILLIAM SELBY. N.B. Any Person securing said Runaway, and will give Information thereof to JOHN SELBY, in Sudbury Street, Boston, shall receive the forementioned Reward."[6] The musician John Selby's address was indeed Sudbury Street, as seen in a concert advertisement.[7]

John's only known composition dates from May 1762, when William Riley, a London singing teacher, published a book of psalm tunes entitled *Parochial Harmony*. Both John and William Selby are in the list of subscribers to this collection. William's name is followed by the churches where he served as organist, but there is nothing after John's name, which suggests that he had no such position as yet. In 1764 he was elected to succeed John Reading (1677–1764) as organist of St. Mary Woolnoth. He tried also to "inherit" Reading's second position at St. Dunstan in the West, but he was defeated there by 133 votes to 108 on January 2, 1765, after demanding a poll.[8] All this hints that he had been Reading's deputy and perhaps apprentice.

In September 1771 John Selby arrived in Boston to take up a position as organist of King's Chapel. A concert, to be given at Concert Hall for the benefit of Josiah Flagg on October 4, was announced in the *Boston Evening Post* on September 30 and was to include "an Organ Concerto by a Gentleman lately arrived from London, Organist of the Chapel." The *Massachu-*

setts Spy (October 3) called it an "Organ Concerto by Mr. Selby."[9] The chapel records show a payment for three months' service ending December 22, 1771.[10] He kept his options open by retaining his position at St. Mary Woolnoth, which was presumably discharged by a deputy until he resigned it on January 3, 1772.

In Boston, concerts for John Selby's benefit, and presumably under his direction, were given at Concert Hall on October 26, 1772, and September 22, 1773. The first was for the anniversary of the king's accession, the second for the anniversary of his coronation, and in both cases the Band of the 64th Regiment took part, all suggesting that Selby was more loyal to George III than were many leading Bostonians at this time. Both programs included "Handel's Coronation Anthem," probably (as Owen suggests) "Zadok the Priest." These were unusual events, perhaps the last great Loyalist spectaculars in Boston. John played harpsichord at concerts in 1774 and 1775, on three occasions contributing a concerto. Lambert and Owen do not mention a concert for the benefit of Morgan and Stieglitz on May 18, 1775, which included "Harpsichord Concerto, Mr. Selby."[11]

All these events were attributed by earlier writers to William Selby. In fact, it is John Selby who shares with Josiah Flagg, William S. Morgan, and David Propert the credit for developing Boston's concert life at this period.

John's last payment as King's Chapel organist was made on January 30, 1776, for one quarter's salary. Owen has discovered that he left with the retreating British army in the summer of 1776 and migrated to Halifax, Nova Scotia, "where he began a new life as a customs official and organist of St. Paul's Anglican church." He died there in 1804 or early 1805, at age sixty-nine, which confirms his probable identity as William's elder brother, born in 1734 or very early 1735.[12]

William Selby, as we have seen, was probably born in December 1738. He married Mary Dixon at St. Luke, Old Street, Finsbury, London, on November 19, 1757. Less than four months later, on March 8, 1758, their son William was baptized at the same church.

On April 18, 1765, also at St. Luke's, Selby took a second wife, Sarah Owen. They had three children while he was living in London (see table 1). Again, there is some slight evidence that the first child, John, was conceived before marriage. The record of his burial at Trinity Church, Boston, on July 31, 1779, gives his age as fourteen; if correct, this means that he was born on or before July 31, 1765, that is, within four months of his parents' marriage. It was not unusual to wait for up to a year before having a child baptized.

Sonneck found that a Sarah Selby was listed in a Boston directory for 1800

Table 1. William Selby's Children

Name	Baptized	Later History
By Mary Dixon		
William	1758, Mar. 8, at St. Luke, Finsbury	?Died before 1768
By Sarah Owen		
John	1766, Feb. 8, at St. Mary, Staining	Buried Trinity, Boston, July 31, 1779
William Thomas	1768, May 16, at St. Ethelburga, Bishopsgate	?Died before 1774
Ann	1770, Apr. 4, at St. Botolph without Aldersgate	?
?William	1774, Mar. 5, at Trinity, Newport	?Died before 1777
Mary Frances	?	Married Benjamin Brown, Mar. 28, 1796
William Howell	1777, July 25, at Trinity, Boston	Buried Trinity, Boston, Sept. 30, 1777
Elizabeth Wakeman	1778, Nov. 8, at Trinity, Boston	Death announced, July 22, 1795
William Joseph Price	1780, Nov. 12, at Trinity, Boston	Died Boston, July 27, 1798

Sources: IGI database; Mason, *Annals of Trinity Church, Newport;* Oliver and Peabody, *Records of Trinity Church, Boston; A Volume of Records relating to the Early History of Boston; Columbian Centinel,* July 22, 1795, April 1, 1797, and July 28, 1798; Worcester, Mass., Massachusetts Historical Society, MS. Records of King's Chapel, Boston; private correspondence with Barbara Owen.

at the same address (Tremont Street) at which William Selby himself had resided in 1796 and 1798.[13] It seems probable, then, that William brought his pregnant second wife, Sarah, and young children with him to America in 1773, that this Sarah was the mother of all his (legitimate) children except the eldest, and that she outlived him.

Selby was evidently determined to have a son who bore his name. The repeated use of the name William indicates that any child previously given that name had died. This is the basis for assuming the deaths of the first three Williams, in table 1. The William Selby baptized at Newport on March 5, 1774, while Selby was organist there, seems likely to have been another son, though there is no proof of this since the parents' names are not given in the baptism register. This William cannot have been a child of Selby (legitimate or otherwise) by a local woman, since Selby was still in London five months before the child's baptism. Records show the marriage of a William Selby to Susannah Parker at Boston in 1792. The only one of the five sons named William who could have been living and of marriageable age then (though only about eighteen) is this one. However, if this William survived infancy, we have to assume that his parents were prepared to name another son William while he was still living. It seems more likely that the William Selby who married Susannah Parker was unrelated to, or anyway was not a son of, William the musician.

The three baptisms at Trinity, Boston, are all recorded as "son/daughter of William Selby by [blank] his wife," as if the clerk could not remember the wife's name and planned to fill it in later but never did so. The newspaper announcement of Mary Frances's wedding in 1796 calls her "2d. daughter of Mr. Wm. Selby of this town," which suggests that she was born between Ann (1770) and Elizabeth (1778); but Elizabeth had died in July 1795.

On June 21, 1798, Mary Deering, daughter of Benjamin Brown and his wife Mary Frances, was baptized at Trinity Church, Boston; this was William's only known grandchild. His sole surviving son died a few weeks later.

On December 12, 1798, the *Columbia Centinel* carried the following notice: "DIED]. . . . In this town, Mr. WILLIAM SELBY, Æt. 59." This was certainly William Selby senior. At least five sons and a daughter had predeceased him; he left a widow, probably two daughters, and a granddaughter. The wardens of the Stone Chapel voted fifty dollars toward his funeral expenses.[14] (King's Chapel was renamed Stone Chapel during the War of Independence.)

SELBY'S LONDON CAREER

In November 1753, when still only fourteen years old, Selby was a candidate for organist of St. Edmund, King and Martyr, London, though he received no votes.[15] The successful candidate, Edmund Gilding, received 58 votes out of 107 cast by members of the vestry. These contests were generally decided by influence (corrupt or otherwise) rather than merit.

In May 1756, at age seventeen, Selby was elected organist of All Hallows, Bread Street.[16] (Table 2 gives all available information about his posts as organist.) In the first poll he received 23 votes to Jonathan Battishill's 26; as neither had received an absolute majority, a runoff was held in which Selby

Table 2. Organist Posts Held by William Selby

Church	Annual Pay	Commencement	Termination
All Hallows, Bread Street, London	?	Elected, May 1756	Resigned, Oct. 14, 1773
St. Sepulchre, Holborn, London	£20	Appointed jointly with Samuel Jarvis, Mar. 20, 1760	Resigned, early Oct. 177?
Magdalen Hospital Chapel, London	?	Appointed, 1766	Dismissed?, 1769
Trinity Church, Newport, R.I.	£30	Elected, Dec. 20, 1773; pay backdated to Oct. 1	Resigned?, 1776?
Trinity Church, Boston	£26 13s. 4d.[a]	Appointed, 1776	Resigned?, March 1780
Stone Chapel, Boston	£66 13s. 4d.	Appointed, 1782	Died, early Dec. 1798

a. Augmented by an annual collection.

won by 40 votes to 30. This was a considerable victory, though not necessarily on merit. Battishill (1738–1801), an exact contemporary, was to become one of the most prominent of London's organist-composers. In 1760 Selby was appointed to another London church, St. Sepulchre, Holborn, jointly with the blind organist Samuel Jarvis (c. 1742–84), "during their good behaviour."[17]

A third position came his way in 1766, that of organist to the Magdalen Hospital, which was then in Whitechapel, adjoining the City. All three buildings in which Selby had to officiate were within a mile of his probable residence in Wood Street. Plural appointments were common enough among organists at that time (as they were for more exalted officials in the Church of England). Nevertheless, it would have been difficult for him to play services at all three places twice every Sunday, and it may be that he employed a deputy for at least one of them or had an arrangement whereby Jarvis always played at St. Sepulchre.

An organist's stipend was barely a living wage. Selby received £20 per year for the post at St. Sepulchre. The average wage for a building craftsman at that date was about £36 per year, for a laborer £24.[18] As organists' duties were generally confined to Sundays and Christmas Day, it was assumed that they would seek other employment on weekdays.

Selby was now one of a group of London organists that included a number of well-known men, Battishill among them. He may have played a harpsichord concerto (presumably of his own composition) at a benefit concert for a Mr. Roberts at Hickford Rooms, Brewer Street, the main concert hall in the West End, on February 21, 1760.[19] He had been admitted a member of the Royal Society of Musicians in 1762, but this cannot truly be regarded as evidence of either his musical ability or his reputation.[20]

In February 1766 he was made a freeman of the Company of Musicians "by patrimony," that is, on the grounds that his father, Joseph Selby, was a freeman of another company, the Fishmongers'.[21] One had to be a freeman (i.e., citizen) in order to carry on any art, trade, or occupation in the City, but Dawe points out that church appointments did not qualify. (The "City of London," of course, refers not to London as a whole, but to the ancient walled city, which in the period under discussion contained seventy-six parish churches in addition to St. Paul's Cathedral.) Therefore very few organists joined the Company of Musicians unless there was a specific reason to do so: it had little prestige, being made up largely of City waits and fiddlers.[22] Why did Selby bother? The position at the Magdalen Hospital does not explain it, for Whitechapel was a suburb, outside the ancient jurisdiction of the City proper.

A possible reason is to be found in a report that he was appointed to play the organ at Christ Church, Newgate Street, for the annual meeting of the Charity Children of London. The information comes from an unlikely source. Carl Ferdinand Pohl, in *Mozart und Haydn in London*, says that Selby, organist of St. Sepulchre, accompanied an anthem by "Kiley" (William Riley?), sung by the children, with the whole congregation joining in three times (this sounds like a psalm tune rather than an "anthem").[23] Pohl cites no source for the story, and I have been unable to confirm it. The annual meeting of the Charity Children of London was sponsored by the Society for Promoting Christian Knowledge, but the archives of the society, now at Cambridge University Library, do not include minutes of the committee for the annual meeting, and its printed annual reports do not name the organists.

If Selby indeed received this appointment, it may have required full citizenship. In a parallel case of 1724, the Musicians' Company had brought an action against an organist named Henry Green "for his exercising the Science of Musick in the City without being free thereof" because he had played the organ at the annual Festival of the Sons of the Clergy.[24] Green acquiesced by becoming a freeman of the Leathersellers' Company. Selby may have decided to forestall a similar action by claiming his patrimonial right to become a freeman.

A more cogent reason, however, would have been the opportunity to earn money by playing harpsichord at some of the more than one hundred concert venues that existed within the bounds of the City.[25] If so, this is an indication that Selby's income prospects were on the rise in the mid-sixties, though the western suburbs of London housed more fashionable concerts. Another likely way of augmenting his income was by teaching instruments, singing, and dancing; he would claim such experience in an advertisement soon after he arrived in America.

London organists were generally appointed for life, assuming good behavior, and most held on to their salaries if they possibly could, appointing deputies (at a much lower rate) if they were unable to carry out their duties. Therefore the fact that Selby gave up his position as organist of the Magdalen Chapel in 1769 suggests that there was a good reason. Unfortunately the records are missing.[26]

However, it is possible to make a plausible conjecture. The Magdalen was a charity for penitent prostitutes, most of whom were very young girls. The choir was drawn from these inmates, who sang from behind specially constructed screens to shield them from the gaze of the congregation (fig. 1). They were trained and rehearsed by the organist. Selby was the last male organist

Figure 1. The Magdalen Chapel, London, 1808 (From Ackermann's *The Microcosm of London*, courtesy Guildhall Library, London)

appointed to the hospital, being replaced in 1769 by a Mrs. Smithey. A later bylaw laid down that the organist must always be a woman.[27] The clear implication is that Selby had made sexual advances to one or more of the girls in his charge.

We have already seen that Selby had no strong scruples about extramarital sexual relations. Of course, getting a girl pregnant and then marrying her was hardly unusual in eighteenth-century London, or anywhere else, and would not have been particularly scandalous. London was tolerant of sexual peccadillos at this period. But taking advantage of the Magdalen girls was another matter; they were little more than children, and he had been placed in a position of trust by an institution whose very purpose was to lead its charges back to a respectable life. The scandal would have been a considerable blot on his record and could have led wealthy parents to dismiss Selby as a teacher of their daughters. This in turn may have prompted him to consider the possibility of emigrating, though it took him four years to make up his mind to do so.

Meanwhile, in about 1770, Henry Thorowgood published *A Second Collection of Psalms and Hymns use'd at the Magdalen Chapel . . . The Musick Compos'd by D'Arne [, and by] M'Will'''' Selby and M'Adam Smith Late Organists of the Chapel.*[28] It contained nine tunes by Selby, two by Smith (Selby's predecessor as organist), and one arranged from the overture to Thomas Augustine Arne's *Artaxerxes*. Each tune was scored for treble voices and figured bass (with occasional organ symphonies); at the end of the book are arrangements of all the tunes for guitar (that is, English guitar, or gittern), presumably for home use.

A preface explains that "the favourable Reception the Magdalen Psalms and Hymns have met with from the Public, has induced the Publisher to procure from the late Organists of the Chapel, some new Tunes (which are occasionally perform'd there) to the after-mentioned [or rather, afore-mentioned] Psalms and Hymns, . . . never before publish'd." That is to say, these are alternatives to tunes set to the same texts in the first book. It seems quite likely that Selby was the musical editor, if only because three-quarters of the tunes are his own. Although he may have been out of favor at the hospital, this would not have stood in his way, since Thorowgood's editions were purely commercial and were in no way under the authority of the hospital governors.[29]

By far the most successful piece in the collection was an adaptation of the Larghetto from the overture to Arne's *Artaxerxes*, which may well have been done by Selby. It was reprinted as a hymn tune, in original or revised form, in 115 British or American publications by 1820.[30] The book itself was reissued by Thorowgood, about 1775, as part of *A Companion to the Magdalen Chapel*, and subsequently by his successors Longman and Broderip, Broderip and Wilkinson, and Muzio Clementi and Company, the last reprint occurring in about 1810.

EMIGRATION

I have suggested reasons why Selby may have begun to think about emigration after his dismissal from the Madgalen Hospital. In 1771, his brother John moved to New England and may have encouraged William to join him there, telling him of opportunities for trained musicians in the thriving and still peaceful colonies. John may have begun negotiations for a church position for William. Unfortunately, no correspondence between the brothers is extant.

At any rate, William resigned his two remaining London posts in Octo-

ber 1773. The vestry minutes of St. Sepulchre have the following entry for
October 27: "A Letter from Mr William Selby late joynt organist of this parish together with Mr Samuel Jarvis Junior Importing that he was to quit this
Kingdom the 10th Instant and Returning thanks for the favours he had Received Was Read[.] And it was thereupon Ordered that the said Mr Samuel
Jarvis be sole Organist of this Parish with a Salary of £30 per annum."[31] Presumably the letter, though read out at a meeting on October 27, was dated
between October 1 and 9, to make sense of "the 10th Instant" as a date in
the future.

Selby had received a provisional offer from Trinity (Anglican) Church,
Newport, Rhode Island. Transatlantic crossings took six to eight weeks at that
time, so he may have arrived in Newport in late November or early December. The record of a meeting of the congregation of that church on December 20, 1773, includes the following: "Whereas, Mr. William Selby is arrived
in town from London, in consequence of an application made to him by the
Wardens of the Church, and now offers himself as an organist, and the congregation having heard him officiate, and think him a suitable person to
sustain said office, it is therefore voted: that he be received as organist of the
Church, and that he be paid at the rate of £30 sterling per annum, to commence from the first day of October last; and that the Wardens be requested
to collect by subscription, ten guineas or more, for him, towards paying his
passage to America."[32] This reasonably generous treatment is a sign that the
wardens were pleased with Selby's playing and demeanor.

There is no evidence that Selby played a role in the concert life of Newport, despite McKay's claim of "his Court-House concert of August 3, 1774."
The notice of a concert of that date in the *Newport Mercury* gives no details and does not say who organized or directed it; it says only that tickets
are "to be had of Messrs. Samuel and John Bours, of Mr. Selby, and at the
Printing-Office."[33]

He tried to augment his income in January 1774 by offering "to instruct
young gentlemen and ladies to play upon the violin, flute, harpsichord, guitar and other instruments now in use" and to open a dancing school "for
young Masters and Misses," claiming that "he had been entirely bred to these
genteel professions."[34] Later the opening of the dancing school was postponed
until May 9, with "Teaching days on Mondays and Thursdays, at 4 o'Clock,
P.M.," but there is no evidence that it actually opened. Selby also, as we have
seen, took at least one "apprentice," presumably to train her as a musician.
At some unknown date he seems to have been dropped by Trinity Church,
without any stated reason; by September 1776 a Mr. Knoetchel was function-

ing as organist.[35] Again, it seems unlikely that Selby would have voluntarily relinquished the post unless he had another source of income.

Eventually this was forthcoming from Trinity Church, Boston, probably as early as the summer of 1776. The records do not mention any salary until April 20, 1778, when it was fixed at £26 13s. 4d. for the "ensuing year" (this works out at exactly £80 for three years). But on March 31, 1777, the proprietors had voted "that in Consideration of Mr. William Selbys having acted as Organist for the greatest part of the year past, there be a public collection for his Benefit on such a day as the Revd. Mr. Parker shall appoint." The collection yielded £41 3s., and two more in 1778 produced £85 3s. and £100, respectively—large sums for an organist, as table 2 illustrates.[36]

Yet Selby in April 1779 wrote a letter "expressing Dissatisfaction with the Salary paid him last year." The wardens' response is difficult to comprehend. On May 2, 1779, they reappointed him and resolved "that his Salary be £20 sterling to be made good according as Mr. Parkers Salary be settled." Parker's salary was later settled at £3 per week. In November 1780 there is an entry, "To Mr. Selbys 1/2 year Salary, 188.16"—surely in some unit other than pounds, or it would have been more than twice the minister's salary and incredibly high for an organist at that time. That is the last reference to Selby as organist at Trinity Church. John Cutler, who had served as organist at various times since the 1750s, was appointed for a full year on March 27, 1780.[37] This time, Selby had no other appointment to go to. Since January 1780 at least he had been running a wine shop in Boston.[38]

Twice, it seems, Selby's Magdalen experience had been repeated: he was dropped and replaced by another organist. This could hardly have been due to incompetence, for it is generally conceded that he was the best-trained musician in New England at this time, and the amounts collected for him at Trinity, Boston, rule out the possibility that his work was unsatisfactory. It is true that Anglican churches were depleted during the War of Independence (1776–81), when many clergymen left the country and loyal church members were suspected of siding with Britain. Yet at both churches, another organist was appointed in Selby's place, showing that services continued there. It seems more likely that he was let go because of some moral failing that the church authorities were too discreet to write into their records. Looking again at the newspaper announcement about Jane Fontena quoted on page 13, one begins to see why the young apprentice might have run away from her master.

Selby's final appointment was his most successful one. Services at King's Chapel had been suspended during the war, but they were resumed in 1782. (After the war the former King's Chapel was, for a time, variously called the

"Chapel Church," the "Stone Chapel," or "First Episcopal Church.") Selby, who had played an organ concerto in April 1782 at a concert "For the Benefit of the Poor of Boston," was playing for the chapel services by October of that year. He received an excellent salary and retained the job for the remaining sixteen years of his life.[39]

SELBY IN BOSTON'S MUSICAL LIFE

It is not until 1782, the year of his appointment to the Stone Chapel, that we have any concrete record of Selby as a public performer. In that year, he suddenly emerged in Boston's musical life as a composer, arranger, choir director, and keyboard player. To do so he had first to establish himself as an American patriot, especially since John Selby was known to have been a Loyalist. His proposal for a musical publication called *The New Minstrel* (to be discussed later), dated January 20, 1782, contained this vehement declaration: "The promptness of this young country in those sciences which were once thought peculiar only to riper age, has already brought upon her the eyes of the world. She has pushed her resea[r]ches deep into philosophy, and her statesmen and generals have equalled those of the Roman name. And shall those arts which make her happy be less courted than those arts which have made her great? Why may she not be 'in Song unequall'd as unmatch'd in war'[?]"[40]

For the details of this part of Selby's musical career, David McKay provides an excellent account, which is filled out by the documents transcribed in Barbara Lambert's edition. McKay lists and summarizes the concerts in which Selby figured as either performer or composer from 1782 to 1793.[41] His benefits in Boston's Concert Hall, discussed below, did not begin until 1786. Before then his performing activities, at least as far as they were reported in the newspapers, were confined to the Stone Chapel. In April 1782, before the chapel services had resumed and before he had been appointed organist, he offered: "Musica Spiritualis, or Sacred Music: being a Collection of Airs, Duetts and Choruses, selected from the Oritories of Mr. [John] Stanl[e]y, Mr. [John Christopher] Smith, and the late celebrated Mr. Handel; together with a Favourite Dirge, set to Music by Thomas Augustine Arne, Doctor in Music [i.e., "To fair Fidele's grassy tomb," from *Cymbeline*]: Also, a Concert[o] on the Organ, by Mr. Selby. . . . The whole to be conducted under the direction of Mr. William Selby, Professor of Music, in Boston."[42] This historic event, postponed to April 30, raised a profit of over £150, which Selby passed on to the Overseers of the Poor. Much of the music seems to have been new to

Boston. We know from a publication announcement (discussed below) that Selby's *Jubilate* was also on the program.

After an interval of nearly four years, on January 10, 1786, Selby directed a very different type of charity event in the Stone Chapel: a modified Anglican service (morning prayer and ante-communion), read by the minister of the chapel, the Reverend James Freeman, and preceded, interspersed, and concluded by various pieces of music with orchestral accompaniment, some of them composed by Selby himself.[43]

The plan was described in exceptional detail in an announcement in the *Massachusetts Gazette*, which has been transcribed several times and need not be fully reproduced again here.[44] A very similar event took place a year later. The two programs are summarized in table 3.

It has not been appreciated how closely these events were modeled on British choral festivals. For over a century it had been the custom in London, Oxford, Salisbury, and elsewhere to hold a special festival on St. Cecilia's Day (November 22). There was an evening concert, but the centerpiece was an Anglican service of morning prayer held in a cathedral or parish church, departing in no way from the normal liturgy as laid down in the *Book of Common Prayer*, but adorned by an orchestra, joining with the organ both for voluntaries and for accompanying the anthems and service settings, and by prominent professional solo singers. The choir might also be augmented by singers from neighboring churches. A similar practice developed at the Festival of the Sons of the Clergy (from 1698), the Three Choirs Festival (from 1724), and other early choral festivals. The service, rather than any oratorio performance, was the centerpiece of these events. It was an effective compromise, allowing as much of a "concert" as possible while never straying from the structure and rubrics of the Anglican service. Some people objected to the musical trappings; partly for this reason, a sermon was often preached giving biblical and rational justifications for the use of instrumental music in worship. At the Three Choirs Festival, it was only in 1759 that a performance of *Messiah* was added to the morning events. Long after this date, British choral festivals continued to include a full Anglican cathedral service, with orchestrally accompanied music and solos by leading opera singers. The Birmingham Festivals of the 1820s included services strikingly similar to the ones described here.[45]

It now fell to Selby to introduce this custom to Boston, the Puritan capital of Massachusetts, at a time when Anglicanism was hardly able to raise its head because of its association with Loyalism. As we have seen, Selby had been at pains to assert his own support of Independence by public pronouncement.

ble 3. Programs of Services/Concerts Given at the Stone Chapel, Boston, 1786–87

rder of Service	Interpolated Musical Numbers	
	January 10, 1786	January 16, 1787
	Handel, Overture, *Occasional Oratorio* Handel, "Comfort ye" and "Ev'ry valley" (*Messiah*)	Piccinni, Overture, *La buona Figliuola* Handel, "Comfort ye" and "Ev'ry valley" (*Messiah*)
pening prayers and responses, said]ᵃ		
nite (Ps. 95), sung or said		
roper psalms for the day, saidᵃ	Avison?, Concerto, Op. 7, No. 4	a violin concerto
rst lesson		
Deum, chanted (1787: setting by Samuel Arnold [in A major?])		
cond lesson		
bilate [Ps. 100], set by Selby		
postles' Creed, said		
	Handel, "The trumpet shall sound" (*Messiah*)	Felsted, "Out of the deep" (*Jonah*)
ersicles and responses, said		
rst Collect, said		
	Handel, "Let the bright seraphim" (*Samson*)	Handel, "Let the bright seraphim" (*Samson*) Handel, "Hallelujah chorus" (*Samson*)
econd and third Collects; prayers		
	Handel, Organ Concerto No. 2	an organ concerto
eneral thanksgiving; prayers		
ffertory sentences read, collection taken	Soft solo on the organ by Selby	
rayer for the church militant; concluding prayers; blessing		
	[J. C.] Bach, Overture	Dittersdorf, Overture

a. Followed by a new doxology composed by Selby.
Note: The newspaper advertisements give the names of several composers and pieces in garbled form. These ave been corrected or interpreted here; the original spellings can be found in any of the transcriptions listed 1 note 44. "Avison" seems the most likely interpretation of "Amizon"; Charles Avison's concerti grossi were opular in England, but there was not one numbered Op. 7, No. 4. The original description reads "That the 4th Concerto of *Amizon*, musica de capella. opa. 7 be performed by the organ and all the instruments, as and for he Voluntary."

Furthermore, the Stone Chapel, though its congregation included many of the same people who had been members before the war, was no longer strictly Anglican (or Episcopalian). A new, semi-Unitarian liturgy had recently been prepared for use there, probably by John Freeman.[46] It was a modification of *Common Prayer,* and it was followed at the festival services of 1786 and 1787.

The preface expresses the hope that "the Liturgy, contained in this volume, is such, that no Christian, it is supposed, can take offence. . . . The Trinitarian, the Unitarian, the Calvinist, the Arminian will read nothing in it which can give him any reasonable umbrage. God is the sole object of worship in these prayers; and as no man can come to God, but by the one Moderator, Jesus Christ, every petition is here offered in his name. . . . The Gloria Patri . . . is not in this Liturgy. . . . Instead of that doxology, doxologies from the pure word of God are introduced." The doxology for Morning Prayer is the one set to music by Selby: "Now unto the King eternal, immortal, invisible, the only wise God, be honour and glory, through Jesus Christ, for ever and ever. Amen" (based on 1 Timothy 1:17). Selby's setting was published the following year.[47]

As table 3 shows, the service kept as close to the Anglican liturgy as theological changes permitted. The instrumental pieces come at points where it had long been customary to play organ voluntaries (in the case of the Avison concerto, the program says "as and for the Voluntary").[48] The excerpt from *Samson* is in the place provided for an anthem. One choral piece, the *Jubilate,* is part of the service itself, as is Arnold's *Te Deum,* added in 1787. The most startling addition in 1786 was "The trumpet shall sound" immediately after the (modified) Creed, but it was not inappropriate after the words "and the life in the world to come" that ended the Creed. In 1787 it was replaced by a quieter selection from *Jonah,* by the Jamaican composer Samuel Felsted.[49] Though the events were billed as "Concert of Sacred Musick," the 1787 overture was taken from an opera.

These performances, called "extravaganzas" by Sonneck and McKay, but not in fact departing from church tradition, were sponsored by the Musical Society of Boston. They were "thronged with all classes of people" and received an unprecedented amount of attention in the press. Everything about them was highly praised, including Selby's efforts as organist and composer. As a contemporary put it: "The first recitative and the first song in the Messiah were sung as to have done no discredit to any capital singer at the theatre in Covent Garden; but the song 'Let the bright cherubims in burning row, etc.' in the opinion of several who had heard the oratorio of Sampson at Covent Gardenhouse, was sung, at least as well, in the Chapel Church, on Tuesday by our townsman, as they had ever before heard."[50] The utmost rapture was reserved for Handel himself.[51] Relatively large sums were raised for the poor.

Despite the success of these concerts on all counts, there were no further performances on similar lines, as far as we know. Subsequent "concerts of sacred musick" directed by Selby look more like conventional concerts, independent of a liturgical service.[52] The programs are set out in two parts, or acts. Where the content is known, it is not unlike that of the 1786–87 events, including overtures or symphonies, organ concertos, Selby's *Jubilate* and other anthems, and the same favorite Handel oratorio excerpts. In two cases the concert was called "Oratorio," probably because it included Felsted's *Jonah* complete (in one act). The October 1787 concert is remarkable for including two anthems by William Billings, a rare bridge between the two musical traditions. Another concert for the benefit of Billings was given at the Stone Chapel on December 15, 1790; McKay assumes, though without evidence, that Selby directed it.[53] For the concert of October 1789 the Musical Society orchestra was replaced by a band from the French fleet.

These sacred concerts, taken together with the two "service concerts," justify Sonneck's claims for Selby as the remote progenitor of the Handel and Haydn Society. This organization, after a similar event directed by George K. Jackson in 1812, held its first public concert at King's Chapel (by then restored to its old name) in 1815.

Clearly the support for these developments went far beyond the old Anglican elite. Many of Boston's Congregational churches had also liberalized their theology and were moving fast toward full Unitarianism. As the old Calvinist doctrines receded, there was no longer any compelling reason to object to elaborate concerts of sacred music. With the professional musicians, who more and more frequently directed these concerts, came the styles and habits of the English anthem and oratorio, and the European music of the London concert halls and theaters.

Selby's activity as a giver of secular concerts is less fully documented and may have been exaggerated by some writers. (As we have seen, the concerts of 1771–75 can no longer be credited to this Selby.) A "Concert of Vocal and Instrumental Musick" given at Concert Hall on April 27, 1786, was sponsored by the Boston Musical Society for Selby's benefit; the society's exact relationship with Selby is unknown, and he may or may not have directed the concert. His ode in honor of George Washington was performed there. A similar event was held on September 10, 1787, with no details given.

The next Selby benefit was on January 24, 1788, with the following program: "FIRST ACT: Overture. A double piece [i.e., for two manuals] on the Harpsichord. Song. Full Piece [i.e., symphony]. SECOND ACT: The Country Courtship, a Musical Entertainment [by James Hook, 1772]. The characters, Dorus, Alexis, and Pastora." Lambert calls this "[one] of the few benefit concerts sponsored by subscription series, . . . specifically organized to aid Selby."[54] This may be a misreading of the announcement: "The Subscribers to the Musical Society, are desired to take notice, that their next Concert is postponed to the 7th of February, as the Hall on Thursday the 24th instant, will be appropriated to the benefit of Mr. Selby, when there will be a Publick Concert of Vocal and Instrumental Music."[55] That is, Selby's benefit *replaced* the society's subscription concert. Sonneck said that Selby was "undoubtedly the musical guide" of the Musical Society of Boston, which, he said, was "presumably founded in 1785,"[56] but I can find no evidence for either claim.

The Musical Society gave six concerts in 1788–89, but again there is no documented connection with Selby. There is nothing more until 1792, when an announcement appeared in the *Columbian Centinel* for March 15: "Mr. SELBY'S CONCERT. The Subscribers to the Concerts are hereby notified, that the sixth and last Concert . . . is postponed until the first Wednesday in April." Selby had evidently offered a series of six subscription concerts, perhaps on alternate Wednesdays, during the winter season of 1791–92. (The word "concert" in the singular, as in "Mr. Selby's Concert," was capable of meaning what would now be called a concert series, as in London's "Concert of Antient Music.") No details of the programs are known. Advertisements show that there was another series on Thursday nights, beginning on March 22, 1792.

Next season, a meeting of "the Subscribers to Mr. Selby's Concert" was called for October 2, when "something of importance will be proposed." This confirms that there had existed a regular subscription series directed by Selby. The subscription concerts that were subsequently announced, however, do not mention Selby at all; and as they took place on Thursdays they are more likely to have been those of the rival series.[57] Possibly the "something of importance" was a proposal to amalgamate the two series.

The final reported event was on June 20, 1793, when a single concert of "Instrumental Musick" (but with one vocalist) was announced "For the benefit of Messrs. *Selby* and *Pick*" at Concert Hall. Jacobus Pick was a French player of the glass harmonica. The program is an interesting one, consisting chiefly of French music.[58] It begins with "The Overture of Henry IVth" (probably that by Jean-Paul-Gilles Martini);[59] includes concertos for violin, clarinet, and flute, a "Duetto on the Harmonica," and a "Piano Forte Sonata by Mr. Selby"; and ends with a symphony by "Pichell" (probably the Bohemian composer Wenzel Pichl).

Selby also appeared as a keyboard player at a few benefit concerts given by others; the last was Mrs. Pownall's benefit at Concert Hall on July 22, 1794, when he again played a "Sonata on the Piano Forte."[60]

It seems, on the whole, that Selby's efforts on the secular side were less successful than his sacred performances. The exact extent of his participation in and direction of these concerts cannot be ascertained; it may have been as little as a single annual benefit, or as much as an annual series. In any case, few of the concerts seem to have attracted much attention in the press. They do not quite support Sonneck's claim that Selby "prepared the musical future of Boston more than any other musician before or after him."[61]

SELBY AS EDITOR AND PUBLISHER

Selby's Boston publishing enterprises were less prosperous than his London volume of Magdalen hymns. In 1782, the year of his rehabilitation, he advertised a proposal to print by subscription "a collection of original compositions" called *The New Minstrel,* in ten monthly numbers at $1.50 each, beginning on March 1, 1782, "if a sufficient number of subscribers appears." Evidently this did not happen. Each number was to have had a preface consisting of sixteen pages of Charles Avison's *Essay on Musical Expression* (London, 1752) and "at least one composition for the Harpsichord, Piano Forte, or Spinett, one for the Guittar, and one for the german Flute, also, of one song in French, and two songs in the English language."[62] At this stage Selby was hoping to appeal to the secular, domestic market.

Later in the same year, perhaps realizing that his reputation was founded chiefly on sacred music, he published *Two Anthems, for Three and Four Voices.*[63] In announcing this in the *Boston Gazette,* Selby further described the two pieces: "One taken from the 100th Psalm, for Four Voices (that was performed at the Stone Chapel, Boston, on the 30th April last), the other taken from the [1]17th Psalm, for Three Voices, composed in an easy and familiar Stile, and adapted for the Use of Singing Societies."[64] The first anthem was indeed his *Jubilate,* which became quite popular and was many times reprinted. Whether the publication was financially successful is more doubtful. It was not reissued, and only one copy is now extant.

In the same announcement, Selby declared his intention "(if encouraged) periodically to publish Anthems, Cantatas, Songs, Pieces of Music for the Harpsichord, Spinnet or Forte Piano, Violin, German Flute, and Guitar." He made one more attempt in this direction in 1790, when he advertised a proposal to print by subscription *Apollo and the Muses: Musical Compositions by William Selby,* in six bimonthly numbers at three dollars each (with a seventh free number for those who subscribed to all six). The issues would include anthems, voluntaries, sonatas, songs, and chamber pieces. The plan was to be put into operation "As soon as 200 Copies are subscribed for."[65]

McKay reports that Selby issued a modified proposal in 1791, with the significant addition of "Choruses and Songs from the Oratorios of the late celebrated Messrs. Handel, Boice [William Boyce], [John] Stanley, and [John Christopher] Smith."[66] This is much the same repertory that he had drawn on for his sacred concerts of 1786–87. McKay has shown that an untitled collection of printed music in the Massachusetts Historical Society, which Sonneck had identified with the 1790 proposal, represents the first two issues of the revised series, and he plausibly argues that they appeared in October and December 1791.[67] One contains the song "Yes, Adam, yes" from John Christopher Smith's *Paradise Lost,* and the other includes "Would you gain the slender creature" from Handel's *Acis and Galatea,* both arranged on two staves for keyboard accompaniment. The rest of the pieces are unattributed, but the announcements leave no room for doubt that they are Selby's own compositions; indeed, one of them, the song "When from my Sylvia I remove," had already been published by him in London (see table 6, p. 41).

The series was then probably abandoned. As we shall see, a few of his secular vocal pieces had appeared in magazines shortly before this time, and some of his anthems were reprinted during the 1790s. But there is no record of any further attempt at musical publication by Selby himself.

SACRED COMPOSITIONS

In his London years, Selby's few known sacred compositions were psalm and hymn tunes, eleven in all, arising naturally out of his position as organist, first in parish churches and then at the Magdalen Chapel. Six of them were reprinted in America, in *The Massachusetts Compiler* (Boston, 1795), Samuel Holyoke's *Columbian Repository* (Exeter, N.H., 1803), John Cole's *Divine Harmonist* [Baltimore, 1808], Oliver Shaw's *Providence Selection* (Dedham, Mass., 1815), and Charles Southgate's *Harmonia Sacra* (New York, 1818). All these books tended to favor music of British origin. Incidentally, one of the tunes, "Psalm 19," also reached G. van Rooyen's *Selection of Hymns for the Use of the English Presbyterian Church in Rotterdam* (Rotterdam, [1810]).[68]

Two of the tunes, composed for Riley's *Parochial Harmony,* are in four-part harmony with the melody in the treble. The other nine tunes, for the Magdalen Chapel, are more like solo songs with an instrumental bass. All are quite elegantly written, being ornately melodious in the fashionable *galant* style. They lack the religious solemnity and austerity of many of the tunes in the first book of the "Magdalen Collection."[69] As they are not known to have been in regular use at the Magdalen Hospital, they were probably meant for domestic use. The harpsichord is the most likely choice among the accompanying instruments mentioned on the title page. Several tunes have short keyboard introductions, and one, "Psalm 23," is made into a more extended composition by interludes between each pair of lines as well as a prelude and postlude (fig. 2). If Selby's tunes show one individual trait, it is a tendency to modulate to the relative minor toward the end, after the conventional mid-cadence in the dominant. This feature, not common in tunes of the time, is found in six of Selby's ten major-mode specimens.

Selby seems to have been encouraged by the concert at the Stone Chapel in 1782 to create more elaborate church music. Only five compositions of this type have survived: four anthems and a doxology (see table 4).

"O be joyful in the Lord" was performed in the Stone Chapel at the concert of April 30, 1782, according to the title page of *Two Anthems,* when it was no doubt accompanied on the organ. As a canticle setting (the *Jubilate*) it includes the Christian doxology, Gloria Patri. It was singled out for praise by the Boston correspondent of the *Pennsylvania Herald,* who said it "has not disgraced the inspired, royal author of the 100 psalm."[70] At the liturgical concerts of 1786 and 1787 it was heard again, "accompanied by all the instruments," when, as we have seen, the Gloria Patri was replaced by "Now to the king eternal" from the new Stone Chapel liturgy.[71] Selby's setting of this New Doxology is in the same key.

Table 4. Selby's Anthems and Service Music

First Line (Text Source)	Key	Scoring	Number of Measures	Performed	Publication (Number of Reprints)
O be joyful in the Lord (*Jubilate:* Ps. 100)	C	SATB	119	1782	*Two Anthems,* 1782 (10)
O praise the Lord, all ye nations (Ps. 117)	D	ATB	114	?	*Two Anthems,* 1782 (0)
Behold, he is my salvation (Isaiah 12:2, etc.)	D	SATB	234	1783	*Worcester Collection,* 1786 (8)
Now to the king eternal (Freeman, Doxology)	C	SATB	13	1786	*Worcester Collection,* 1786 (4)
The heavens declare (Tate and Brady, Ps. 19, 45, 89)	D	satb/ATB, org.	176	?	*Apollo and the Muses,* 1791 (0)

Figure 2. Selby, "Psalm 23"

..tend, And all my Mid..night hours de..fend.

2

When in the fultry glebe I faint,
Or on the thirfty mountain pant,
To fertile vales and dewy meads
My weary wandering fteps he leads,
Where peaceful rivers foft and flow,
Amid the verdant landfkip flow.

3

Though in the paths of death I tread,
With gloomy horrors overfpread,
My ftedfaft heart fhall fear no ill,
For thou O Lord art with me ftill
Thy friendly crook fhall give me aid,
And guide me through the dreadful fhade.

4

Though in a bare and rugged way,
Through devious lonely wilds I ftray,
Thy bounty fhall my pains beguile,
The barren wildernefs fhall fmile,
With fudden greens and herbage crown'd,
And ftreams fhall murmur all around.

Figure 2 (cont.)

But the published versions of both pieces are for voices only, without even bass figures. The *Jubilate* is evidently modeled on the verse service of English cathedral music. It seems incomplete without the accompaniments that we know existed, and it cannot fairly be judged in that form. The same is true of the New Doxology, accompanied "by the Organ and all the instruments," in 1786.[72] Nevertheless, they must have been at least acceptable to the unaccompanied choirs of singing schools and Congregational churches, since, as we have seen, they were reprinted in several collections intended for such use.

"O be joyful" (ex. 1) is hearty and extrovert.[73] Compared with hymn tunes such as that in figure 2 it is startlingly plain and bare, with very unsophisticated melodic lines. It seems that Selby was deliberately shedding his London manner and adopting something closer to the country style that was familiar in Boston. But he adds his usual modulations to the dominant and the relative minor, followed by triumphant returns to the main key. However obvious this effect may seem today, it was excitingly novel to Bostonian ears in the 1780s. The art of modulation was not one that had been mastered by Billings or other American-born psalmodists, and it must have reminded the hearers chiefly of the excerpts from Handel's *Messiah* that they had been hearing for some fifteen years in local concerts. There is a more direct reminder of Handel later in the piece (ex. 2). Selby achieved a certain cohesion by the simple but effective device of recalling the opening phrase, beginning with four eighth-notes on C, at two later points.

"O praise the Lord, all ye nations" had a different purpose. Selby distinguished it from "O be joyful" in announcing the publication of *Two Anthems*, pointing out that it was "for Three Voices, composed in an easy and familiar Stile, and adapted for the Use of Singing Societies."[74] In fact, however, it is a much more difficult piece, with a very large range for all three voices and a number of imitative entries. Daniel points out a "piquant detail," the "use, in three different passages, of a descending succession of triads in first inversion, a latter-day fauxbourdon." This was also a favorite device of Handel's.[75]

The word "adapted" in the announcement could mean that it was originally written for a different medium. Perhaps it was part of a verse anthem, with organ accompaniment, that Selby had brought with him in manuscript from England and now tried to launch in a new context. If so, he was unsuccessful. Unlike its companion, the piece was never taken up by American compilers of music for the use of singing societies in the many books published for this purpose during the next twenty years.

"O praise the Lord," like "O be joyful," has a middle section in the relative minor and in triple time, a common enough procedure in the Georgian

Example 1. Selby, Anthem, "O be joyful in the Lord," mm. 1–16, with editorial organ accompaniment

verse-anthem. The final buildup is effective (ex. 3). It will be observed that Selby seems quite unaware of any rules proscribing consecutive fifths or octaves, a point that would have brought him censure had these anthems been performed or published in England.

"Behold, he is my salvation" (reprinted in some sources as "Behold, God is my salvation"),[76] with a text compiled from "sundry scriptures," was

Example 2. Selby, Anthem, "O be joyful in the Lord," mm. 74–82

Example 3. Selby, Anthem, "O praise the Lord, all ye nations," mm. 91–108

composed for the rededication of Old South Church, Boston, on March 2, 1783,[77] presumably without organ accompaniment. It was revived in the same church as late as May 9, 1830.[78] It is a long work, with many solos; even the choruses have stark sections in which the text is broken up and thrown from one unaccompanied voice to another (ex. 4). There is nothing to indicate whether single or massed voices are meant to sing each part. The last section, "Hallelujah: For the Lord God omnipotent reigneth," has obvious echoes of Handel's *Messiah*. The harmonies are not always "correct" by the standards of art music.

"Behold, he is my salvation" has another element as well, one that gives some countenance to McKay's characterization of the anthems as "commendable imitations of Billings's 'fuguing tunes.'"[79] It was the only one that was custom made for a Congregational church, without an organ, and it is clearly tenor-led (see, for instance, the cadence at the end of example 4, with its upward resolution of a seventh in the top voice). The bare harmonies, and especially the passages for a single unaccompanied voice, are indeed reminiscent of Billings's fuging tunes, and also of his early anthems. It seems unlikely that Selby, given his background, was a true admirer of the New England school of church music, which must have reminded him of the country psalmody of his home country, held in low regard by professional musicians there. But it may be that in this case, and at this time, he thought it expedient to imitate Billings's style.

Ralph Daniel made a study of these three anthems. His conclusion was that "many of the stylistic features . . . suggest that Selby's vocal music was

Example 4. Selby, Anthem, "Behold, he is my salvation," mm. 31–42

more strongly influenced by instrumental music of the later eighteenth century than that of [his American contemporaries]."[80] However, although Selby was himself an instrumental performer, the bulk of his compositions are for voices, and cathedral music is the likely ideal of his sacred choral music. If there was any other model, it was surely Handel, whose "Hallelujah chorus" finds an echo in more than one of Selby's anthems. There is little sign here of the *galant* style we observed in his Magdalen psalm and hymn tunes.

"The heavens declare" (titled *Anthem for Christmas*), not considered by Daniel, is the one anthem of Selby's with an extant organ part. It is quite different from the others, being much more "polite," in a *galant*, Italianate art-music tradition, with appoggiaturas and other pretty ornaments. In style it resembles his Magdalen psalm tunes and his solo songs.

The text is metrical and is a curious selection from Tate and Brady's *New Version of the Psalms,* having no connection with Christmas—a fact that suggests the anthem had been composed earlier, for some other purpose, before Selby decided to use it in his *Apollo and the Muses* for December 1791. The original advertisement of *Apollo and the Muses* mentioned a "Thanksgiving Anthem" in the second number, due to appear in November 1791, as McKay points out.[81] Probably this was the same work under a different name; however, it is not much more suitable for Thanksgiving than for Christmas. It would have been well suited to a wedding. It starts with general praise of the Creator (Psalm 19:1, 3), then goes on to four verses of the amorous Psalm 45 (verses 1, 2, 10, 11), headed "A Song of Loves" in the King James version of the Bible, though traditionally interpreted as an expression of Christ's relationship with the church. The last stanza, based on Psalm 89:17–18, returns to general praise. It is in long meter where the rest are in common meter. All are from Tate and Brady's *New Version of the Psalms.*

Each four-line stanza is set as a separate movement (see table 5). The resulting form is more complex, and with a wider range of tonalities, than in any other extant work of Selby's, sacred or secular. Perhaps because of the metrical form and the rhymes, it is chiefly made up of a succession of binary tunes, with a middle cadence in the dominant or relative major of the prevailing tonality, each half being rounded off by a short organ symphony. The opening (ex. 5) and closing movements, as befits their texts, have a more triumphal character. The four "amorous" stanzas from Psalm 45 are set as a dialogue between treble and tenor soloists (ex. 6 shows an opening gambit), each singing a recitative and binary song, and this portion is quite operatic.

le 5. Structure of Selby's *Anthem for Christmas*

s	Stanza	Key	Meter	Voices	Description
∙0	1. The heav'ns declare thy glory, Lord	D	¢	t	Short phrases echoed by organ
-63	2. Their powerful language to no realm or region is confined	d	3/2	b	Binary tune with repeats
-69	3. While I the king's loud praise rehearse			s	Recitative
-87	4. How[a] matchless is thy form, O king	C	6/8	s	Binary tune (siciliano)
-93	5. But thou, O royal bride, give ear			t	Recitative
-26	6. So shall thy beauty charm the king	G	2/4	t	Binary tune
ʔ–52	7. For in his strength they shall advance	D	3/4	a, t	Binary tune
∫–76	8. The Lord of hosts is our defence	D	3/4	ATB	Similar binary tune

ɑ. "How" is misprinted "Know."

Example 5. Selby, Anthem, "The heavens declare," mm. 1–19

Example 6. Selby, Anthem, "The heavens declare," mm. 70–78

SECULAR VOCAL MUSIC

Selby's output of secular songs is slender, but it is a little more substantial than has been thought. David McKay listed only five songs in his "Checklist of Extant Published Compositions by William Selby," under "Vocal solos . . . Secular text settings." It is now possible to augment this number to nine, plus one duet ("To musick be the verse addrest"), which McKay classified as a "secular choral work" for soprano, alto, and bass. It is more properly called a song for one or two sopranos with instrumental bass.

There is a clear division between Selby's London songs of 1759–c. 1765 and the Boston songs of a quarter-century later (table 6), though one of the former was reprinted at Boston in 1791. All have several stanzas to the same music, and that music consists of the voice accompanied by an unfigured bass (the right hand to double the voice) with an introduction, middle symphony, and coda on two staves. This was the normal format for keyboard songs in London, and in most of Europe, at this time; independent keyboard accompaniments on two staves were rare before 1790. (This point will be discussed more fully in relation to Rayner Taylor.)

le 6. Selby's Secular Songs and Duet

t Line (Title)	Key	Acct.	Publication
eauty's pow'r so potent be	D	kbd.	In *Clio and Euterpe* 2 (London, 1759)
en from my Sylvia I remove	E	kbd.	In *Clio and Euterpe* 3 (London, 1762)
	D	kbd.	Repr. *The Musical Magazine* 3 (London, 1769)
	F	kbd.	Repr. *Apollo and the Muses* ([Boston], 1791)
ɡ from the force of beauty's			
arms (The Conquest)	A	kbd.	London, [c. 1765?]
r the bowl we'll laugh and sing	F	orch.	London, [c. 1765?]
. Drinking Song)			
you hear, brother sportsman, the	F	kbd.	London, [c. 1765?]
und of the horn (The Chace of	F	kbd.	In *A Choice Collection of Favourite Hunting*
e Hare: A New Hunting Song)			*Songs*, 1 (London: [1772])
	F	kbd.	In *The Sportsman's Companion* 1 (London: [c. 1775])
musick be the verse addrest	F	bass[a]	In *Massachusetts Magazine* 1 (1789)
ɹıet)	F	bass[a]	Repr. *American Musical Miscellany* (1798)
ewell my Pastora, no longer your	D	kbd.	In *Gentlemen and Ladies Town and Country*
ᴠain (Psalemon to Pastora)			*Magazine* (March 1789)
ɹdy groves and purling mills			
The Rural Retreat)	B♭	kbd.	In *Massachusetts Magazine* 1 (1789)
end, dear maid, thy patient ear			
The Lovely Lass)	A	kbd.	In *Massachusetts Magazine* 2 (1790)
e fair Eliza's living grace			
Addressed to Miss D. by a Lady,			
oth of Boston)	G	kbd.	In *Apollo and the Muses* ([Boston], 1791)

a. Plus a second melodic part for voice or instrument.

The songs are generally in binary form, with a middle cadence in the dominant key; in many cases the second half includes Selby's characteristic modulation to the relative minor. The first two songs were published in a miscellany called *Clio and Euterpe, or British Harmony,* elegantly printed with engraved illustrations. They are chaste pastoral love songs of the kind that were sung and played by ladies in many a drawing room, with florid melismas including the "Scotch snap." "If beauty's power," in D major (ex. 7), Selby's earliest known composition, takes a surprising turn to E major for its halfway cadence, but it is smoothly brought back to the normal A major by the middle symphony. In other respects it shows an easy mastery of the midcentury song in the general idiom of Arne. "When from my Sylvia I remove" has a sweet simplicity and must have achieved some popularity. It was reprinted in another London magazine, transposed down to an easier key; and Selby used it yet again in 1791, this time in a higher key. "The Conquest" is of the same general class.

Example 7. Selby, "If beauty's power so potent be," mm. 4–17

The other two London songs, by contrast, are clearly addressed to a male audience. "A Drinking Song" is in a hearty 6/8, with accompaniments for violin, two horns, and figured bass, all accommodated on two staves. Such as it is, this is our sole example of Selby's writing for orchestra. "The Chace of the Hare" is in the same key and meter, and although for keyboard only, it has many conventional horn imitations, perhaps reduced from an orchestral original (ex. 8). The vocal style is direct, with few ornaments. Both songs depict the kind of vigorous, extroverted "John Bull" that Englishmen liked to see in themselves. This hunting song seems to have remained in the repertory, along with some of his hymn tunes, after Selby's departure from London.

When in 1789 Selby again offered keyboard songs to a magazine, he returned to the innocuous pastoral idiom. The six-stanza song "To Musick" has two melodic lines moving mostly in parallel thirds and sixths, in the manner of many an Italian *canzonetta a due* (such as those of Johann Christian Bach, London, 1765, 1767). In "Psalemon to Pastora" Selby reduces his harmonies to a drone bass, suggesting a bagpipe, a device that was becom-

Example 8. Selby, "The Chace of the Hare," keyboard introduction

ing conventional for Scottish and Irish airs. "The Rural Retreat" works the Alberti bass with a vengeance. But in the equally pianistic "The Lovely Lass," perhaps Selby's best song, he achieves a fine flow and balance between voice and accompaniment (fig. 3). "The fair Eliza's living grace" is "by a Lady," but this must refer to the text, which is a tribute to the beauty of another lady of Boston (Miss D) and to "Her Wit, her Sense refin'd." The song has charm, but again Selby overdoes the rattling accompaniment, this time in left-hand triplets. Selby's achievement in songs is by no means negligible, however, and in my view equals that of his American-born contemporary Francis Hopkinson (1737–91).

Selby wrote several occasional pieces under the title of Ode (table 7). The amount of music in each of them is quite small, because, like the solo songs, they are designed for strophic repetition with several stanzas. All are patriotic in content, with a chorus after each verse. The "Ode to Columbia's Favourite Son"—a mere twelve bars of music—was performed at Selby's benefit on April 27, 1786, the program calling it "An Ode in Honour of General Washington." The "Ode to Independence" followed an oration given at the Stone

Table 7. Selby's Choral Odes

First Line (Title)	Key	Scoring	Performance and Publication
Great Washington the hero's come (Ode to Columbia's Favourite Son)	G	t, TTB	Performed: Apr. 27, 1786 Published: *Massachusetts Magazine* 1 (1789)
Hail! sublime she moves along (Ode to Independence)	?	?	Performed: July 4, 1787
Behold the man whom virtues raise (Ode performed before the President of the United States)	F	t, SATB	Performed: Oct. 17, 1789 Published: *Apollo and the Muses* (1791)
Hark! notes melodious fill the skies (Ode for the New Year, January 1, 1790)	A	t, TTB	Published: *Massachusetts Magazine* 2 (1790) Reprinted: *American Musical Miscellany* (1798)

Figure 3. Selby, "The Lovely Lass" (Courtesy American Antiquarian Society)

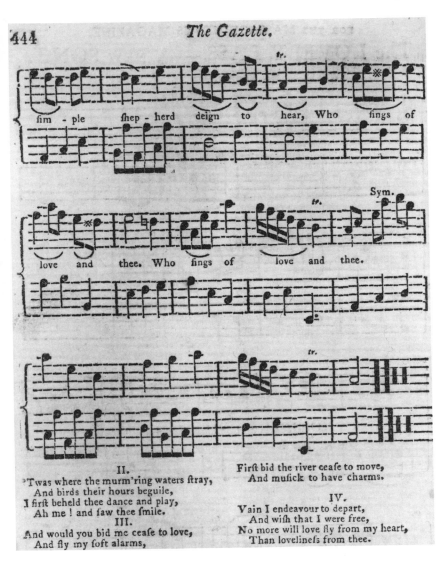

The Gazette.

simple shepherd deign to hear, Who sings of love and thee. Who sings of love and thee.

II.
'Twas where the murm'ring waters stray,
And birds their hours beguile,
I first beheld thee dance and play,
Ah me ! and saw thee smile.

III.
And would you bid me cease to love,
And fly my soft alarms,

First bid the river cease to move,
And musick to have charms.

IV.
Vain I endeavour to depart,
And wish that I were free,
No more will love fly from my heart,
Than loveliness from thee.

Figure 3 (cont.)

Chapel on Independence Day 1787, and its text was published in the "Castalian Fount" department in the *Massachusetts Centinel* (July 7, 1787); but the music has not been found.

A second ode in honor of Washington was published in *Apollo and the Muses,* with the heading "As performed at the Stone Chapel, Boston, before the President of the United States of America. Words by Mr. Brown of Boston." This was almost certainly the piece called "A congratulatory ODE to the

Example 9. Selby, "Ode to the President," mm. 43–50

PRESIDENT" in the program of the concert of October 27, 1789, printed in the *Massachusetts Centinel*. A subsequent stanza contains a clear reference to the French Revolution:

> Thy glory beams to Eastern Skies,
> See Europe share the sacred flame,
> And hosts of patriot heroes rise
> To imitate thy glorious fame.

When published, this ode had a pianistic introduction that could possibly have been played on the organ at the Stone Chapel, but it does not suggest the orchestral accompaniments that were probably used there. The chorus (ex. 9) is unusually bold in its clashing passing notes.

No performance of the "Ode for the New Year" is on record. It is in verse-chorus form, and like the "Ode to Columbia's Favourite Son," it is in a boisterous style befitting its content. The chorus goes into 6/8 and recalls Selby's earlier hunting and drinking songs.

INSTRUMENTAL MUSIC

Selby is on record as having played organ concertos at various Boston concerts, but one work might have been sufficient for all these occasions. One was announced for publication in *Apollo and the Muses,* but the series folded before it could appear, and it has not survived.

But a Lesson by Selby did appear in that series, in 1791. The word "lesson" in English usage at this period was often synonymous with "sonata,"[82]

and this specimen could easily have been called a sonata. It is quite probably the sonata that Selby played at Boston Concert Hall in 1793 and 1794.
In any event, it is roughly contemporary with what are usually regarded as
the earliest sonatas composed in America, the superior "Philadelphia" sonatas of Alexander Reinagle. But unlike them, it was printed (however unsuccessfully) for the American public. It is in three movements, all in the
key of C, and all on a small scale. The opening Allegro (ex. 10) and the
concluding jig are each in a concise sonata form, while the middle movement is an expressive Andante in rondo form (ex. 11), with episodes in G
major and C minor (ex. 11b).

Example 10. Selby, Sonata in C Major, first movement, mm. 1–11

Example 11. Selby, Sonata in C Major, second movement

Unlike those English contemporaries who stayed in their home country, Selby did not experience the influence of C. P. E. Bach and Haydn, and he was still writing in the thin textures of the midcentury. A comparison can be made with the 1766 sonatas of John Burton (1730–85).[83]

There are two Selby voluntaries extant, one published in London, the other in Boston.[84] Neither is likely to have been the one played at the service/concert of 1786. They are fugues of the kind that was often played before the First Lesson or at the end of the service; a likely model was Handel's *Six Fugues or Voluntarys* (1735). At the 1786 event, on the other hand, it was announced that "Mr. Selby will then play a Solo, Piano, on the organ; during which the sentences in the Offertory will be read." He would have done the same thing many times in London, Newport, and Boston. We have no example of this type of quiet improvisation by Selby, or indeed by any contemporary organist-composer.

The two voluntaries have been treated in some detail by Clark.[85] The Voluntary in A (fig. 4) was published in *Ten Voluntaries* (London: C. and S. Thompson, [c. 1770]), with attribution to "Mr. Selby." (In theory it could have been the work of John Selby, but this seems unlikely, since his only known composition is an undistinguished hymn tune.) It is in two sections, recalling a French overture. There are thirteen measures of slow chords for full organ, in a chord sequence passing through the keys of A, E, B, and C-sharp minor, followed by a fifty-nine-measure "Fuga." The fugue has six entries in the tonic and closely related keys, with noncontrapuntal, sequential episodes between them; it seems competently written, except for a weakness in the modulations returning from F-sharp minor to A major.

The "Fuge or Voluntary" in D was published in *Apollo and the Muses* (1791). It is a single movement of 107 measures. There are only four contrapuntal entries of the longish subject (ex. 12), but they are followed by an extensive passage that successfully develops the main motive of the subject to a climax, where the full subject enters in unison before cadential chords round off the piece.

In both works, though Selby's contrapuntal skill is modest, he successfully adopts the learned manner of fugal writing, complete with suspensions and diatonic sequences. In these he is only following earlier English models, including Handel. Naturally, there are no pedal parts, and there is also no indication of registration or dynamics. Both pieces could be played on the harpsichord with little loss of effect.

Figure 4. Selby, Voluntary in A Major, from *Ten Voluntaries* (Courtesy British Library)

Example 12. Selby, "Fugue or Voluntary" in D Major, mm. 1–27

THE SIGNIFICANCE OF WILLIAM SELBY

Recent discoveries have narrowed William Selby's period of importance in Boston concert life to a span of perhaps nine years (1786–94) and cast some doubt on his dominance of secular music-making. But his sacred concerts at the Stone Chapel still stand out as a landmark, and there can be little doubt that he raised the standards of performance to a point where Bostonians could, for the first time, fully appreciate the grandeur of Handel's masterpieces.

As a composer Selby does not deserve the neglect he has suffered. His output was small, but it was skillful, serviceable, and melodious. Two of his anthems are not fairly represented in their published state, deprived of their original accompaniment. In some of his songs and in the Magdalen psalms he had enough control of his medium to convey a tender expressiveness.

In England, Selby might have made an adequate living as a middling musician, if he had not got himself into trouble. But in ability he fell far short of the leading English musicians of the day, not to mention the many prominent Continental musicians living in London. In New England, on the other hand, he found himself at the top of the heap, once the war was over. He was one of the first resident performers and composers proficient in European art music—a style that Americans were beginning to prefer to that of Billings, even though by today's values Billings was certainly the greater man of the two. Selby's competence in the desired idiom was sufficient for the purpose. He could play, direct, teach, and compose European-style music better than anyone else in the region. There were no real masters present to compare him with. And thus, at the end of his career, he achieved a degree of esteem and renown that could never have come to him had he stayed in London.

THREE

Rayner Taylor

Rayner Taylor (1747–1825) was already forty-four years old when he crossed the ocean, and had come closer to achieving eminence in Great Britain than any other America-bound musician. Possibly the most gifted of our three composers, he arrived in Philadelphia too late in life to make the mark he deserved in the competitive musical world of that thriving city. He won esteem as the most brilliant organist in America; yet the theater, rather than the church, was the center of his career. Another factor that distinguishes him from Selby and Jackson is the French element in his background and thinking, revealed here for the first time.

Taylor has attracted the attention of several modern scholars. John A. Cuthbert's dissertation of 1980 remains the most complete study of his life and works. Victor Fell Yellin has written a perceptive essay on Taylor's career, adding some new facts. Shorter notices have also appeared.[1]

All modern writers take as their starting point the biographical sketch that appeared in the Boston journal *Euterpeiad* on January 5, 1822, near the end of Taylor's life. It was "No. 3" in a series of "Musical Reminiscences. Or Biographical Notices. Of several eminent musical characters, who have either merely visited or domesticated in America, and who are deceased, returned to Europe, or have declined [i.e., retired from] their professional avocations." Most have assumed that it was the work of John Rowe Parker, editor of the journal, since it was later reprinted, without the original footnotes, in Parker's *Musical Biography*. But Parker only "collated and compiled" this book, according to its title page; and in the journal he introduced, but did not write, the biographical sketch, hoping that it would be "recorded for posterity by a far more abler pen than mine." He wrote only the introductory paragraphs, pointing out that the subject of the biography "is too permanently established in a neighbouring city, to allow us to hope of ever benefitting by [his abilities] here." Indeed, he used part of this introduction, in revised form, in his biographical sketch of George K. Jackson.[2]

Cuthbert discovered that the real author of the main text of the sketch was Benjamin Carr (1768–1831), the composer's close friend, junior colleague, and compatriot. In a letter to Parker dated "Phil[adelphia], Dec[embe]r 7 1821," Carr wrote: "I did myself the pleasure of forwarding to you this day by the Eliza Jane [under] Captain Milton bound to your port a package containing some sketches of Musical Biography." Later in the same letter he remarked: "I have been thinking it may [be] as well not to give the title 'Musical Gossip' to the Biographical notices—for fear they may suspect who the author is—there is a sentiment in one or two of them, that I hope will not give offence, which is—that they were the greatest in their line—in giving this opinion, I had not the smallest idea to deteriorate the talent of any [other] individual . . . but if you think them calculated to give the least offence—pray soften down the sentences—they occur in Menell (violoncello) Gillingham (violin) Garrelli (vocal) as also in Mr Taylor (organist) but he is so universally allowed to be beyond all competition as an organist & Man of Science that this will inflict no wound whatever."[3]

The heading of the articles, which had been "Musical Gossip" for Nos. 1 and 2 in the series, was duly changed to "Musical Reminiscences" with No. 3, the one devoted to Taylor. Subsequent installments contained sketches of Gillingham, Garrelli, and Menell among others. In an earlier letter (June 30, 1821) Carr said that he could "lay no honest claim" to the articles, "as a literary friend is kind enough to re-write the whole from my bungling notes of the same." Nevertheless the content was presumably Carr's, and this confers considerable authority in matters of opinion as well as fact. For Carr was not only thoroughly acquainted with the subject of the notice, but was himself the preeminent musician then active in Philadelphia, with long and broad experience in all the main branches of musical performance and composition. Carr's knowledge of Taylor and his work extended back to the London years. His sketch in the *Euterpeiad* will be a frequent point of reference in this chapter.

THE TAYLOR FAMILY

Rayner Taylor was baptized at the church of St. Anne, Soho, in Westminster, on November 29, 1747.[4] His distinctive and frequently misspelled first name makes it almost certain that this baptism entry (where the name is correctly spelled) refers to the musician who is our subject. Moreover the date agrees well with the inscription on his tomb at St. Peter's Episcopal Church, Philadelphia, which stated that he "died August 17th 1825, in the 78 year of his age"—that is, at the age of seventy-seven. The two sources combine to determine that he was born between August and November 1747.

His parents, according to the baptism record, were William and Susan Taylor. These names, unlike his, are common. But an announcement of a 1767 concert, in which Taylor took part, stated that tickets were "to be had of Mr. Taylor at Mr. Taylor's Senior, in Great Maddox-Street, Hanover Square," and a later publication of Rayner Taylor's, dated around 1770, was also "to be had of Mr. Taylor in Great Maddox St., Hanover Square." Cuthbert found that a William Taylor paid taxes at that address until 1772, making it certain that he was Rayner's father.[5] This, in turn, identifies Rayner's father, in all probability, as the William Taylor who was married at the parish church of St. George, Hanover Square, on January 11, 1746. His bride's name was Susanna Petit.

The church where Rayner was christened is less than half a mile from Hanover Square. The parish of St. Anne's housed a large population of French Huguenots, who had their own chapel there. "Many parts of this parish [St. Anne's] so greatly abound with French that it is an easy Matter for a Stranger to imagine himself in France," wrote William Maitland in 1739.[6]

Susanna (Susan, Susanne) Petit, Rayner's mother, was a Huguenot by background. She was born September 22, 1725, a daughter of Jacob Petit and Marie Toueillet, and christened at the French Church in Threadneedle Street, London, on October 10. Her paternal grandfather, Samuel Petit, was probably one of the thousands of refugees who came from France after Louis XIV's revocation of the Edict of Nantes (1685), since his baptism is unrecorded in the London Huguenot records.[7]

Soho was near the center of London's entertainment world. It seems probable that one or both of Taylor's parents belonged to a theatrical family. This is the best explanation for his given name, with its unusual spelling. A family named Rayner dominated the art of rope-dancing in London theaters in the mid-eighteenth century.[8] One of them could well have been the boy's godparent, or at least a friend or relative of his parents.

A Mr. Taylor offered benefits at Drury Lane Theatre from 1728 to 1743, and from 1739 onward tickets for these events could be had at "Mr. Taylor's Grocer, in Greek-street, Soho."[9] Evidently this grocer was either the benefit giver, or his father or other relative. It is possible that one of these was William Taylor, Rayner's father. There is no evidence that his mother was a theater performer, but a member of her family may have been the subject of these lines printed in 1761: "What can have harm'd our gay Italian Belles / To make sweet Petit dance at Sadler's Wells?"[10]

Rayner seems to have been his parents' eldest child. His younger brother, William, was baptized on January 17, 1749, also at St. Anne, Soho. This time the parents' names are given as William and *Susanna* Taylor. Nothing more is known of this younger William, and there is no record of any further children of the marriage.

CHILDHOOD AND YOUTH

Benjamin Carr, in writing about the youth of a man twenty-one years his senior, must have based his information chiefly on what the composer told him. He says that Taylor became a Child [choirboy] of the Chapel Royal: "In this capacity he often attended occasions which have since become historical events, such as the funeral of Handel in 1759—that of George the Second in 1760—as well as the marriage and coronation of George the third and his estimable consort (which occurred in 1761)." Carr added the following anecdote relating to Taylor's attendance at Handel's funeral: "On this memorable and solemn occasion, his hat accidentally fell into the grave, and was buried with the remains of that wonderful composer. As Mr. Taylor's higher works of composition are of the Handelian school, the following remarks of a gentleman to whom he related this extraordinary occurrence, were highly complimentary: 'Never mind, he left you some of his brains in return.'"[11]

It was usual for boys to be recruited to the Chapel Royal at the age of seven or eight. Up to the year 1755, their names were printed in successive editions of a work called *Magnae Britanniae Notitia*. Taylor's name is not among those listed in the last edition, published in that year.[12] But he must have been admitted by 1757.[13] Official records show only that one "Reynard Taylor" left the choir on March 16, 1763, on the changing of his voice, at which time he received "the usual Allowance of One Suit of plain Cloth one hatt and band two holland Shirts two Cravatts two pair of Cuffs two handkerchiefs two pair of Stockings two pair of Shoes and two pair of Gloves," plus a cash payment of £20.[14]

The ten Children of the Chapel Royal were recruited, taught, fed, and boarded by the Master of the Children. Taylor began his term as chorister under the elderly Bernard Gates (1686–1773), but his principal teacher would have been James Nares (1715–83), who succeeded Gates as master in October 1757 and who trained many prominent musicians of the next generation, including George K. Jackson. The choristers led a spartan life; until reforms were enacted early in the next century they were bullied, exploited, and often half-starved. The master was allowed to profit from their talents. According to an observer in 1785, "The Children of the Chapel Royal made Dr Nares £100 a year by going out at 10/6 each. He gave them sixpence among them for Barley Sugar. He made of their clothes £50 a year."[15] "Going out" meant performing for hire at public concerts or theaters. R. J. S. Stevens (1757–1837) remembered that the boys frequently sang at the Italian opera house.[16] It was only in 1804 that new regulations, drawn up by the dean of the chapel, specified that "the Boys shall not be allowed to sing at either of the Play Houses and when they return from singing at the *Oratories*, the *Ancient Music* or any other Concert public or private, upon the leaving they shall have a coach to carry them home and a good supper."[17] The "Oratories" were the oratorio concerts, instituted by Handel, held at the major London theaters (in fact, at the "Play Houses") during Lent; the "Ancient Music" was the Concert of Antient Music, but this series did not begin until after Taylor's time.

Thus, membership of the choir was not incompatible with secular performing activity. There were also ample opportunities to study the organ and to learn the principles of music theory. So Taylor may have enjoyed free early training and experience of all the main branches of music in which he was to make his career.

Carr tells us that "upon leaving the school, [Taylor] was immediately in active employment as composer, vocalist, organist, and harpsichord performer." He was indeed engaged in all these capacities for four summer seasons at Marybone Gardens (1765–68). Even before that, a Marybone clipping of June 1764 refers to a song "Say what is Maria like?" by "Mr. Taylor, late of His Majesty's Chapel Royal."[18] He was one of five singers in a performance of William Boyce's serenata *Solomon* on August 6, 1765, when he was seventeen.[19] Vocal engagements continued, and on August 7, 1766, he played an organ concerto (probably of his own composition); the following year a "drinking glee" and a catch "Upon Catches and Glees" by Taylor were heard. Every season until 1768 there were performances of songs, glees, organ concertos, and a "New Cantata" of his composition. A 1767 critique of the Gardens musicians refers to "Mr. Collett, and Mr. Taylor in particular, as[,] not to mention their different excellence on the Violin and Organ, they are particularly happy in their Compositions."[20]

The concert of August 7, 1766, was a benefit offered jointly by Taylor and "Master Raworth." The following summer he joined forces with several other musicians: Thomas Lowe (c. 1719–83), a popular singer and the manager of Marybone Gardens; Mrs. Gibbons, who also sang in *Solomon* in 1767; Mrs. Isabella Vincent (1735–1802); Samuel Webbe the elder (1740–1816), later a prominent composer; and Cecilia Davies (1753–1836), the precocious young soprano.[21] Some songs by Taylor published around this time are stated in their titles to have been sung at the Gardens by one of these benefit partners, or by himself. By the age of twenty, then, he had already made headway in establishing himself as one of a set of prominent performers and as a composer of songs, glees, and organ concertos.

When Samuel Arnold took over the management of the Gardens from Lowe in the spring of 1769, he hired a new cast of performers. We next hear of Taylor in Edinburgh, where on July 29, 1769, Arne's *Artaxerxes* was produced at the New Theatre Royal for the benefit of Giusto Ferdinando Tenducci, the famous castrato. The cast included Tenducci himself as Arbaces, Taylor as Artaxerxes, and Mrs. Rayner Taylor as Mandane.

This is a significant event in several ways. It was the first time on record that Taylor had sung in an opera, and he took a part written for a castrato; this latter point will be discussed later. What is more, this particular opera was the solitary example of *opera seria* in English, on a libretto adapted from Metastasio's *Artaserse*. Thomas Arne, who composed it in 1762, was clearly trying to establish a new tradition, and although he failed to do so, the opera itself was immensely successful. Tenducci had created the very difficult part of Arbaces, which he now repeated in Edinburgh, with the addition of several Scottish airs to please the local audience.[22]

Still more interesting is the first mention of Mrs. Taylor. Who was she? The part of Mandane is spectacularly difficult and was created for the great soprano Charlotte Brent. Unless it was drastically revised for Edinburgh, Taylor's wife must have been a remarkable singer. No record of the marriage has been found, but a conjecture may be offered. A Miss Frederic, billed as a pupil of Arne, had sung the part of Dorinna in a "comic interlude," *Capochio and Dorinna*, attributed in the program to "Dr. Arne" but otherwise unknown in that composer's output, at Marybone Gardens on August 4, 1768. And in Edinburgh on April 9, 1770, at a benefit for "Mr. and Mrs. Taylor," there was performed "a new Burletta, called, Capochio and Dorinna composed by Mr. Taylor," with the beneficiaries in the title roles.[23] Could it be that Rayner Taylor had met Miss Frederic when they were both performers at Marybone, had courted and married her, and that they had gone to Edinburgh, where she not only repeated the role of Dorinna but sang a more demanding role in her former teacher's grand opera?

Against this hypothesis is the fact that *Capochio and Dorinna* was attributed to Arne, not Taylor, when performed in London. But it seems extremely unlikely that Taylor would have offered a new piece with the same name so soon after the premiere of a work by Arne. It is also improbable that Arne composed a work that is not mentioned in any account of that well-studied composer. Perhaps the Taylor attribution was the right one.[24] It is also a fact that no further performances by "Miss Frederic" in London theaters have been traced, though a Miss Frederick occasionally sang at the Haymarket Theatre in the 1770s and 1780s.

On the other hand, Cuthbert discovered the record of a marriage at St. Marylebone parish church on July 20, 1767, in which "Rayner and Sarah Taylor" signed as witnesses, and concluded that Taylor must already have been married to a woman named Sarah at that time. If Sarah Taylor was the former Miss Frederic, she would surely not have called herself "Miss Frederic" in 1768. So the identity of Mrs. Taylor remains uncertain.

Also performed at the Taylors' benefit in Edinburgh was a "Sonata on the Harpsichord by Mr. Reinagle, a scholar of Mr. Taylor's." This was Alexander Reinagle's first recorded appearance in public, at the age of about fourteen.[25]

The Taylors seem to have returned to London soon after these events. The chief evidence for this is the title page of Taylor's *A Collection of Favourite Songs and an Overture*, published by Longman, Lukey and Company, and "to be had of Mr. Taylor in Great Maddox St., Hanover-Square," his father's house until 1772.[26] The usual phrase in such cases was "to be had of the Author." It is of course possible that the "Mr. Taylor" here referred to *was* the father, and that Rayner and his wife did not return to live in London at this time.

CHELMSFORD

The following year they moved to Chelmsford, a prosperous and growing market town in Essex (its population was 2,151 in 1738 and 3,800 in 1801), some fifty miles northeast of London. It is likely that Taylor went there to take up the post of organist of the parish church of St. Mary, but his appointment is not recorded. For the first time since the sixteenth century, an organ had been erected in the church in 1772, built by the London firm Crang and Hancock, and it seems probable that Taylor was carefully selected by the parish vestry as an organist who could bring out the qualities of the new instrument. He was the tenant of a house in Duke Street from 1773 to 1776.[27]

He quickly asserted his presence. "R. Taylor, the organist" presented a summer concert at the White Horse Inn, Chelmsford, in 1773,[28] to coincide with the annual horse races, and this was to be the first of many during the following decade. At first Mrs. Taylor appeared with him, and in 1773 she sang once again the great coloratura aria from *Artaxerxes*, "The soldier tired of war's alarms." But her last recorded appearance was in summer 1775. Cuthbert notes that the following year the concert tickets were to "be had of Mr. Taylor, at Mr. Rayments, near the Black-Boy Inn," instead of "in Duke St." as in earlier years, and concludes that he had moved into lodgings.[29]

Whether his wife had died or simply left him is unknown. There is no record of her burial in the Chelmsford parish registers, nor of any child born to the couple.

Cuthbert provides details of the annual races concerts directed by Taylor. He found that Taylor's name was no longer mentioned in advertisements after 1777. Hilda Grieve assumes that he left Chelmsford that year,[30] but Taylor still described himself as "Organist of Chelmsford" at least until 1781.[31] It is possible that after 1777 he lived in London but commuted to Chelmsford for Sunday services or sent a deputy.

His work had entered a new domain, that of the parish church. Three anthems of the cathedral type by Taylor were published during this period (discussed below). Cuthbert says that they "attest to the presence of a trained choir" and "reveal that conditions at Chelmsford were not unlike those of the larger provincial cathedrals."[32] Had this been so, Chelmsford would have been unique in its time. Parishes, apart from a handful with surviving collegiate churches, had no funds to pay singers. True, many rural churches used voluntary choirs, but the music they sang was a far cry from cathedral anthems. For an unendowed parish church to support a choir and soloists of a caliber that could have attempted Taylor's three cathedral anthems was simply out of the question. Significantly, the anthems were printed in a serial publication called the *Cathedral Magazine*, where they shared the space with works by leading cathedral musicians past and present.

The singing in eighteenth-century town parish churches consisted of metrical psalm tunes, nominally sung by the congregation led by the parish clerk, but frequently led or monopolized by the children of the local charity school.[33] Grieve's history of the town shows that Chelmsford was no exception. It actually had two schools, one for forty-one boys, the other for twenty girls, founded in 1713 and 1714, respectively. As in other charity schools under the general supervision of the Society for Promoting Christian Knowledge, the children were taught psalmody. In 1717 a professional organist from a neighboring parish was hired at £1 per quarter to teach psalmody to both girls and boys: "his brief was to 'perfect' as many of the children as 'are capable of taking a tune,' and to instruct the [School] Master's apprentice . . . in 'Psalmody by Notes,' so that he could take over the teaching of the children."[34] Thus the children, here as elsewhere, learned the metrical psalm tunes by rote and were not taught to read music. They must have sung from the gallery at the west end of the church. There was no organ to accompany them until one was erected in the gallery in 1772. After that, they had to sing from behind the organ, and that must have been the situation during Taylor's tenure. In

1786 galleries were erected on each side of the organ for the children "who before, were hidden."[35]

Like many charity schools, the one in Chelmsford appointed an annual day for fund-raising, for which two visiting preachers were engaged, one in the morning, the other in the evening, and special music was performed at the services in the parish church. In 1772, shortly before Taylor's arrival, the occasion was grander than usual because it coincided with the opening of the new organ by James Hook, organist of Marybone Gardens. During the services four anthems were performed—not by the local children but "by some of the most eminent performers from choirs in London." They were conducted by Samuel Arnold, the manager of Marybone Gardens, who the following morning directed "a complete band of music" at the Black Boy Inn.[36]

The 1773 notice suggests a more modest affair: "On Sunday next, the 5th of September, two sermons will be preached at the parish church, for the benefit of the Charity Children in Chelmsford. . . . The Hymn, for the occasion, is set to music by Mr. Taylor, organist, and will be performed by the Charity Children, under his direction."[37] The charity hymn was an established musical genre in the eighteenth century.[38] It had a metrical text clearly praising the giving of funds to the poor; the setting tended to be rather more than a strophic tune, and to have one or two solo sections. Nothing of the kind by Taylor has survived.

The following year the music was once again elaborate, and evidently beyond the powers of the local choir: "During Divine Service, several Anthems will be performed by some of the most Eminent Vocal Performers from the choirs in London, and the Services of the Day chaunted; accompanied by a Gentleman of the First Eminence in his Profession, on the Organ: Also an Hymn, suitable to the Occasion, set to Music by Mr. Taylor."[39] No doubt Taylor invited Nares, his former teacher and certainly "a Gentleman of the First Eminence in his Profession," to come down with some of the Chapel Royal choir. It is possible, certainly, that one or more of Taylor's published anthems were among those performed, though none have texts specially suited to such an occasion.

The event was similar in the next two years, except that in 1776 the special hymn was composed by Nares.[40] In 1777 there was no mention of outside singers or chanting, but during 1778–80 boys were again sent down from the Chapel Royal to sing at the annual services. Grieve finds it "curious" that the school trustees paid five guineas to "Mr. Taylor . . . for the Chapple Boys" in September 1780, because she assumes that Taylor had left Chelmsford in 1777. But in fact, as we have seen, there is reason to think he kept his post until at least 1781. Cuthbert thinks Taylor remained until 1783, because a hymn of his composition was used in that year at the annual charity services and he sang in one Chelmsford concert.

One anthem of his, "Try me, O God," is in a far simpler style than that of the three cathedral anthems and does indeed suggest parochial use. Apart from an elaborate Amen it is largely homophonic. It is for three voices unaccompanied, the upper two in the treble clef, a scoring derived ultimately from John Playford's *Whole Book of Psalms . . . in Three Parts* (1677) that was occasionally found in tunebooks for urban parish choirs,[41] and that would become more popular after 1790. The two upper voices are in parallel thirds most of the time. The bass part could have been sung by the parish clerk or by one or two volunteers. According to its heading, "Try me, O God" was "set by Mr Rayner Taylor for the Musical Magazine," that is, for *The New Musical and Universal Magazine,*[42] a publication offering music for amateur domestic use. Nevertheless it is quite likely to have been written originally for the Chelmsford choir. It was reprinted in two East Anglian collections designed for parish churches: *The Psalm Singer's Assistant* (London, 1778), by John Crompton of Southwold, Suffolk; and *The Complete Psalmodist,* seventh edition (London, 1779), by John Arnold of Great Warley, Essex. In addition, Ruth Mack Wilson discovered a copy in a manuscript of parochial music.[43]

Parish organists generally had to play only on Sundays and Christmas Day; they did not, as Cuthbert suggests, have "daily church responsibilities."[44] When they did play, they were expected to improvise voluntaries before, during, and after the service, and to perform "givings-out" and interludes for the metrical psalm tunes. As we shall see, a few samples of Taylor's interludes survive in an American publication. It may be assumed that he excelled in this part of his job. On more than one occasion he was asked to play at the opening of organs in neighboring parish churches.

But the most important side of his work at Chelmsford was teaching, if we are to believe contemporary accounts. The anonymous reviewer in the *European Magazine* wrote in 1781: "His later avocations have been at Chelmsford, where he was the organist, and teacher at most of the boarding schools, and private houses, in and about that country." And in 1822 Benjamin Carr said much the same thing: "he was organist at the church and had an immense round of teaching, both at the principal female academies, and in private families."

It was in this way that almost all musicians had to earn their bread. Playing the organ, performing on stage, publishing compositions—none of these in itself brought an adequate income. Instead, such activities served to build up the musician's name, reputation, and standing, so that the wealthy parents of young ladies would pay him a handsome fee to teach their daughters to sing and play. That, no doubt, was the practical reason why Taylor offered three impressively professional anthems to the *Cathedral Magazine*. The first was duly advertised in Chelmsford when published.[45] Of course, I do not mean to rule out an additional, "higher" motive—one of simple pleasure in the act of creation. These three anthems were by far the most serious and ambitious compositions Taylor had yet attempted (unless others existed that have not survived).

Another serious effort was a set of *Six Sonates for the Harpsichord, or Piano Forte, with an Accompanyment for a Violin. Opera Seconda.* Subscriptions were invited in the *Chelmsford Chronicle* on November 3, 1780, for publication "early in the ensuing year." When the sonatas appeared, they carried a list of 118 subscribers, of whom more than half were entitled "Miss" and were presumably his pupils. A few carried titles of nobility. Also among the subscribers were Nares and other leading musicians such as Arnold, Edmund Ayrton, and Thomas Dupuis.

One other substantial composition surviving from Taylor's years at Chelmsford was the burletta *Buxom Joan,* performed at the Haymarket Theatre, London, on June 25, 1778. The libretto was by a Chelmsford draper, Thomas Willett,[46] so it may have premiered in the town, though there is no record of such an event. It was popular enough to achieve publication and to be successfully revived in Philadelphia in 1801.

While at Chelmsford Taylor evidently visited London from time to time, and he kept up with theater life there. It was probably in 1781 that he resigned his organistship, finding too many lucrative opportunities in London. His last recorded appearance at Chelmsford was on May 9, 1783, when he sang in Arne's *Love in a Village.* His charity hymn was performed that September, as already noted, whereas the following year it was replaced by a hymn by "Mr. Rogers."

SADLER'S WELLS

Taylor's next important appointment is described in Carr's knowledgeable account: "From this [his position at Chelmsford] he was called to be the composer and director of music to the Sadlers Wells theatre, a pleasing place of amusement, open during the summer months, which began to rise somewhat above the level of a mere show box for rope dancing, tumbling &c for which it was no less indebted to Mr. Taylor as composer than to [Mark] Lonsdale, who had assumed the office of author, as well as that of stage manager."

Cuthbert provides a well-researched and illuminating account of the entertainments at Sadler's Wells Theatre (fig. 5) before and during Taylor's time there. He shows that Taylor had appeared there as early as April 1784, and perhaps before that.[47] It is not known when he was engaged as full-time composer and director of music, but he was evidently in charge for at least seven seasons (1785–91). Over that period he was responsible for the music of between forty and fifty shows in all, most of them classified as burlettas and pantomimes.[48] It is impossible to know how much of the music was original and how much arranged or adapted from the work of others, or from traditional songs and dances. Several of Taylor's Sadler's Wells songs were published as sheet music (see table 9, below). His most famous achievement at Sadler's Wells was *The Champs de Mars* in 1790, to be described later.

Other London opportunities had also come his way. He sang in the Handel commemorations in May and June 1784. He composed the overture to *Circe and Ulysses,* produced at the Royal Circus on July 19, 1784. The overture was published in a keyboard arrangement, which was reviewed (harshly) in the *European Magazine.*[49] He hoped to continue his career as a church organist,

Figure 5. Sadler's Wells Theater, London, 1809 (From Ackermann's *The Microcosm of London,* courtesy Guildhall Library, London)

competing unsuccessfully for positions at two city churches, St. Giles, Crip-
plegate (1785) and St. Andrew Undershaft (1790). The preceding organist at
St. Andrew's was one of the leading executants of the day, John Worgan (1724–
90); at the trial, Taylor lost to a Miss Mary Allen, 64 votes to 59.[50]

He left Sadler's Wells at the end of the 1791 season. His music continued
to be performed there for several years. His only known activity during his
remaining year in London was at a new pleasure garden. He had played the
organ at the opening of the Apollo Gardens on May 16, 1791, and several songs
of his were published or reprinted at this time with title pages recording their
performance there. Yellin points out that Taylor later claimed to have composed "The Heaving of the Lead," a song that was included in William Shield's
popular burletta *Hartford Bridge*, premiered at Covent Garden on November
3, 1792, well after Taylor's departure.[51]

EMIGRATION

Taylor crossed the Atlantic some time in the late summer of 1792; no record
of his voyage or arrival has been traced. Another ship that had left Graves-
end, in the Thames estuary, on June 28, 1792, bound for Norfolk, Virginia,
carried a number of musicians and actors recruited by the Old America
Company of New York. They included John Hodgkinson and his wife, Bene-
dict Bergman, Joseph (Jean) Gehot, Francis Phillips, William Young, and the
composer James Hewitt.[52] But Taylor did not accompany them. Nor did he
share their fixed purpose or their assured future.

The first contemporary record of his presence in the United States is an
advertisement for a concert to be given at the Eagle Tavern, Richmond, Virginia, on September 12, 1792, by "Mr. Taylor, Music Professor, lately arrived
from London . . . and his pupil Miss Huntley, late of the Theatre Royal, Covent Garden."[53]

Miss Huntley, whose first name is not known, was probably the daughter of a male acrobat named Huntley and his dancer wife, who had frequently
performed at Sadler's Wells during Taylor's time there. Her debut was as
recent as December 20, 1790, when she sang at Covent Garden in an afterpiece called *The Picture of Paris, Taken in the Year 1790*, one of the many representations of events in France: it included the scene of Louis XVI's oath
on the Champs de Mars,[54] which may well have used Taylor's music for that
same scene as performed at Sadler's Wells (to be described later). Her next,
more prominent role was that of Polly in Shield's comic opera *The Woodman*, which actually achieved mention in *The Times*: "The character of POL-

LY, though prettily sustained by Miss *Huntley*, is yet totally uninteresting and ought to be taken out of the piece."[55]

Presumably Taylor and Huntley traveled to America together, and it is difficult not to see their flight as an elopement, and as the likely reason for Taylor's surprising emigration. We know nothing of the circumstances, nor even whether his wife was still living. If he was a widower, it does not seem very likely that Miss Huntley's parents would have objected to the match. For, although Taylor was probably more than twice her age at forty-three, he was a successful musician with considerable standing in the world they knew best—the world of the theater.

Carr's account says: "About 1792, he emigrated with his family to America." No trace or mention of any children born to Taylor in England has been found, so it must be assumed that "his family" was here a euphemism for Miss Huntley—as Yellin has also concluded. She continued to appear with him under that name in concerts until June 1798.[56] The U.S. census of 1800 shows Taylor living with a woman between twenty-six and forty-five years old, who was probably the same person as Miss Huntley (whether married to Taylor or not), but without children.

The 1810 census, however, shows him living with two women between sixteen and twenty-six, a girl under ten, and a boy under ten, without any older woman. Yellin found a record of the death in October 1811 of a boy aged one year and two months named Rayner Taylor, "Son of Rayner & Mary Taylor." He asks, "Was Mary Taylor, Rayner's wife and the mother of Rayner, Jr., the same person as Miss Huntley?"[57]

To answer this question we must return to the 1810 census report. Census day that year was August 6. The baby who died at one year and two months in October 1811 could have been the boy under ten recorded in the census, if born shortly before August 6, or could have been born shortly after, and thus not recorded. In either case it seems certain that his mother would have been living at home on August 6. Therefore the mother, Mary Taylor, must have been one of the two women between ages sixteen and twenty-six who were then in Rayner's household.[58] This age range is too young to accommodate Miss Huntley. We must conclude, therefore, that Miss Huntley had either died or separated from Taylor between 1800 and 1810. The mother of the girl under ten living with him in 1810 could have been Miss Huntley, or more probably the younger woman, Mary, who was (or became) Taylor's wife and the mother of Rayner Jr.

To return to Taylor's arrival in America in 1792: it is evident that he did not come to take up any prearranged position and that nobody (not even his former pupil, Alexander Reinagle, now living in Philadelphia) was ready to help him find his feet professionally. He and Miss Huntley moved quickly from Richmond to Baltimore, where they gave "a musical entertainment on a new plan, the whole of which will be entirely original, and his own composition" on October 1, followed by similar entertainments later in the month. They evidently intended to settle in the Baltimore area, for Taylor placed the usual advertisement offering to teach "Piano Forte, Harpsichord, etc."[59]

Yet on the very same day (October 18) he advertised in the Annapolis *Maryland Gazette,* agreeing to become organist of St. Anne's Episcopal Church, Annapolis, and to offer instruction in music in that city, by the end of the "ensuing month."[60] This suggests that he planned a weekly commute; the two cities are less than thirty miles apart, closer than Chelmsford is to London. He was responding to an advertisement by the vestry of St. Anne's Episcopal Church for an "industrious mechanic capable of teaching psalmody and act[ing] as clerk, sexton, and organist."[61] The wording may have given him pause, but he hoped for the best.

Once installed as organist, he must have tried to make improvements that were unpopular with the parishioners, or perhaps he declined to perform menial tasks. A movement was organized against him as one of those "pretenders who make themselves greater than they are." In May 1793 he announced his intention to leave Maryland, after attempting to collect the money due from those who had agreed to subscribe to his salary.[62]

There is no positive record that Taylor ever lived in Annapolis as his principal residence. Whether he was living there or in Baltimore, he now left the state of Maryland with Miss Huntley and traveled to Philadelphia, where he was to spend the rest of his life.

PHILADELPHIA

His first move was to advertise a "Nouvelle Entertainment, or Musical Extravaganza," of exactly the same kind as he had offered in Richmond and Annapolis, at Oeller's Hotel on June 28, 1793. As before, he and Miss Huntley were the sole performers. A few weeks later he placed the customary advertisement offering his services as a teacher of voice and keyboard to "the Ladies of Philadelphia." At the same time he offered for sale a grand piano made by Longman and Broderip of London.[63]

Unluckily, this was the time when a terrible epidemic of yellow fever struck the city. Most of his likely pupils left town to escape it. His response was to offer "An Anthem. Suitable to the present occasion, for public or private worship," for sale by subscription at a price of one dollar. He gave his address as 96 (North) Sixth Street. This was to be his residence until 1813, when, after a brief stay at number 62 on the same street, he moved to number 72, where he remained for a further nine years.

Significantly, the anthem was also for sale "at Carr and Co's Musical Repository, No. 122, Southside of Market Street, where may be had, composed by the same author, various comic, serious, and pastoral Songs, Overtures, lessons, etc. for the harpsichord, or piano forte."[64] Most of these must have been London editions that Taylor had brought with him.

Benjamin Carr had arrived from London in April 1793.[65] Twenty-one years younger than Taylor, he too had been a choirboy at the Chapel Royal and had begun a career as a singer and composer; he had also worked at his father's music publishing shop in London. He advertised the opening of his "Repository" in Philadelphia on July 25, 1793, and was to become one of the most important American music publishers, editors, and composers of the age. His long American association with Taylor now began. In the next decade he was to publish many compositions of Taylor's.

When the epidemic subsided, Taylor again appeared in public with Miss Huntley, this time with "another young lady" as well, at Oeller's Hotel on January 18, 1794. The principal work was "An Ode to the New Year."

A great effort was under way at this time to open an ambitious theater company under the management of Thomas Wignell, of Lewis Hallam's American Company, who had gone to London to recruit a large number of actors and musicians. For several months, the company had been waiting for the end of the fever epidemic to begin its operations at the New Theater on Chestnut Street, Philadelphia (fig. 6).

Taylor may have been approached by the company from the beginning of its first season in February 1794. However, it already had an able director in the person of Alexander Reinagle, who normally supplied and directed the music until 1808, when he was succeeded by Victor Pelissier. Taylor would be called on only occasionally.

The first documented instance of his working for the company is not until May 11, 1795, when, at William Darley's benefit, *The Brother* was produced as an afterpiece, "the music by [Charles] Dibdin, the accompaniments, with an introductory symphony, composed by R. Taylor."[66] For the many shows imported from London, normally the theater had only the printed libretto to work with, or only the libretto and a piano/vocal score. In the former case, someone had to compose or adapt new music; in the latter case, someone had to provide "accompaniments," that is, orchestrate the music found in

Figure 6. New Theater (Chestnut Street Theater), Philadelphia, 1794 (Courtesy American Antiquarian Society)

the score. Taylor was called on to perform one or other of these tasks several times during the next few seasons. In some cases, as Cuthbert has shown, he adapted music from his own English works.

One of his most successful efforts was the five-act play *Pizarro, or, The Spaniards in Peru*, premiered on May 12, 1800. This drama, written in German by August Friedrich Ferdinand von Kotzebue, had been translated into English (with much new material) by Richard Brinsley Sheridan, the foremost British dramatist of the age, and performed with music composed and compiled by Michael Kelly at Drury Lane, London, on May 24, 1799. The Philadelphia company had no access to the music used in London, so new music had to be supplied—in this case jointly by Reinagle and Taylor (in that order on the advertisement). Cuthbert plausibly conjectures that Taylor reused some of his music for *The Incas of Peru*, which had been produced at Sadler's Wells in 1790.[67]

Another significant event was the revival of *Buxom Joan* ("for the first time in America") on January 30, 1801, a considerable success.[68] In March 1805 a three-way collaboration took place, when Reinagle, Carr, and Taylor each composed the music for one act of another musical drama, *The Wife of Two Husbands*, adapted by James Cobb from a French play by Guilbert Pixéré-court.[69] Their music replaced Joseph Mazzinghi's of the 1803 London production. After about 1806 Taylor's name rarely appears in advertisements for productions at the Chestnut Street Theater.

Lacking regular employment at the most prestigious theater in Philadelphia, Taylor found work in several other venues. For a few years he had continued to give mixed entertainments or "olios." At one, in Oeller's Hotel on April 21, 1796, a violin concerto by Taylor was played by George Gillingham with an orchestra containing four other violins, a viola, a cello, a double bass, an oboe, a bassoon and a trumpet (the two last played by the same man), and two horns.[70]

There are traces of his activity in Philadelphia circus productions.[71] One of the earliest and most explicit had been on February 27, 1797, when he provided music for a new pantomime, *The Weird Sisters,* produced by a visiting French troupe called Lailson's Circus. The music was "partly selected from the works of Arnold, Arne, Matthew Locke, Shield, Dibdin, etc., etc." No doubt it included the century-old "Macbeth" music, then attributed to Matthew Locke, but actually by Richard Leveridge (1670–1758). This was still a great favorite for scenes involving witches. Taylor wrote "the whole of the accompaniments, introductory symphony, witches song, chorus, and finale."[72] Further performances of the same piece were given at Richmond in 1798 and at Fredericksburg in 1799.

Taylor also performed frequently in the Centre House Gardens, later called Lombardy Gardens (1799–1807), where his comic songs were regularly sung, "Jockey and Jenny" becoming a nightly favorite. Later he was prominent in Philadelphia's Vauxhall Gardens. As for his many appearances in readings with music, benefits, charity concerts, and miscellaneous entertainments, John Cuthbert has scoured the newspapers and found that he was an almost ubiquitous presence in the musical life of Philadelphia. But there are only a few cases where details of the music were provided, and virtually none where it is available for our inspection.

An interesting aspect of Taylor's career was his association with the University of Pennsylvania; once again, we are indebted to Cuthbert for uncovering the facts. Taylor directed the music at the university's commencement exercises at least from 1803 to 1815, and also those of its preparatory school, the Philadelphia Academy. A number of his own compositions were performed there, including a *Storm Symphony* in 1809, which unfortunately has not survived.

Taylor was a Freemason. We do not know when he took the vows, but at the consecration of the new Masonic Hall on June 24, 1811, the music included an organ voluntary, a "grand chorus" ("Raise, raise the choral strain"), and a Masonic hymn ("Supreme grand master most sublime"), all composed by "Brother R. Taylor."[73]

Evidently these sporadic opportunities did not yield a good income, for Carr was to report that "the drudgery of teaching and a scanty organ salary have been his only recompense." The salary came from his organistship at St. Peter's Episcopal Church, which has been thoroughly researched by Victor Fell Yellin.[74] Taylor was hired in the second half of 1795 at a salary of £25 per year but replaced in 1796, first by J. H. Schmidt and then by George K. Jackson. But he was reappointed on April 16, 1798, and for each year after that until 1813. Attempts were made to repair the dilapidated organ; in 1811 a subscription was raised for a new instrument, but eventually the vestry decided it could not afford one. This may have contributed to Taylor's letter of remonstrance on September 14, 1813, complaining that his salary of $90.32 was too low. Shortly afterward he was offered the organistship of another Episcopal church, St. Paul's, "with a Salary adequate to my wishes, and an Excellent Instrument to perform on," and he not unnaturally accepted, resigning from St. Peter's.[75] We do not know how much he earned at St. Paul's, but the St. Peter's vestry offered (too late) to raise his salary there to $150.

He closed the gap by teaching and miscellaneous services. The fullest information about this side of his work comes from an advertisement of 1800, offering to teach ladies "piano-forte, singing & guitar." He did not set up schools, like Jackson in New York, but assured potential pupils that they would be "punctually waited on," presumably in their own homes. He also offered to copy music from his "good stock, both vocal and instrumental (particularly for the Piano Forte)," which included "several of Handel's Oratorios, &c. and all Oratorio Songs; many of Dr. Arndt's [i.e., Arne's], Dr. Arnold's[,] Abel's, Dr. Boyce's, [J. C.] Bach's, Clamenti's, Edelman's, Goirdani's, Nicolai's, Playel's, Schobert's works &c." These names, often misspelled, referred to composers popular in London in the 1770s and 1780s; it is a little surprising that Haydn is not among them, for his music was well known there long before his visits of the 1790s. This "good stock" was also presumably Taylor's chief resource for teaching pieces. In addition, the notice offered pianos and guitars for sale, and a number of his own compositions.[76]

On October 6, 1809, Taylor became a naturalized American citizen,[77] a fact that probably spared him from internment during the war with Britain in 1812–15. Indeed, he played a marginal part in the war by arranging the military music used in 1814 by the Advanced Light Brigade at Camp Dupont, near Wilmington, Delaware. The camp existed only from September 29 to

November 30, 1814. It is known that there were bands as well as fifes and drums there, but Taylor's arrangement, *The Martial Music of Camp Dupont,* is for two flutes and piano. The publication announcement in the *Daily Advertiser* (June 29, 1815) states: "Such a volume will be very acceptable to a great proportion of our Volunteer Amateurs, as it will excite the recollection of many pleasing scenes and adventures, which were familiar to them in the tented field."[78]

By this time, in his late sixties, Taylor's thoughts might well have been turning toward retirement. But he seems to have retained his energy for several more years. On January 1, 1814, a "New Grand Romantic-Opera" by Taylor was produced, called *The Æthiop, or, Child of the Desert.* Once again, it was a British import that had arrived without its music. William Dimond's drama had been performed at Covent Garden in October 1812 with music by Henry Rowley Bishop. Only the libretto was published, and Taylor had to compose a completely new score. The show was one of the most successful of its era, being performed eleven times in its first year, revived in Philadelphia three years later, and produced in other American cities.[79]

Meanwhile he was still appearing as a singer at the Handelian Society (discussed below), as an organist at various concerts, and as an entertainer. He continued to compose at least until 1817 and to perform until 1819: the last recorded instance found by Yellin was at Mrs. De Luce's concert on February 15 of that year.[80]

The 1820 census found Taylor living alone, still at 72 North Sixth Street. In February 1820 he became a founding member of the Musical Fund Society of Philadelphia, whose object was "the relief and support of decayed musicians and their families"; funds were raised principally by the sale of concert tickets. But Taylor, though appointed one of twelve "directors of music," was too frail to participate in the society's concerts, and in 1823 he became its first beneficiary, when he was voted the sum of two hundred dollars per year. John C. Hommann Sr. (1760–1842), who was also a founding director and had "for some years acted as the trustee and Banker of Mr. Taylor[,] . . . consented to continue in the performance of the same friendly offices."[81]

Rayner Taylor died on August 17, 1825. A brief notice appeared the following day in the newspapers. He was buried in the churchyard of St. Peter's. The inscription on his tombstone is no longer legible, but its wording has been recorded: "In Memory Of RAYNER TAYLOR A distinguished professor of music, and many years Organist of St. Peter's Church who died August 17th 1825, in the 78 year of his age. This tribute of respect is erected by the Musical Fund Society of Philadelphia."[82]

TAYLOR AS PERFORMER

Taylor began his career as a singer and continued this activity to a surprisingly advanced age. After the breaking of his voice, the first definite record of his singing in public was at Marybone Gardens on August 6, 1765, when he was seventeen. The last was in 1815, when he was sixty-seven, and he may have continued for a few more years after that.[83]

A question arises as to the range and type of his voice. In later life it was undoubtedly tenor: in 1815, for instance, he sang three tenor arias from Handel's *Judas Maccabaeus*. But at Edinburgh in 1769, when he made his operatic debut in Arne's *Artaxerxes*, he took the title role. This was written as a castrato part in the alto range, with a combined range of g'–c." Was the part transposed or rearranged for a tenor, or sung at pitch by a countertenor?[84]

In 1765 he sang in Boyce's *Solomon*, and he was joined in it by four other singers: Cecilia Davies, Isabella Vincent, Jonathan Legg, and Thomas Lowe. This is puzzling at first sight, as the work calls for only two soloists: a soprano and a tenor. But perhaps the SSATB "chorus" was rendered by a quintet. Lowe was undoubtedly a tenor, and is likely to have sung the tenor solos as well as the chorus part. With both women needed for soprano parts in the chorus, it looks as if the alto part fell to Taylor, with Legg on the bass line.

In 1784 Taylor sang in the Handel commemoration. Burney's *Account* of this famous event lists the chorus singers by voice type, but it does not help us here, for a "Mr. Taylor" is listed under each of the headings "Counter Tenors," "Tenors," and "Basses."[85] Sometimes Taylor sang one of his own songs that survive in published editions. Two songs specifically printed as "sung by Mr. Taylor at Marybone" are *Bacchus* and *Sound the Brisk Horn*. They have high tenor ranges (f'♯–a" and e'♭–a"♭, respectively), but these ranges were possible for a countertenor.[86]

Some English singers used both tenor and countertenor ranges,[87] as Haydn noticed in 1791 when commenting on Charles Incledon's singing in Shield's *The Woodman*: "The first tenor has a good voice and quite a good style, but he uses the falsetto to excess. He sang a trill on high C and ran up to G. The 2nd tenor tried to imitate him, but could not make the change from the falsetto to the natural voice."[88]

In the absence of definitive information, it seems entirely possible that Taylor began his adult career as a countertenor, but that when he went to America, the high male voice was too unfamiliar to be acceptable in public,[89] so he turned himself into a tenor. He could still sing falsetto in private, according to Carr, whose account is the most reliable evidence we have of the style and quality of Taylor's singing:

> As a vocalist, Mr. Taylor has not met with that approbation to which his talents so justly entitle him. This, in a great measure, is supposed to arise from his always selecting comic songs for his public exhibitions, and the circumstance of his singing not being in the fashion of the day. In short, many of his warmest admirers have regretted that so much talent should stoop to the performance of a Vauxhall ballad; yet his merriment and vivacity in glees and catches of a humourous nature, have often led to social merriment. Sometimes among particular friends he would in perfect playfulness, sit down to the piano forte and extemporize an Italian opera, giving no bad specimen, though a highly caricatured one, of that fashionable entertainment. The overture, recitative, songs and dialogue, by singing alternately in the natural and falsetto voice, were all the thought of the moment, as well as the words, which were nothing but a sort of gibberish with Italian terminations. Thus would he often in sportive mood, throw away ideas sufficient to establish a musical fame.

Since real Italian opera was unknown in Philadelphia during this period, these satires must have been chiefly for the benefit of his English "particular friends." In public, his comic olio-type entertainments ceased in 1794, but he continued to appear as a popular singer in the circus and elsewhere for more than twenty years. Some of his later performances were serious. He may well have come into his own with the formation of the Philadelphia Handelian Society in 1813 or 1814, when his knowledge of Handel's music and the proper way of performing it must have been unequaled on the local scene.

Taylor's career as a keyboard player was equally long, and more distinguished. He directed countless performances from the keyboard in theater, concert room, and church. He played solos and organ concertos and accompanied himself and others at concerts and other entertainments throughout his life. Like all harpsichordists of his generation, he switched to the piano when the time came. Though detailed accounts of keyboard playing are rare in the newspapers of the period, Taylor gained a few plaudits, the earliest (already quoted) from 1767.

Above all, he must have been a brilliant solo organist. In those days, solo organ playing was largely improvisatory, and there are few records of Taylor's playing a work by another composer. (One such case was on March 2, 1815, when he played a Handel organ concerto for the Handelian Society, Philadelphia.)[90] For the quality of his playing, we must again rely on the judicious testimony of Benjamin Carr, who had succeeded him as organist of St. Peter's Church: "As an organist, he is second to no one. Any person acquainted with the true style of organ-playing, who has ever heard Mr. Taylor, will testify to this. Not his voluntaries alone, but each passing interlude to a common psalm tune was full of taste and ingenuity. But on various occasions, after church service, when he has obliged a favoured few who remained for the purpose with extemporaneous effusions, a never failing strain of harmony and science would burst upon the senses. Subject follows subject in quick succession, through all the mazes of modulation by the hour together."

Reinagle, Taylor's pupil, "declared unequivocally, that he conceived [one of Taylor's extemporizations] to be equal to the skill and powers of [C. P. E.] Bach himself," while "an eminent professor lately from England has often affirmed, that he considered Taylor in no degree inferior, as an Organ performer, to the celebrated S[amuel] Wesley."[91] It may be argued that Reinagle exaggerated a little out of loyalty to his old teacher. But Carr was under no such obligation. No mean organist himself, he knew very well what he was talking about and was generally discriminating in his judgments. His remarks about Taylor's singing, as we have seen, are far more moderate in their praise, which makes one the more ready to accept his high assessment of Taylor's organ playing at face value.

THEATER MUSIC

John Cuthbert has compiled an admirably comprehensive list of all Taylor's compositions that are known to him, whether or not any of the music has survived.[92] It shows that theater music was the most important and prolific branch of Taylor's composing activity, but no precise quantitative assessment can be given, because in most cases we do not know how much original music was involved in a production.

Table 8 summarizes his output in this field. Not unnaturally, the bulk of it occurred during the eight years when he was musical director at Sadler's Wells Theatre, London, and was required to provide (though not necessarily compose) music for all productions there. A fairly high rate of activity continued during his early years in America, when he was still in demand as a theater composer. Both Cuthbert and Yellin were struck by one of the few surviving contemporary comments on Taylor's music, in a detailed account of the pantomime *The Restoration of Hymen,* and the burletta *The Gates of Calais,* both premiered on April 15, 1786: "Though his music has merit, it is to be wished he would make more use of old airs."[93] In our eyes this amounts to a compliment.

Table 8. Summary of Rayner Taylor's Known Output of Music for the Theater

Years	Place	Number of Theater Works	Number from Which Any Music Survives
1770	Edinburgh	1 (*Capochio and Dorinna*)	0
1773	Chelmsford	1 (*The Midnight Mistake*)	1
1778	London	1 (*Buxom Joan*)	1
1784–91	London	19 (documented) 46 (assumed)	6
1792–93	Richmond; Annapolis	5	0
1794–1807	Philadelphia	19	2
1814	Philadelphia	1 (*The Æthiop*)	1

Among these ninety-three shows, there is not one for which orchestral parts or scores have survived. Theater fires in both London and Philadelphia destroyed most of the performing materials of the period, which of course would have been in manuscript only. Consequently our knowledge of the music is limited to what was published for domestic use with keyboard accompaniment and has survived in one or more copies: table 9 gives the complete list. It has been slightly augmented by Yellin's discovery that "The Heaving of the Lead," publicly credited to William Shield, was in fact composed by Taylor, as a manuscript of the song in the Library of Congress bears a handwritten note: "Mr. Willig: This is my last composition of which I told you. R. Taylor."[94]

What was published depended, in turn, on what was popular. It was not a case of a single publisher promoting Taylor as a composer. Various firms took on what they thought might be profitable. So his published work was not necessarily his best, either from a modern standpoint or in the view of connoisseurs of the time. "Ching Chit Quaw," for example, is very slight indeed, and could be called silly. But Carr's glowing reminiscence suggests that there was more substantial music to be heard at the theater when Taylor was in charge: "Eminent professors of music who visited this place of amusement to pass a leisure hour were astonished to find the little orchestra well disciplined, correct and effective, and were delighted with the pleasing yet scientific style of the music." The term "scientific" was customarily used in the sense of "learned" in English writings on music. It suggests dissonance, modulation, thematic development, counterpoint, and harmonies venturing beyond the I–V–IV of much popular music.

But Carr singles out three of the published pieces for special mention: "Mr. Taylor's song of '*A sailors life at sea*,' in a piece which represented the distress and return of the Guardian Frigate in most impressive dumb show,

Table 9. Surviving Music from Taylor's Theater Works

Production	Premiere	Surviving Music	Publication
Chelmsford production			
The Midnight Mistake	Dec. 13, 1773	Song, "Chelmers Banks"	London: New Musical and Universal Magazine, 1774 Repr. Philadelphia: Young's Miscellany, [1793?]
London productions			
Buxom Joan	June 25, 1778	Complete	London: Longman & Broder [1778]
The Fortune Tellers	Apr. 12, 1784	Song, "The Female Ballad Singer"	Philadelphia: Carr & Schetky [1800]
Circe and Ulysses	July 19, 1784	Overture	London: Longman & Broder [1784]
The Gates of Calais	Apr. 17, 1786	Symphony	Southwark: T. Williams, [1786?]
		Song, "La petite Savoyarde"	Southwark: T. Williams, [1786?] Repr. Paris: Imbault, [1790?]
The Mandarin	June 30, 1789	Trio, "Ching Chit Quaw"	London: S. A. & P. Thompson [1789?]
The Guardian Frigate	May 10, 1790	Song, "Jack the Guinea Pig"	London: Longman & Broder [1790?] London: Bland & Weller, [1790?] Repr. Philadelphia: Young's Miscellany, [1793?]
The Champs de Mars	July 26, 1790	"Solemn Chaunt"	London: Longman & Broder [1790?]
		Chorus, "Vive la loi"	London: Longman & Broderi [1790?]
		Song, "John Bull"	London: Longman & Broderi [1790?]
		Song, "Ça ira"	London: S. A. & P. Thompson [1790?]
Hartford Bridge	Nov. 3, 1792	Song, "The Heaving of the Lead"	London: Longman & Broderi [1792?] Repr. Philadelphia: Young's Miscellany, [1793?]
Philadelphia productions			
The American Tar	June 17, 1796	Song, "Independent and Free"	Philadelphia: Carr, [1796]
The 63rd Letter	Jan. 24, 1803	Ballad, "Edward"	Philadelphia: Carr & Schetky, 1803
The Æthiop	Jan. 1, 1814	Complete	Philadelphia: G. E. Blake, [181

and the ear-tickling and comic trio of '*Chin chet quaw*' sung in a pantomime exhibiting chinese manners and scenery[,] received for several seasons, on every night, a certain *encore;* and in a spectacle founded upon events then passing in France, the solemn and impressive solo and brilliant chorus that was sung upon the scene representing Louis the XVI. as taking the oath in the champ de mars constantly produced peals of applause."[95] One notices that Carr does not actually praise the first two songs but merely reports their popularity. The "scientific" music appreciated by "eminent professors of music" was evidently not well represented in these two published specimens.

The "Champs de Mars" scene, however, is praised by Carr as a "solemn and expressive solo and brilliant chorus." This extraordinary piece has survived in an edition by Longman and Broderip and is worth detailed discussion.[96] It concerns the momentous celebration in the Champs de Mars outside Paris of the first anniversary of the storming of the Bastille, July 14, 1790, when Louis XVI, in the presence of the National Assembly, the newly federated municipal authorities, and a vast crowd of spectators, publicly accepted the goals of the Revolution in exchange for a guarantee of his sovereignty. We know, of course, that this attempt to buy his safety would ultimately fail, for he was executed on January 21, 1793. At the time, however, the event seemed historic and appeared to bring an end to the Revolution. It was likely to appeal particularly to the majority of the British public, since the French king had accepted the form of government that they believed was the best guarantee of freedom and stability: constitutional monarchy.

Like other great events before the days of newsreel or television, it was quickly represented on the London stage in a spectacle called *The Champs de Mars, Or, Loyal Fœderation.* According to *The Times,* Taylor's score was "interspersed with a variety of the most popular Chansons now sung among the Citizens of Paris, and the original French Airs, Marches, and other Music made use of on that occasion."[97] One of these, "Ça ira," was published in Taylor's version.

For the concluding, climactic scene, both Taylor and the librettist, Mark Lonsdale (d. 1815), rose above their usual frivolities in a bold effort to capture the sublimity of the occasion (fig. 7). After grave introductory chords, the High Priest intones the "solemn chaunt":

Thus pursuing Freedom's Plan,
Kings confirm the rights of man:
Mighty shall the Monarch be,
Who nobly makes a People Free.

The first part, leading to a pause on the dominant, uses largely common chords in what was sometimes termed the "ancient style"; the second part, in halved note-values, uses more modern harmony. A quartet then repeats the chant, with the same harmonies in full four-part chords. This striking melody, simple but avoiding triteness, curiously anticipates "The heavens are telling" from Haydn's still-to-be-written *Creation*.

Then suddenly the shouts of the crowd burst forth with the words "Vive la Loi! vive la Loi! vive la Nation! vive le Roi!," each phrase answered with excited triplets in the orchestra. This must have been an electrifying moment, and it galvanized the theater audience into participation. *The Times* reported thus: "The rapturous burst of applause bestowed on the four lines chaunted in the concluding scene of *Loyal Fœderation*, at Sadler's Wells, is a tribute justly due to the respective merits of the Poet, the Composer, and the Performer—so great is the impression created by this particular part of the ceremony, that Pit, Box, and Gallery, catch the enthusiasm of the moment, as if by electricity, and *Vive le Roi! Vive le Roi!* seems to be echoed from the very hearts of every spectator."[98]

The word "chaunted" is striking. It reinforces the description of the first part on the title page ("solemn chaunt"). As the music appears to be strictly metrical, the word suggests that the lines must have been sung very slowly, making the following *vivace* section all the more exciting. Carr mentioned that "this has since had religious words adapted to it, and forms a truly valuable addition to the stock of sacred music." It was indeed quite appropriately set to a *Prayer for the Commonwealth* ("Save, O Lord, the Commonwealth; / Let thy people's rights prevail").[99]

Apart from this one case, the few surviving single songs or movements, whatever their merits, can give little idea of Taylor's methods and skills as a dramatic composer. "La petite Savoyarde," from *The Gates of Calais,* is a solo scene of some dramatic point, where the girl sings part French, part English, to her father, whom she rebuffs. The modified ternary form has a middle section that is itself a coloratura aria with long melismas. It is arranged in the published score on three staves for pizzicato violin, voice, and figured bass.

But we are fortunate in having the complete music (though not the orchestral scores) of two of his theater works, *Buxom Joan* (Theatre Royal, Haymarket, London, 1778) and *The Æthiop, or The Child of the Desert* (Chestnut Street Theater, Philadelphia, 1814). Vocal scores of operas were commonplace in England: over a hundred were published between 1762 and 1800;[100] but they were still a rarity in America. Of course, even a complete vocal score gives little idea of the full sound. The voice has to share the two-stave score

Figure 7. Taylor, "The Solemn Chaunt in the *Champs de Mars*" (Courtesy Bibliothèque nationale de France)

2

Figure 7 (cont.)

Figure 7 (cont.)

with the accompaniment. "So often in these operas the music looks inept because only the skeleton got printed and none of the flesh," as Fiske has remarked.[101] The score of *Buxom Joan* does have bass figures, which serve at least to clarify the intended harmonies.

The two works are widely spaced, from near the beginning to near the end of Taylor's long theatrical career; and, as table 9 shows, each is an isolated achievement, separated by several years from the periods in which he was most active as a theater composer. Both are products of London theater traditions, but they are poles apart in character and structure. *Buxom Joan* is an all-sung comic afterpiece in one act, set in the village life of its time, as were many contemporary works, starting with Arne's *Love in a Village* (1762). It offered familiar types and situations that would raise a ready laugh from an English audience, and later, from an American one. *The Æthiop* is a high-flown spoken romantic melodrama, with musical interludes that do little to advance the main plot. It too belonged to a fashionable genre, but fashions had altered greatly in thirty-five years. Yet there is no striking advance in Taylor's compositional style and approach between the two works, except in the overtures. If anything, the later work is musically the simpler of the two.

Buxom Joan is dismissed by Roger Fiske as "a poor burletta." Fiske points out that Willett's libretto is "based on Ben's bawdy song in Act III of Congreve's *Love for Love,* but it is dulled by bowdlerization."[102] Of course, it is also expanded from a "ballad" into a viable drama with distinct characters. If we compare *Buxom Joan* with works by Taylor's contemporaries Arnold, Dibdin, and Shield—let alone Arne, the master of English comic opera—we may well find that Fiske's assessment is valid. *Buxom Joan* has no striking or memorable song (or perhaps one, which will be mentioned below), the recitatives are wooden, and the ensembles, as in most operas of the time, are few.

Yet the writing is professionally competent, the piece is concise and well constructed (especially when we remember that the librettist was an obscure Chelmsford shopkeeper), the harmonies are often sophisticated, and Taylor succeeds in providing music to suit each character, though the characters themselves are stereotypes. He seems to be in his element in this brisk and sprightly comedy.

The story is simple, straightforward, and free of distractions. Along the lines of Goldonian *dramma giocoso,* the heroine is the only serious character; the rest are comic. Joan is a young girl whose lover, the Sailor, has gone to sea. Her mother opens the action with a recitative and bipartite aria urging Joan to marry one of her suitors, lest she become an "old maid." Joan sings, first, a pert number telling her mother she is in no hurry, then, left alone, an aria of sentiment (E flat, *amoroso*), revealing her heart's indomitable feelings for her absent lover.

The suitors come to her one by one, following the order of the old rhyme "Tinker, Tailor, Soldier, Sailor."[103] The Tinker sings cheerfully to a background of metallic clinks and bumps (presumably on plucked strings and percussion); it takes Joan only four bars of recitative to dismiss him. The Tailor, according to custom, is depicted as a melancholy wimp, and sobs while he sings; but for whatever reason, the song Taylor wrote for his namesake rises to unexpected heights of originality and skill (ex. 13). In her dismissal Joan predictably questions the tailor's virility. The Soldier, of course, enters to a march in D major (no doubt supported by trumpets and drums) and sings a technically demanding aria of empty *braggadocio*. In the scene that follows, the three suitors insult and threaten each other in an amusing catch-like Trio eight measures long. Curiously, this is printed in two forms, one "For a Bass, two Tenors or Countra Tenors," the other "For three Tenor Voices, or the highest Voice a Countra Tenor." It is to be sung "three or four times over, faster and faster."

The Sailor now makes a well-timed return to land. Joan welcomes him to her arms, and he sings the typically English, extroverted song of a "rough honest Tar" (ex. 14). After the love duet, the other three men accept the situation with surprising equanimity. Mother remains out of sight. In a tense D-minor passage, Joan accepts the sacrifices that will be demanded of a sailor's wife:

> Tho' at home I'm left to languish
> Trembling, anxious and dismay'd
> I will bear my heartfelt anguish
> When old England needs your aid.

The Sailor responds in an equally patriotic but more positive vein, switching back to D major, the key of trumpets:

> Our foes can never have their will
>   If we're at home united.
> They'll find we'll fight like Britons still
>   Till all our wrongs are righted.

This forthright reminder of the American war segues into an energetic tribute to George III, in which Joan joins her four admirers, and so the opera ends.

Example 13. Taylor, *Buxom Joan*, No. 6, mm. 31–42, and following recitative

When *Buxom Joan* was revived at the Chestnut Street Theater in 1801, it seems that some Philadelphians found it "wholly unworthy of the stage," because of the slightly risqué elements that remained even in the cleaned-up text. Presumably the loyal plaudits at the end were either omitted or drastically modified.

Ironically, the premiere of Taylor's *The Æthiop* (or *The Ethiop* or *The AEthiop*—the spelling varies) had to be postponed to make way for stage representations of the American victory over Britain at the Battle of Lake Erie

Example 14. Taylor, *Buxom Joan*, No. 8, mm. 8–12

in September 1813. But the work itself has no patriotic element. It was based on an English play by William Dimond, which had been put on at Covent Garden, London, as a "grand romantic drama" in 1812 with music by Henry Bishop (1786–1855). It belongs in a long line of operas set in the exotic lands of the East, depicting Western travelers exposed to the mercies of evil Ottoman or Arab functionaries, who generally want the heroine for themselves or for the ruler's harem. Mozart's *Die Entführung aus dem Serail* (1782) and Boieldieu's *Le Calife de Bagdad* (1800) are famous precursors, and there were several English ones also. Dimond's libretto is pretentious and often obscure, deliberately introducing obsolete words such as *boon* ("How boon are the hours after set of the sun") and *thrid*. Bishop's opera was an expensive failure, and his score was not printed until a collected edition of his works was brought out. But the book was published, and Taylor was soon commissioned to provide new music for it.

The work falls into a category that was generally called a "musical drama" on the London stage of the period, in which the principal characters did not sing, but in which there were "some ten or twenty musical numbers including several choral or concerted ensembles."[104] There is little point in recounting the complex story here, since hardly any of it was set to music, but the libretto has been reproduced in facsimile as a prelude to Victor Fell Yellin's imaginative realization.[105] Some of the numbers are untexted marches and dances (including a graceful "Pas seul"); others are short pieces of action music, with or without voices (eight to sixteen measures). The "Finale" is a mere eighteen measures of bland C-major harmonies. Presumably, audiences were not prepared to tolerate any lengthy musical numbers going beyond simple songs or dances. The same was true of London audiences in this period, as the librettist John Robinson Planché (1796–1880) remembered: "Ballads, duets, choruses, and glees, provided that they occupied no more than the fewest number of minutes possible, were all that the playgoing public of the day would endure. A dramatic situation in music was 'caviare to the general,' and inevitably received with cries of 'Cut it short!' from the gallery, and obstinate coughing and other signs of impatience from the pit."[106]

The most substantial numbers of The Æthiop,[107] apart from the overture (which will be considered in its own right), are three strophic songs and one duet, and a few short scenes where music and action advance simultaneously. The songs and duet are in a pleasant but innocuous style, with little or no attempt to depict the situation, character type, or geographical context. "The Camel's Bell" has a cheerful, catchy tune and imitates a bell in the accompaniment; the singer (Zoe) is hoping to hear that sound, which would herald the return of her husband, Alexis, but the music shows no trace of the anxiety expressed in the text. Instead of Alexis, the wicked *cadi*, Benmoussaff, enters, and clearly has designs on Zoe. A trio follows: Zoe cries "Mighty man! if I surrender, Pledge me first a solemn vow," Benmoussaff swears eternal love, and Alexis secretly observes Zoe's apparent acceptance of the *cadi*'s advances. Again, Taylor did not seize the opportunity offered by this dramatic situation. He wrote a pretty tune over an Alberti bass (ex. 15), with no vocal ensembles except a unison "Fal la la." (Of course, the Alberti figure may be merely a pianistic arrangement of an orchestral texture.) A dance between Zoe and Benmoussaff leads to a scuffle when Alexis intervenes, but the music for this is merely a short dance marked "Faster by degrees."

Example 15. Taylor, *The Æthiop*, Trio, mm. 5–18

Another scene, headed "Musical Colloquy" in the score, comes at a high point in the subplot, where Benmoussaff has Alexis arrested by guards (who sing in three-part chorus), and Zoe rushes in to plead for his release. Taylor's music does convey a sense of urgency here, less through harmony or declamatory singing than by the rapid-fire rhythm of the short vocal exchanges (see ex. 16). But it is only "Allegretto." Here the restriction to two staves is particularly oppressive, and it is possible that the full score would show a richer and more dramatic musical scene such as Yellin has devised in

Example 16. Taylor, *The Æthiop*, Musical Colloquy, mm. 1–11

his reconstruction. Yet it is curious how little resourcefulness Taylor shows here in either melody or harmony. He was limited not by his own capabilities but by the audience's patience and comprehension.

A much more glowing assessment of this scene, and of the whole work, is offered by Yellin in the introduction to his edition.[108] It must be said that Bishop's setting of the same libretto for the London stage is not much more adventurous than Taylor's, and, unlike his, was a complete failure with the public.

The only place in Taylor's published score where he attempts to write even faintly exotic music is in a short chorus entitled "The Bezestein" that depicts the colorful bustle of a bazaar. Here (ex. 17) he may have drawn inspiration from Osmin's song "Ha! wie will ich triumphiren" in *Die Entführung*,[109] though without Mozart's telling avoidance of regular four-bar phrases. In an even shorter "Subterranean Chorus" he conveys romantic gloom by means of C-minor unisons (ex. 18), a convention that may also derive ultimately

Example 17. Taylor, *The Æthiop*, "The Bezenstein," mm. 1–13

Example 18. Taylor, *The Æthiop*, "Subterranean Chorus," mm. 1–8

from Mozart (specifically the Fantasia in C Minor, K. 475)[110] and which he had already presented in the slow introduction to the overture.

As it happens, the stock of surviving Taylor overtures is somewhat larger, although they too exist only in piano reductions. They will be considered under "Instrumental Music," below.

DOMESTIC SONGS: ENGLAND

Taylor composed songs prolifically; and since there was a sure market, a great many of them were published. As many as seventy-one (including two duets) are extant in printed form, covering a period of more than half a century. Although at least twenty-three of these were composed originally for public performance in the theater or pleasure gardens with orchestra, their publication was obviously for domestic use, and thus they are generally arranged for keyboard accompaniment.

It is clear that in both Britain and the United States amateurs often accompanied themselves on the harpsichord, piano, or possibly harp, and the scores are designed for this mode of performance. Before 1800 they are generally restricted to two staves, the upper stave carrying both the vocal melody and the right-hand part, which largely doubled the voice. In some London publications a third stave carrying an independent violin part is present as well. If there is room on the last page, there is often an arrangement of the melody on one stave for English guitar (gittern), "German flute" (flute), or clarinet.

Songs were nearly always strophic, with additional stanzas of text printed after the music. The preferred form is binary, with "symphonies" before, between the two halves, and after. A handful of Taylor's songs, instead, are sectional, with two or three sections in contrasting tempo and meter.

In the English phase of his career, Taylor published twenty-nine songs.[111] Twenty of these were performed publicly: thirteen at Marybone Gardens (1756–58) or Apollo Gardens (1791–92), four in the theater, and three at other unknown public events. Most of these show clear signs that their accompaniments were originally orchestral. There are two written apparently for drinking clubs.

Perhaps because most of the songs were designed, in the first instance, for public performance, they seem to be aimed principally at male rather than female tastes. If women were beginning to control music-making in the home, men were the more likely frequenters of theaters and public gardens, not to mention clubs. Most of the texts revel in the pleasures of life—one, sung at Marybone Gardens, is actually called "Invitation to Pleasure." There are four "Anacreontic" or drinking songs and three hunting songs—both widely popular genres at the time, almost stereotypes. Six are pastoral, invoking either the familiar classical arcadia with its Damons and Chloes, or a slightly more contemporary world of streams and village greens, but with the general message that we should cast aside our worries and inhibitions and enjoy ourselves while we can. Most of these are essentially comic and imply casual and promiscuous sex. Three songs are about naval or military heroism. Finally, one ("Summer") is simple nature description. Perhaps because of its universal appeal, it was the most reprinted of any of Taylor's songs, and he repeated its pretty imitations of birdsong in later songs throughout his life.

Arguably the best of these "public" London songs is *Tomorrow. A Favorite Song, Written and Sung, by Mr Jefferys*, published by Longman, Lukey and Company in about 1770. Nothing is known about the author, Jefferys, or when or where he sang the song. It is of the comic-pastoral variety, about a coquettish Chloe who is brought to yield to Damon only when he feigns interest in Phyllis. It is one of the few that retains its violin line, giving a better idea than usual of how it would have sounded when sung in concert.

The twelve-measure introduction has an energetic violin part that is not always easy to play on the keyboard (ex. 19). The vocal melody is strong and cheerful, modulates as expected to the dominant (where the violin resumes its running sixteenths in a four-measure interlude), then to the relative minor. The extended ending (ex. 20) uses the title word with telling effect. The repeated phrase "I'll tell you to-morrow" well expresses the character of "the pert one," and the last four measures of example 19 round off the song. The plot develops in the three following stanzas, and the concluding line is Chloe's "Today if

Example 19. Taylor, "Tomorrow," mm. 1–13

you please—we'll ne'er think of Tomorrow." The theatrical nature of the song
is obvious and could be imitated to some degree in the drawing room. It also
shows how much Taylor's art depends on full realization of his harmonies.

In contrast, the six songs Taylor published in *A Collection of Favourite
Songs and an Overture adapted for the Harpsichord* (c. 1772) seem to represent a new decision to cultivate purely domestic songs and to publish them
himself. The title page says "Book 1ˢᵗ," though no sequel is known to have
appeared. Its wording is ambiguous as to whether the songs, as well as the
overture, were "adapted" for the harpsichord, but none of them are known
to have been publicly performed. Some do suggest orchestral effects; the last
even specifies "Flutes." But that need not imply that they are arranged from
orchestrally accompanied songs. It was becoming increasingly fashionable
to imitate orchestral effects in keyboard music, and Taylor's accompanied
sonatas have been singled out for mention in this respect by Stanley Sadie.[112]

What is striking is that the texts of this set seem on the whole much more
calculated to appeal to feminine tastes than those of the public songs, apart

Example 20. Taylor, "Tomorrow," mm. 32–40

from one hunting song. Two of them, "A Scotch Song" (ex. 21) and "Never doubt that I love," express constancy and romantic love rather than casual sex. The other three are comic-pastoral, but two refer distinctly to a wedding as the desired consummation. "A Scotch Song" has a delicately perfumed melody in the fashionable pseudo-Scots idiom of the day, but Taylor shows that he is a real composer by "scientifically" extracting a motive from the melody and using it in various ways in the accompaniment.

DOMESTIC SONGS: AMERICA

Nicholas Tawa, in an admirably thorough study of the American parlor song of the period 1790–1860, has classified songs by subject matter.[113] By far the commonest type, he says, is the song of affection, which he breaks into five

Example 21. Taylor, "Scotch Song," mm. 1–18.

subdivisions. He notes a gradual progression, after 1810, away from light-hearted sex: "Love turns serious. Its sadder aspects dominate."[114] His other categories (mortality and time; death and lamentation; alienation; sacred songs; criticism of society; praise of nature; moral lessons) are all much less common, and nearly all his examples of these, with the exception of those in praise of nature, date from after 1830.

This aversion to sexually suggestive songs is summed up in the title of a song book published at Boston in 1808: *The Nightingale, or Polite Amatory Songster.* The antipathy seems to have been already strong in America well before 1800. Several categories of Taylor's London songs do not appear at all in Tawa's classification of all American songs. After he came to Philadelphia Taylor virtually gave up publishing songs devoted to drinking, pleasure, or sexual license. The eleven London songs known to have been reprinted in

Philadelphia consist, according to my classification, of three heroic, three comic-pastoral, two hunting, two romantic, and one in praise of nature.

Of the comic-pastoral ones, which tend to condone free love, two ("De tout mon coeur" and "En verité") have not survived in their American editions, which are known only through advertisements. But in the third case, "Jockey and Jenny," originally sung by Miss Wingfield at the Apollo Gardens, London, we can make an interesting comparison. The song's plot is similar to that of "Tomorrow." For the American market the text was sanitized, regardless of the damage done to rhyme, scansion, grammar (shaky enough even in the original version), and musical accent. It is no longer about carefree sex, but about respectable courtship leading to love and marriage:

JOCKEY AND JENNY

London version
Printed for the Author, [1791–92]

Philadelphia version
Printed for the Author, [1794]

In a secret wish'd for Bow'r,
  With fair Jenny playing,
Jockey pass'd the noon-tide Hour,
  Both had been a maying;

Near a shady Myrtle Bow'r
  JOCKEY once was straying
JENNY chanc'd to pass that way
  JENNY had been a maying

Love had made the Shepherd bold,
  And her charms were killing;
Yet the Nymph was coy and cold,
  Never to be willing.

Love had made the Shepherd sad,
  Her disdain was killing
For the Nymph to hear the swain
  Seem'd never to be willing.

How can am'rous Jockey gain
  All the Joys of Leisure?
Ev'ry Art he tries in vain,
  Jenny's deaf to Pleasure.

How can hapless JOCKEY now
  Improve this fair occasion?
JENNY still, what e'er he says
  Is deaf to all perswasion.

See says he yon turtle dove
  Cooing chaste, & billing;
But to hear the faithful swain
  Still she was not willing.

Now to leave her seem'd inclin'd,
  Says he'll fly to Molly;
He prefers the Nymph that's kind;
  Pride is nought but Folly.

Now to leave her seems inclin'd
  Says he'll fly to MOLLY
He prefers the Nymph that's kind,
  Pride, he says is folly.

Fearing to be left alone,
  Jenny grew relenting;

JENNY, knowing well his truth
  Her mind with fear now filling

Rather than have Jockey gone,	Soon resolv'd to hear the Youth
Sweet she smil'd consenting.	While he to wed was willing.

'Tis as well, says she, to stay,
    Parting is but Sorrow;
Love shall conquer here to-day,
    Rivals may tomorrow.

In the two-stave format lies another difference between the English and American situations. In England, most song basses were provided with figures, or with additional notes for the right hand in small print, or both. Whether they were or not, a moderately well taught English amateur could be expected to fill in the necessary harmonies. As Sadie says, the singer "could easily accompany herself at the keyboard, playing the independent right-hand part when not singing, and otherwise supplying a bass and perhaps some intermediate harmonic support from the figures."[115] He does not say that she also doubled the voice part with her right hand, but I suspect that this was normally the case.

In America, also, "One can be reasonably certain the amateur vocalists usually accompanied themselves," Tawa states. But the ability to realize a figured bass was not to be assumed. Moreover, most songs had only the voice part in the upper stave. Tawa writes, "Apparently, the singer first studied the song by playing the bass part with the left hand and the melody with the right. Once learned, the vocal line could then be sung while both the treble and bass parts of the accompaniment were played on the piano."[116]

Tawa is inclined to attribute this practice to the composers' desire "to avoid the performing difficulties that would discourage players living in an America where competent keyboard instruction was unavailable or scarcely come by in most communities." When after 1800 some songs appeared on three staves, with an independent treble part for keyboard, he attributes the change to the increasing number of keyboard teachers from Europe.[117]

But this is an unconvincing explanation. For one thing, the same change had taken place in Europe a few years earlier. Haydn's songs were printed on two staves until his English canzonets were published in London in 1794. The earliest firmly datable set of songs published in London with a fully written out two-stave keyboard accompaniment seems to have been Bonifacio Asioli's *Twelve duettos* (London: Birchall, [1792]). Publishers in Paris, Mainz, and Vienna were little, if at all, ahead of London in this move.

Furthermore, the left-hand parts in many eighteenth-century songs are quite active, and in the "symphonies" some songs also have elaborate right-hand parts. If Americans could play these, why couldn't they also play more difficult right-hand accompanying parts? The more likely explanation is that whereas English amateur singers were used to filling in accompaniments under the vocal line, Americans, brought up on English songs printed in a largely two-part texture, but unable to make use of the bass figures, had become accustomed to the thin sound that resulted when they were played as written. Their deficiency was not in the fingers, but in the mental capacity (derived from training and experience) to conceive a vocal line and a full accompaniment simultaneously. Indeed, Tawa himself supplies evidence supporting this conclusion. Even after full accompaniments on two staves had become the norm, a writer in 1822 still had to urge singers to play the right-hand part as written, "never to play the song part, as is generally done."[118]

Thus, a musician such as Carr or Taylor coming from England would feel frustrated at being compelled to impoverish the harmony of his songs. It was Carr who took the lead, in America, in the printing of songs on three staves with independent right-hand parts; he published a set in this format at Philadelphia as early as 1794. In his *Musical Journal for the Piano Forte* (1800–1803) he allowed Taylor one song with figured bass ("The Faded Lily")—the only such concession in the entire journal—and one with a full two-stave accompaniment ("Sophrosyne"). Otherwise Taylor had to be content with the old format, with perhaps a few added notes in small print.

Example 22 compares the original figured-bass accompaniment for part of Taylor's song "Never doubt that I love," one of the "romantic" songs from his c. 1772 *Collection*, with the revised piano accompaniment that he provided when the song was printed in Carr's *Musical Journal* in 1800. (Staves 1 and 3 are from the London edition, with the figured bass editorially realized in stave 2. Staves 1 and 4 represent the Philadelphia edition.) One sees how much of the intended harmonies was lost, and also how Taylor attempted to reduce the loss by means of a few added notes in the left-hand part, and to lessen the gap between voice and bass by transposing part of the bass to a higher octave. In another republished song Taylor used a broken-chord figure to fill in missing harmonies.[119] A set of eight songs published in the *Philadelphia Repository* (1800–1803) was even more restrictive. The songs are limited to one small page each, and all but one are typeset rather than engraved, which further hampered the possibility of a complex keyboard texture.

However, in some of the new songs Taylor wrote for the American public, he clearly tried to make the best of the situation by writing two-part harmony that would not sound as if something was missing, but would be complete in itself. An interesting example is "The Kentucky Volunteer,"[120] one of

Example 22. Taylor, "Never doubt that I love," mm. 1–19: London and Philadelphia versions compared

his first American songs and certainly the first of them to express heroic patriotism in the American context (ex. 23).

"The Faded Lily," mentioned above, was published in the *Musical Journal* in 1801. It is much more original and sophisticated than most of Taylor's published songs, venturing on an unfamiliar kind of chromaticism as well

Example 23. Taylor, "The Kentucky Volunteer," mm. 9–17

Example 24. Taylor, "The Faded Lily," mm. 1–11, with editorial realization

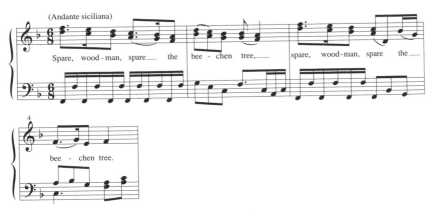

Example 25. Taylor, "The Beech Tree's Petition," mm. 7–10

Example 26. Henry Russell, "Woodman, spare that tree," mm. 15–18

as attempting to illustrate the drooping lily in its melodic contour (ex. 24, with editorial realization). This was one of two Taylor songs singled out by Carr for praise, and it may also have been one of "the best of his compositions" that Carr said were "consigned to his shelves," until he rescued it from oblivion, more as a personal tribute to his older contemporary than out of any hope that it would be profitable.

After the *Musical Journal* ceased publication in 1804, Taylor's activity in song publication slackened off considerably. John Aitken published three of his songs singly between 1807 and 1810; George Willig published two more around 1810, of which one, "The Beech Tree's Petition," was commended by Carr. Its words, by the Scottish poet Thomas Campbell, began "O leave this barren spot to me, Spare, woodman, spare the beechen tree." They anticipated the famous Victorian ballad "Woodman, spare that tree" by Henry Russell, which was to be an instant success when published in 1837. Both songs are sentimental, in the sense that they exaggerate the emotional significance of the subject, but the sentimentality is more discreet in Taylor's version of the key phrase (ex. 25, p. 99) than in Russell's of a quarter-century later (ex. 26, p. 99). Taylor's version, like his other songs from this period, is still printed on two staves.

Taylor's final effort was *A Collection of Favorite Songs, from the celebrated new poem Lalla Rookh, written by Thomas Moore Esq*[r], published by G. E. Blake, Philadelphia, in 1817 as "No. 10 of Blake's Musical Miscellany" (fig. 8). To write three songs on texts taken from a poem by a major contemporary author shows a newly serious approach, a late and tentative step toward the Romantic art-song. It can also be seen as an answer to Carr's highly regarded *Six Ballads from the Poem of The Lady of the Lake* (1810) and *Four Ballads from . . . Rokeby* (1813), both selected from romances by Sir Walter Scott. Moore's poem itself, written under pressure from his publisher, was in a sense an answer to Scott. Longmans and Company (London) in 1814 had offered Moore three thousand guineas on delivery of "a metrical romance on an Eastern subject, which should contain at least as many lines as Scott's *Rokeby*."[121] *Lalla Rookh, an Oriental Romance,* issued in 1817, exploited the craze for the East that had swept Europe for two or three decades and was also making its way in America (*The Æthiop* being another instance). The romance won instant popularity, and several British composers quickly mined it for the lyrics that Moore had interspersed among the narrative prose and poetry, probably with musical settings in view.[122] Taylor wasted little time in following suit.

The kind of nostalgic melancholy that was Moore's specialty was not, perhaps, the mood that suited Taylor best. In the first song, "The Maid of Bendemeere," he fell back on his birdsong imitations, taking full advantage of the piano's new high notes (ex. 27), though he added this footnote: "N.B. In the second Verse leave out the Symphonys the words not requiring those Bird tones." In the second song, "Come hither," he ignored the voluptuous aura of the harem and wrote a good specimen of his pretty, cheerful manner.

Example 27. Taylor, "The Maid of Bendemeer," mm. 5–9

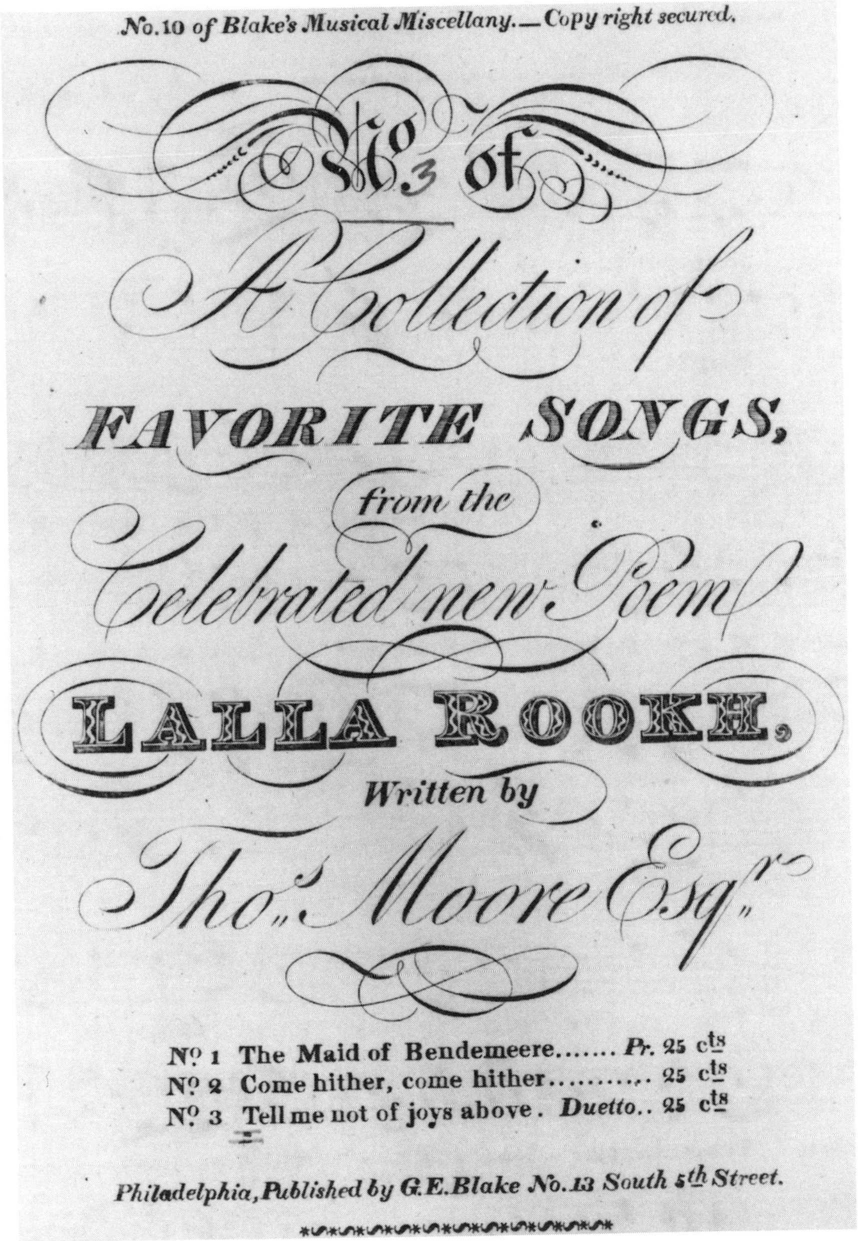

No.10 of Blake's Musical Miscellany.—Copy right secured.

No. 3 of

A Collection of

FAVORITE SONGS,

from the

Celebrated new Poem

LALLA ROOKH,

Written by

Thos. Moore Esqr.

Nº 1 The Maid of Bendemeere....... Pr. 25 cts

Nº 2 Come hither, come hither.......... 25 cts

Nº 3 Tell me not of joys above. Duetto.. 25 cts

Philadelphia, Published by G.E.Blake No.13 South 5th Street.

Figure 8. Taylor, "Tell me not of joys above," title page (Courtesy American Antiquarian Society)

The third song, "Tell me not of joys above," is the most significant. In Moore's romance, the Princess, mounted on horseback,

in passing by a small grove heard the notes of a lute from within its leaves, and a voice, which she but too well knew, singing the following words:

Tell me not of joys above,
If that world can give no bliss,
Truer, happier than the love
Which enslaves our souls in this!

Tell me not of Houris' eyes;
Far from me their dangerous glow,
If those looks that light the skies
Wound like some that burn below!

Who that feels what Love is here,
All its falsehood—all its pain—
Would, for ev'n Elysium's sphere,
Risk the fatal dream again?

Who, that midst a desert's heat
Sees the waters fade away,
Would not rather die than meet
Streams again as false as they?

The tone of melancholy defiance in which these words were uttered, went to Lalla Rookh's heart;—and, as she reluctantly rode on, she could not help feeling it as a sad but sweet certainty, that Feramorz was to the full as enamoured and miserable as herself.

Despite the context, Taylor chose to set the poem as a duet for two equal voices (surely sopranos). But this time, though he could not uproot the classical basis of his style, he matched his music well to the serious, disillusioned self-questioning expressed by the poem (fig. 9). Accompanied songs by now were printed on three staves as a matter of course, but Taylor still indicated orchestral instruments, and even wrote *Tasto solo* at certain points, suggesting that pianists in America, at least, were still in the habit of filling in chords, even in a fully realized accompaniment.

Carr spoke of two of Taylor's songs as "delightful specimens of that melodious flow of air and harmony which formed the style of the last century." Picking up on this, Charles Hamm wrote that "the reasons for his lack of success as a song writer here are clear: he offered Americans a type of song harking back to the generation of Thomas Arne, now old-fashioned in music and text, in no way addressing itself to new moods and tastes in this coun-try. . . . Taylor is an attractive and interesting figure to historians, but his songs held little interest for postwar Americans."[123]

In fact Taylor was notably successful as a songwriter in the United States. Americans at this time, or at least many of them, seem to have looked to British musical leadership, and to like what they heard, whether old-fashioned or not. Only the coarser, male-oriented features of some British song texts had to be avoided. There was a demand for patriotic and heroic songs, which Taylor met quite well, using a musical *topos* that was just as suitable in the United States as in Great Britain. Besides the eleven British songs reprinted in Philadelphia, forty-two songs by Taylor were newly published there, one of the largest totals for a resident composer,[124] and at least five of these were reprinted, including two patriotic ones, "Vive la liberté" and "Citizen Soldiers." Although his friend Benjamin Carr may have indulged him in a few cases, no publisher throws away money on this scale, and we must conclude that Taylor's songs met with an appreciative American public.

GLEES, CATCHES, CHORUSES

Taylor made a modest contribution to the repertoire of the glee and the catch, genres primarily associated with male drinking clubs. About a dozen of them were published in London, mostly in collections or periodicals, and mostly for three male voices (atb or ttb). The subjects are the usual ones of hunting, drinking, the pleasures of love, and nature. There are also three satirical "Epitaphs" in catch form, such as "Under this ground Lies Thomas Round," misleadingly listed by Cuthbert under "Sacred Vocal Works." This was the only one reprinted in America. One apparently newly composed glee by Taylor was published in *The Philadelphia Gazette* in 1800. Another, "Sophrosyne, thou guard unseen," survives only in an arrangement for solo voice and piano. The music of these pieces is craftsmanlike but in no way distin-guished or unusual.[125]

Extended works by Taylor for voices and orchestra are known to have been performed at Chelmsford, London, and Philadelphia—occasional pieces, usually under the generic title of hymn, ode, or cantata. Perhaps the most interesting is the one composed jointly with Reinagle in memory of George Washington, to accompany a monody read by Thomas Wignell at the Chest-nut Street Theater in late December 1799.[126] Unfortunately, the music of all these works is lost.

The same is true of his *New Morning Hymn*, a work for two "Ladies

Figure 9. Taylor, "Tell me not of joys above" (Courtesy American Antiquarian Society)

Figure 9 (cont.)

Amateurs," two professional soloists, semichorus, chorus, and orchestra in at least six movements, which was performed at the Philadelphia Handelian Society's Concert of Sacred Musick on March 20, 1815.[127] Its text was a poem by Michael Fortune beginning "Behold the grey ey'd morning dawn."

CHURCH MUSIC

Taylor never directed a trained, professional church choir, and the anthems he composed with such a choir in view may never have been performed. On the other hand, he was involved with parochial church music through much of his career. Once again, there was a clear difference between his English and American experiences.

In England he was chiefly in demand as an organist. Indeed he was apparently hired at Chelmsford to take advantage of a new instrument. His powers are known to have been considerable, and he would have improvised interludes between verses of metrical psalms as well as voluntaries. We can gain an idea from examples 28 and 30 (discussed below) of the type of interludes that he might have played at Chelmsford and elsewhere. They do not seem particularly remarkable today, but for a country congregation used to singing unaccompanied they must have had a brilliant effect.

As far as vocal music was concerned, he would have been expected to see to the correct performance of existing metrical psalm tunes, led by the children's choir, rather than to provide new compositions. Some years after he had left Chelmsford, three or four tunes by him were published in a collection for dissenters, Thomas Williams's *Psalmodia Evangelica* (London, 1789).[128] One was named "Chelmsford." There is no direct evidence that he had used any of them at Chelmsford parish church, and if he did they would have had different texts (old metrical psalms rather than new hymns). It is quite likely that they were commissioned by Williams, who included new tunes by a number of leading musicians of the day, including one by Arnold.

All these tunes reached American collections, and one of them, "Stepney"—a fuging tune—gained considerable popularity on both sides of the Atlantic with the text "Hark, hark, how all the watchmen cry."[129] When Carr, with Taylor's assistance, began publishing collections of church music to demonstrate the proper Anglican traditions, he included one of Taylor's English tunes with a full prelude and interludes for organ, "Limehouse," now set to Psalm 95 from Tate and Brady's *New Version of Psalms* (ex. 28)—a text that might have been used with this tune at Chelmsford, if indeed he composed it when he was there. The prelude establishes the firm, upbeat character

Example 28. Taylor, Psalm 95 ("Limehouse"), mm. 1–21: score order modernized

of the tune. In a nice touch, reminiscent of aria or concerto form, it antici-pates in the tonic key the cadence that will close the first part of the tune in the dominant. The two upper voice parts may have been sung by women's or men's voices, or both.

But when he became organist at Annapolis, his organ playing was so lit-tle appreciated that it seems to have cost him his job. And at Philadelphia, where he was organist of St. Peter's Church from 1796 to 1813, he had to reckon with the views of William White (1748–1836), who was not only rector of Christ Church, Philadelphia (the mother church of St. Peter's), but also bish-op of Philadelphia and the chief architect of the Protestant Episcopal Church. Bishop White, in some respects a high churchman, was a pioneer in the in-troduction of chanting in American worship, where Taylor's advice was in-valuable; but, like many other clergy of his time, he was critical of flamboy-ant organ solos. He wrote: "concerning interludes and voluntaries, nothing contrary to good taste or decency should be tolerated for the gratification of private whim, much less in violation of all regard to religion and decorum," and he condemned "licentiousness . . . conspicuous in some places, in those light airs, which are calculated to send people dancing out of the church."[130] It is difficult to say whether the bishop would have regarded the organ part of example 28 as "contrary to good taste or decency."

Taylor, therefore, joining with Carr and the other musicians connected with Philadelphia's Episcopal churches, concentrated his efforts on chants for the prose psalms and liturgical texts. Ruth Wilson has written a compre-hensive account of the use of chants in American churches at this time.[131] She has shown that Taylor was not only "one of the most important church com-posers of this period," but that his advice and experience were indispensable to Benjamin Carr, the leading publisher of Episcopal music.[132] The other musicians who guided the liturgical music of the American church at this period were George K. Jackson, of New York and then Boston, and the Bal-timore musician and publisher John Cole (1774–1855), also an Anglican im-migrant. Taylor, as the senior member of this group and with his Chapel Royal background, was naturally looked up to as an authority.

It was Cole who first called in Taylor's help, to supply his arrangement of an existing English chant for the Venite for an appendix to the second edi-tion of *The Beauties of Harmony* (1805), where it was printed among the chants and responses "as performed at Christ Church and Saint Paul's Baltimore" (Cole being organist at St. Paul's). The Venite was sung daily at Morning Prayer. Originally identical with Psalm 95, it was shortened in the American church to seven verses, with two verses of another psalm added. Taylor contributed chants and other liturgical music to several other Philadelphia collections published by Aitken and Carr. Most notably, there are eleven of his liturgical pieces in *The Churchman's Choral Companion to his Prayer Book*, compiled by Dr. William Smith, another leader in the liturgical movement.[133]

These compositions are workmanlike miniatures offering little scope for originality, but Taylor set about his task with grace and skill, and in one case with academic learning, when he composed a reversible chant (ex. 29) on the model of Dr. William Crotch's famous chant *per recte et retro*.[134] The bass notes and chords of the first chant, as well as the very simple melody, are heard in reverse order in the second. Several of Taylor's chants were reprinted in later publications.

Taylor was also recruited by Carr to provide service music for St. Augustine's Roman Catholic Church, Philadelphia, where Carr was organist. Jointly the two men compiled a setting of Vespers "composed by R: Taylor & B: Carr with Selections from Purcell, [Samuel] Webbe & others."[135] Taylor's part was to compose new chants for the five Vespers psalms, which he treated as a continuous composition. Example 30 shows his music for Psalm 111,[136] *Beatus vir*, which is essentially an Anglican chant. Nine verses and the Gloria Patri are laid out below it. Then follows the interlude, designed to modulate from the key of Psalm 111 (A major) to that of Psalm 112 (D major). Taylor skillfully touches on the flat side of the new key to expunge any lingering effect of the previous tonality. These interludes are less exuberant than the ones Carr later added to Taylor's Anglican chants.[137] Taylor also contributed an *Ave Maria* for duet, chorus, and organ: it sounds much like a simplified Anglican anthem.

In quite a different class from all this utilitarian church music are the anthems that Taylor composed without any immediate purpose in view. Three appeared in England in the *Cathedral Magazine* between 1776 and 1778,

Example 29. Taylor, reversible chant

Example 30. Taylor, Psalm 111 (*Beatus vir*) and following interlude

and one in America as a freestanding publication in 1793. Here he was unhindered by clerical restraints, or the limitations of parish choirs. He must have relished the chance to try his hand at a form he had known well since boyhood. He could stretch his technical capacities and release his creative impulses to their fullest extent.

The three cathedral anthems are accomplished examples of their genre. They are verse anthems typical of their period. Each has several sections for one or two solo voices, in varying key, tempo, and meter, including declamatory recitatives, and ends with a four-part chorus. There is a contrast in mood and style between the two penitential anthems, "Hear my crying, O Lord" and "Hear, O Lord, and consider my complaint," and the third one, "I will give thanks unto thee," which is essentially a hymn of praise ending with a triumphant hallelujah. In all three, the emphasis is on the solo voice, which is called upon to sing arias of some technical difficulty. The general idiom tends to strike the modern ear as Handelian, but it is well to remember that Handel deliberately modeled his oratorio style in part on the English anthem.[138]

"Hear my crying, O Lord" ends with a fine Amen, a full-dress fugue of ninety-nine measures. But perhaps the most imaginative movement in these three anthems is the final section of "Hear, O Lord, and consider my complaint." The text is taken from two nonadjacent verses of Psalm 17. Taylor had the idea of making them into a dialogue between the alto solo and the chorus. The alto begins, "Mine enemies compass me round about to take away my soul," with an agitated organ accompaniment. When he has finished, the chorus answers, in free counterpoint, "Up, Lord, disappoint them, and cast them down." The alto begins its melody again, but this time the chorus interrupts (ex. 31) in a forceful unison. After a passage over a dominant pedal, suggesting the end of the anthem is near, the alto begins its text a third time, on a new phrase (ex. 32); the chorus interrupts still more impatiently in a rising sequence and then takes control with stabbing contrapuntal entries only a quarter-note apart, over powerful harmony leading to a last-inversion dominant seventh with a fermata. The final phrase ends in a resounding plagal cadence.

In this passage Taylor combines not only his own performing specialties (countertenor and organ) but the best of his composing skills, including those derived from the stage. He is enough in control of his medium to create a quasi-dramatic scene within the confines of a hallowed ecclesiastical tradition. In Carr's words, "Mr. Taylor's talents are various. As a composer, he stands upon the highest ground, both as to science and originality, as well as to knowledge of effect." Such talent found few practical outlets in his career, but it did ensure that whatever musical tasks were required of him could be executed with complete confidence, and with abilities to spare.

Like "Hear my crying," Taylor's only surviving fully fledged American anthem, "The souls of the righteous are in the hands of God," was headed "An Anthem for Two Voices" (meaning two solo voices and chorus) when it was published in Philadelphia in 1793.[139] Although, of course, it could have been written in England and brought over as part of the composer's large music library, this is made less likely by the fact that it is largely homophonic, with simple harmony. It is not, however, a parochial piece. The solo parts are as elaborate as in a cathedral anthem. As Cuthbert puts it, "it seems likely that although the work displays some concessions, the composer had not yet become fully aware of the limitations of Philadelphia's musical capability."[140]

Evidently this publication was not a success, as there was no sequel. Taylor did write further anthems for special occasions, as Cuthbert has pointed out. "Thus say the Lord" was sung at St. Peter's Church on May 9, 1798.[141] "If we believe that Jesus died" was performed at a "Grand Selection of Sacred Music" offered at St. Augustine's on June 20, 1810, which was a kind of

Example 31. Taylor, Anthem, "Hear, O Lord, and consider," closing section

Example 32. Taylor, Anthem, "Hear, O Lord, and consider," conclusion

miniature version of the Handel commemorations in Westminster Abbey. But neither has survived, and it seems likely that in both of them Taylor was forced to submit to the limitations of his musical forces, though he was free to invent elaborate organ accompaniments, since he was to play them himself. A *Hallelujah Chorus* of twenty-eight measures does survive, in a single copy of an edition without imprint; it may have been one performed at Philadelphia in 1814.[142] It is for three voices and keyboard and is an effective piece along Handelian lines.

Example 32 (cont.)

INSTRUMENTAL MUSIC

Considering that the organ was Taylor's main instrument, the amount of his organ music surviving is pitifully small, consisting of a few interludes and the Rondo on the hymn *Adeste Fideles.* The latter was printed in Carr's *Masses, Vespers,* . . . (1805) and has been reprinted in a modern edition.[143] It is a successful specimen of its kind, with considerable variety of key. Indeed, in Bunker Clark's view, it is "the most adventuresome of all his keyboard sets, including those for piano forte."[144]

For harpsichord or piano, Taylor published several sets of variations on popular tunes of the day, including one on his own song "Ching Chit Quaw." They are purely routine pieces, repeating the tune over and over again with different figurations. If they have any charm or interest, it is generally due to the quality of the tune, which is poor in the case of "Ching Chit Quaw." A few marches, dances, and quicksteps survive, both in manuscript and in print, but they are quite trivial in nature. Perhaps the most interesting is "Peace (America and Britannia), A New March," which was published at the close of the war of 1812–15. It takes the form of a new melody that could be played as a counterpoint to Philip Phile's popular "Washington's March," now known as "Hail Columbia" (ex. 33).[145] Though musically insignificant, it may provide a clue to Taylor's political feelings. A Rondo in G, published at Philadelphia in 1796, is a bright and effective piece, with an amusing theme in close canon between the two hands (ex. 34). A Capriccio, performed by Taylor on June 6, 1798, at the Old Southwark Theater, has not survived. One elementary four-hand duet was published at Philadelphia in the 1790s.[146]

The more important keyboard works are those that aspire to some kind of sonata form, with or without "accompaniments" for another instrument. In 1780, having already published several shorter pieces, Taylor decided to begin a numbered Opus series, and on November 3 he placed an advertisement in the *Chelmsford Chronicle* soliciting subscriptions for "Six Divertimentos, with a Ground, Adapted for Young Practitioners, Opus I" and "Six Sonatas for the Harpsichord with an Accompaniment for the Violin. Opus 2." They were to be published "early in the ensuing year." Both duly appeared, printed for the author by Longman and Broderip. The Divertimentos have survived only in a Philadelphia reprint of 1797.[147] They are short and technically undemanding, though surprisingly ornate here and there; most consist of two movements, the first in a miniature sonata form, the second a dance or rondo.

The sonatas appeared with a revised title, noted above, accommodating the piano as an alternative to the harpsichord. They have earned mention by William S. Newman in his magisterial survey, *The Sonata in the Classic Era*. They are well written and substantial, rather "busy," and, unlike many accompanied sonatas of the day, they have some sections where the violin is independent of the keyboard. They consist of two movements (except No. 6, which has three). Only four of the sonatas have a first movement in full sonata-allegro form; in the others it is in ternary form. Example 35 shows the opening of the first sonata. One of the most attractive is No. 3 in B-flat major, with a particularly melodious violin part. It can be said, though, that Taylor did not equal the inventiveness and power shown by his former student Alexander Reinagle in his accompanied sonatas of nearly the same date (London, 1783).

Example 33. Taylor, "Peace," as a counterpoint to "Washington's March," mm. 1–3

Example 34. Taylor, Rondo in G, Allegretto, mm. 1–9

Example 35. Taylor, Sonata for Piano with accompaniment for Violin, No. 1, first movement, mm. 1–5

Example 36. The song "Ça ira"

Example 37. Taylor, *A Lesson . . . to which is added . . . Ça ira:* theme

"A favorite Lesson and Rondo for Harpsichord or Piano Forte with Accompaniments for a Violin and Violoncello" by "Raynor Taylor, Organist of Chelmsford" was advertised by Longman and Broderip in the *Public Advertiser* for August 26, 1776, but no copy is known. The word "lesson," as we have seen, was sometimes used as a synonym for "sonata," though some pedagogical intention no doubt remained. In the case of *A Lesson for the Piano-Forte or Harpsichord to which is added the favorite air of Ça ira with Variations* (London: Longman and Broderip, [c. 1792]) the "lesson" is presumably the first movement, which is followed, after a short *adagio* link, by the variations. But the first movement is itself linked to "Ça ira," the famous signature tune of the French Revolution (ex. 36); its main theme clearly refers to it (ex. 37). We have seen that Taylor had already treated this theme in the theater in *The Champs de Mars*. The popularity earned by that production may have encouraged him to compose the *Lesson with Variations*, and Longman and Broderip to publish it.

This is perhaps Taylor's best sonata-form movement for keyboard, and it is his last. Its second theme is far from conventional, being unsettled by syncopation and chromaticism. There is a full development, featuring both themes and passing through several keys, including G minor, on its way to the recapitulation in G major. The second movement consists of the theme, eight variations on it (including one in the parallel minor and one marked "Largo. Andante"), and a Conclusion—which returns effectively to the theme, meter, and tempo of the first movement.

Surviving in a manuscript at the Library of Congress are six fine sonatas, attributed to Taylor, for violoncello with figured bass, each in three movements. By their nature, these are likely to be early works, for the genre was already old-fashioned in Taylor's youth: Sadie identifies James Hook's Op. 6 (1782) as the last English set of cello solos.[148] Newman says that they "belie their era and the light, witty songs for which Taylor is best known. They come much closer to a late Baroque cross between the styles of Handel . . . James Nares . . . and Samuel Arnold. Put differently, they are elegant, noble, well-conceived pieces composed, without special originality, according to the tried-and-true melodic and harmonic formulas of late-Baroque writing." Newman suggests that they may have been written for Taylor's Edinburgh acquaintance, the distinguished cellist J. C. G. Schetky (1737–1824); this would place their likely date at about 1770.[149] No doubt the manuscript was part of the personal library Taylor brought with him from London.

Of all this music, only the six Divertimentos (Op. 1) and the first of the sonatas (Op. 2, No. 1) were printed or reprinted in Philadelphia. Presumably because of disappointing sales, no further sonatas by Taylor were published there, and few by anyone else.[150]

ORCHESTRAL MUSIC

In the course of his long life Taylor composed much orchestral music. The organ, harpsichord, and violin concertos, and the *Storm Symphony* written for the University of Pennsylvania, are gone, along with most of the operatic overtures. What we do have is a group of six overtures or symphonies (the two terms were often interchangeable in English eighteenth-century usage) spread over much of Taylor's career. All survive as arrangements for keyboard, with at most a few indications of orchestration. They are listed in table 10. While they cannot give us much idea of how Taylor wrote for the orchestra, they do allow us to explore his writing for instrumental textures as well as his approach to form.

The earliest was printed as a sort of introduction to six songs. It may never have been an orchestral piece; as already pointed out, orchestral indications were often added to keyboard pieces, presumably to influence the way they were played. It begins with a "binary sonata-form"[151] movement in the up-to-date *galant* style, with many passages of repeated bass notes, such as the terse second theme shown in example 38a.

Table 10. Taylor's Surviving Overtures and Symphonies

Title	Date	Movements: Tempo, Key, Meter (Number of Measures)	Scoring Indicatio
Overture, in *A Collection of Favorite Songs and an Overture*	c. 1772	Allegro moderato, C, c (71) Andante, F, c (16) Minuetto: Moderato, C, 3/4 (60)	Oboe soli
Overture in *Buxom Joan*	1776	Allegro, B♭, 3/4 (92) Rondeau e Gavotta: Presto, B♭, ¢ (74)	Soli Oboes
Overture to *Circe and Ulysses*	1784	Allegro, G, c (95) Andante, C, 2/4 (83) Rondo: Giga, Vivace, G, 6/8 (79)	Soli
Symphony, *The Gates of Calais*	1786	Vivace, D, c (91)	Flauti Soli
(?Overture, MS., Library of Congress, M1.A1, pp. 123–27)	n.d.	[Rondo], D–d–D, 2/4 (80) Aria grazioso, D, 3/8 (48) March, D, c, & Quick Step, D, 6/8 (52)	Corni Soli
Overture, *The Æthiop*	1814	Larghetto—Allegretto—Allegro— Larghetto, c, ¢ (42) Rondo: Allegro—Andante— [Allegro], C, 2/4 (112)	Clarinetto, Flauto, So Violin, So Violincell

(a) First movement, mm. 22-25

(b) Second movement, mm. 15-16

Example 38. Taylor, Overture (1772)

The Andante, also binary, is in the Scots taste, exemplified by the "snap" rhythms and the characteristic cadence (ex. 38b). The Minuetto is pleasant, and built mainly on six-measure phrases.

The overture to *Buxom Joan* has a crisp opening movement in a very similar style, though in triple time. It is also in binary sonata form, with the extra feature that the first theme (an emphatic descending arpeggio, ex. 39a) is freely inverted when it recurs at the start of the second half (ex. 39b). Inversion is also employed in the hectic rondo, which, despite having three episodes, takes little more than a minute to play. This little overture is a well-conceived introduction to a miniature comic opera.

By 1784, in the overture to *Circe and Ulysses*, Taylor had moved to full sonata form for his main movement, with a twenty-three-measure development touching on minor keys and a recapitulation of both the principal themes. Again, the first movement is strong and incisive. The Andante is scored on four staves for cetra,[152] flute or oboe, and "organized piano forte" (a combined piano and organ);[153] but it is not entirely clear whether this is how it was played in the theater or is merely an innovative arrangement for domestic use. The texture is interesting, but the tune is commonplace, as is the concluding rondo.

For *The Gates of Calais* Taylor wrote a one-movement "Symphony" that is a simple rondo, with prominent parts for two flutes. It is still essentially in the *style galant*.

(a) mm. 1-6

(b) mm. 39-44

Example 39. Taylor, *Buxom Joan*, Overture, first movement

The overture, if that is what it is, that survives in a five-page copyist's manuscript at the Library of Congress, with its title no longer decipherable but "Composed by R Taylor," is also in the *style galant*. But its concessions to popularity—a rondo replacing the usual sonata-form opening movement, and a march and quickstep at the end—plus the location of the manuscript, combine to suggest that this was a piece written for America, perhaps to introduce one of Taylor's entertainments in the Philadelphia circuses or pleasure gardens. Or it could have been played on the piano at one of his appearances with Miss Hunter, with the "Corni Soli" passages representing mere imitations of two French horns. The D-minor episode in the first movement adds a touch of seriousness, and it is followed by a chromatic cadenza link that suggests a piano rather than a solo violin.

The overture to *The Æthiop* is of a different order from the early group and is the only one that strives to set a mood for the drama that is to follow. The most original part is the introduction (fig. 10). Romantic gloom and mystery—feelings seldom met with in Taylor's music—are immediately captured by the C-minor opening for unison (presumably strings), soon repeated in the still darker key of E-flat minor. Faster sections lead quickly to an agitated climax, followed by a return to *larghetto* and a half-close using an augmented-sixth chord (the octave bass in the last measure should obviously be G, not B flat). The rondo that follows is in Taylor's more habitual manner, but it has some surprises in it. A clarinet introduces the amiable theme in C major, a version of the tune Taylor had used for the 1796 Rondo (see ex.

OVERTURE.

Figure 10. Taylor, *The Æthiop*, Overture (Courtesy Eda Kuhn Loeb Music Library of the Harvard College Library)

34, above).[154] An episode in A minor starts with *pizzicato* strings. Another shifts to A major, and to *andante*, where a solo violin plays an ornate melody that sounds at first like a variation on the main rondo theme. A link returns to C major, where a cello solo plays a bona-fide variation. The next episode returns to C minor and touches on E flat. Finally the main tune is heard in a loud orchestral unison, followed by a brief coda. Although not without flaws, this overture shows an effort of imagination on Taylor's part and a desire to move beyond classical norms.

THE SIGNIFICANCE OF RAYNER TAYLOR

Taylor was a musical all-rounder. From quite early in his career until near the end, he was in demand as an organist and a singer, and pursued careers in both the theater and the church. In America he was considered an authority on both the traditions of Anglican service music and the practices of the London theater. In his composing, too, he developed many different styles: cathedral and parochial church music, comic songs for the theater and public gardens, domestic songs and glees for all tastes, serious keyboard and chamber music, classical orchestral music, melodramatic opera. And, like all his colleagues, he earned his daily bread as a teacher.

The high plateau of his career was certainly in London, where he was the indispensable musical factotum at Sadler's Wells for eight seasons. His triumph came in 1790 with *The Champs de Mars,* when his music was greeted with shouts of applause night after night and the *Times* so far forgot itself as to praise a native English composer. Coming to Philadelphia at a relatively late time in his life, he never quite established the leading position that might have been his due on grounds of merit and experience. That place was already shared by his junior compatriots, Reinagle and Carr.

Taylor was a truly gifted composer. This is quite evident from the few cases where he had the opportunity to give of his best, such as the three cathedral anthems, some of the sonatas and overtures, and a few serious songs. It is tantalizing to think that some of his choicest theater music was probably burned, while the "best of his compositions were confined to his shelves," according to Carr's account, and are now mostly gone. Surviving instead are numerous published compositions, especially songs, most of which involve concessions to the limited skills of amateurs, to the parsimony of publishers, and to the narrowness of popular taste.

FOUR

George K. Jackson

George Knowil Jackson (1757–1822) was one of the most talented composers among the group of British immigrants. In America he was venerated as a learned musician, but he failed to translate this reputation into financial success, and his motive for coming to America is hard to discern.

Until Charles H. Kaufman's 1968 thesis,[1] the fullest biographical account was that of H. Earle Johnson,[2] who like all earlier writers had largely relied on the only contemporary notice, the one published by John Rowe Parker two years after the composer's death.[3] In this case, Parker himself is the likely author. He had lived in the same city as Jackson for many years and was in a position to interview his children. The last two paragraphs of the essay are adapted from the introduction to the biography of Rayner Taylor in *Euterpeiad*,[4] which was also probably written by Parker, though the biography itself was by Benjamin Carr.

Kaufman, on the basis of primary sources, corrected many errors of the earlier writers and produced the first accurate and complete account of Jackson's life. In particular, Parker had given Jackson's year of birth as 1745, which was universally accepted until Kaufman found the record of his baptism.

FAMILY AND EARLY LIFE

George Knowil Jackson was baptized at the parish church of St. Cross, Oxford, on April 15, 1757, as the son of Joseph Jackson, musician. He was probably born a few days earlier. While it was not unknown for parents to wait a year or two after the birth of a baby before presenting it for christening, this is unlikely to have been the case here, for Kaufman reports that another child of the same father was baptized at St. Cross in the spring of each of the years 1758, 1759, and 1760. That was the end of the matter, for the father had died in October 1759, and his last child was baptized several months after his death.

No record of Joseph Jackson's marriage has been found, and his wife's name is not known. He was a prominent violinist in Oxford musical life, leading the orchestra in the concerts at Holywell Music Room, under university

auspices, from 1748 until his death. In his last year, in March 1759, he introduced the first benefit concert there, in which he played "a Concerto and Solo
on the Violin."[5] He was granted "privileged" status by the university, which
was awarded to "certain . . . townsmen on the grounds that [it] provided a
necessary background for academic studies."[6] He did not, however, hold the
degree of bachelor of music, although he is credited with that honor in the
entries recording the baptism of one of his sons and his own burial.[7]

Joseph Jackson was also a composer, who published several songs. A volume consisting mostly of his manuscript compositions has survived.[8] They
include songs with accompaniments for strings and continuo, music for an
untitled pastoral opera, keyboard pieces, an overture in full score dated 1753,
and "Fire Work Music" for winds and timpani. Though only three works are
individually attributed to Joseph Jackson, many unattributed ones are in the
same hand, and the spine of the volume has a red leather label with gilt let-
tering: "M.S.S. I. Jackson."

After the elder Jackson's death in October 1759, Handel's *Alexander's Feast*
was performed at Oxford "for the Benefit of Mrs. Jackson (Widow of the late
Mr. Jackson, first Violin) and her Family."[9] A set of six of his sonatas for violin and continuo was published, also for the benefit of the widow, whose
financial situation must have been precarious.

Little is known of George Jackson's childhood. His education and prep-
aration for a musical career became assured when he was appointed one of
the Children of the Chapel Royal, under James Nares (1715–83), who was
Master of the Children throughout Jackson's time there. There is no record
of the date of his admission, but it was most likely around 1765, some eight
years after Rayner Taylor's. Parker states that he was made a "surplice boy"
at the Chapel Royal in 1773. This is misleading. It was in that year, on October 22, that he was dismissed from the choir after the changing of his voice,
receiving the customary outfit of clothes and the sum of £20.[10] But he left
the royal service at that time and did not return as a "gentleman" (adult singer) of the chapel.

He may have been the Jackson who was an unsuccessful candidate for
organist of All Hallows, Barking by the Tower, in 1770 (thirteen-year-old City
organists were not unknown; on the other hand, Jackson was a very common name). It was certainly he who was elected organist of St. Alban, Wood
Street, on December 2, 1774, defeating his opponent, John Jee, by eighty-two
votes to twenty-six. At this time Jackson was seventeen, while Jee was about
twenty-eight.[11] This post brought Jackson an income of £24 per year.[12] In 1779

he was made a member of the Royal Society of Musicians, still under the single Christian name George.[13]

According to Parker, "Dr. Jackson was married in the year 1787 to the eldest daughter of Dr. Samuel Rogers, Physician, London, by whom he had eleven children." When his wife died in New York in 1822, her name was listed as Jane and her age as fifty-six.[14] A Jane Rogers, daughter of Samuel and Jane Rogers, was baptized at St. Botolph Bishopsgate, London, on March 25, 1764; this is likely to have been the future Mrs. Jackson, despite a two-year discrepancy in her age. However, no record of the marriage has been traced.

Samuel Rogers had been married to Jane Bosworth at St. Botolph Bishopsgate on October 11, 1749. Seven children of the marriage were baptized at the same church, as follows: Samuel (1750), Mary (1750), Ann (1752), Thomas (1753), Jane (1764), William Barnabas (1765), and Margaret (1767). This agrees with the list of subscribers to Jackson's 1791 *Treatise* (discussed below), where the following are listed after Samuel Rogers M.D.: Wm Rogers Esqr King Street, Miss Rogers Newington, Miss M. Rogers [Newington]. However, it is unlikely that Jane was the *eldest* daughter in 1787 (as Parker stated), because the Miss Rogers listed in 1791 must have been either Mary or Ann. It was customary to list the eldest living unmarried daughter of a family without a first name or initial. Miss M. Rogers was the youngest daughter, Margaret.

Jackson's record of public performance in London is meager. Simon McVeigh's exhaustive database of London concerts from 1750 to 1800 lists nearly five thousand events in all. As McVeigh says in the guidelines to the database, "While further searches may reveal further concerts, it is unlikely that there will be a significant number of these." Jackson's name appears only twice. In each case, he was performing a harpsichord concerto (probably his own) at a tavern in the City of London.[15]

He was certainly an active composer in his youth, but the chronology is difficult to establish because neither the published nor the manuscript sources of his music can be exactly dated. The bulk of his musical library is preserved at Illinois State University. One volume, already mentioned, was clearly inherited from his father and is mainly made up of Joseph Jackson's compositions. But it also contains a "Lesson" and "Minuett" by "Geo. Jackson" and an unfinished song, "Ye myrtle wreaths," by "G. J.," all evidently dating from George's youthful period before he had started to use his middle name or initial. And at the end of the volume, in a different hand, are three sonatas for two violins and bass. They are immature in style and belong to a genre that was on the way out in George's youth. He may well have composed them in his Chapel Royal years as a pupil of Nares and entered them in blank pages of his late father's volume of music.[16]

There are many later compositions in his own hand in other volumes of the collection. The most numerous are songs, hymn tunes, and canons, but with a few exceptions it is difficult to be sure which of them belong to his London period. His arrangement of "God Save the King" for chorus and orchestra obviously does, and it was probably performed, since the instrumental parts were copied.[17] Later, certainly before 1789 (although it is impossible to know exactly when), he began publishing his compositions

No doubt Jackson, like most musicians, gained his livelihood from teaching. Some light is thrown on his teaching career by one of his publications, *A Treatise on Practical Thorough Bass*. It was in print by 1790. It contains an "Advertisement," which explains that "This Treatise . . . was written for the Improvement & exercise of my Scholars," and the dedication, to the earl of Rochford, begins: "Your Lordships acknowledged taste & judgment in Music would naturally have led me to solicit your Patronage even if I had not some claim to it from the honor of having assisted your Lordship in this Part of Polite Education." It seems then that his teaching was at least in part devoted to thorough-bass, or, as we would put it, harmony and counterpoint (though in the case of Lord Rochford's "polite education" this is not entirely clear). Thorough-bass, unlike piano playing and singing, was considered to be a male branch of the art of music, so it is likely that many of his pupils were boys and men.

Analysis of the list of 145 subscribers to the *Treatise* suggests how he may have built up his teaching connection. There are a few parish organists, and a number of people with addresses in East London and the adjoining suburbs, which was the area of his residence and of the church where he was organist. The more influential subscribers were Samuel Arnold (1740–1802) and Edmund Ayrton (1734–1808), Nares's successors at the Chapel Royal;[18] Philip Hayes (1738–97), professor of music at Oxford; and several other Oxford connections, including the music seller Richard Firth, Hayes's publisher. The Reverend Robert Nares (1753–1829), son of Jackson's teacher and a distinguished writer on language and history, was also a subscriber, and it is interesting to note that he attended Westminster School from 1767 to 1771.[19] So did William Henry Nassau de Zuylestein (1754–1830), later fifth earl of Rochford, dedicatee of the *Treatise*, who was at the school from 1768 to 1771.[20] A third name, "Revd Mr Lindsey, Newington," probably refers to the Reverend James Lindsey (born 1756/57), who also attended Westminster School before entering Trinity College, Cambridge, in 1773.[21]

All three of these Westminster alumni were slightly older than Jackson, but it seems likely that as a gifted boy in the Chapel Royal, with a particular competence in thorough-bass, he was brought in to teach music at nearby Westminster School, perhaps on the recommendation of Dr. Nares. This might have started as early as 1770, when he was about thirteen years old. In 1786 the younger Nares became usher (assistant master) at Westminster and perhaps recommended Jackson to other Westminster boys who wanted to study music.

Several clergy are listed among the subscribers. Among them, surprisingly, are three prominent Baptist ministers: Samuel Stennett (1728–95), his son Joseph, and John Rippon (1751–1836). Jackson's affiliation was otherwise Anglican/Episcopal throughout his life. The origin of the Baptist connection is not known. It could be linked to his earliest publication, *Dr. Watts's Divine Songs* (since Isaac Watts's hymns were popular in Independent and Baptist circles rather than among Anglicans). This work was probably intended for private use, as it includes several songs of a clearly secular (though moral) variety. It is quite possible that Jackson assisted Rippon in the production of *A Selection of Psalm and Hymn Tunes*, which eventually appeared in about 1792, and that he asked for Rippon's support in return. Against this, however, it must be said that Rippon did not use any of Jackson's own tunes, unless anonymously.

JACKSON'S MUSIC DEGREE

In 1791 Jackson received an honorary doctorate from the University of St. Andrews. The circumstances of this degree are somewhat veiled. Degrees in music, unknown on the Continent, had been a peculiarly English (rather than Scottish) phenomenon. At Oxford and Cambridge the doctorate could be earned by submitting a substantial composition, which had to be approved by the professor of music and then performed at the expense of the candidate. It did not imply in any way that the recipient had been educated at the university; indeed, no university offered a course of instruction in music at the time. The minutes of the Senatus at St. Andrews record the following:

Library. Jan^ry 8th 1791
Sederunt Rector, D^r McCormick, Dr Forrest, Dr Flint
The university agree to confer the Degree of Doctor of Music upon George Knowil Jackson Author of a Treatise on practical Thorough Bass with general Rules for its Composition and Modulation dedicated by Permission to the Earl of Rochford.[22]

The date of this minute was just five days before the *Treatise* was deposited at Stationers' Hall. It must be assumed, therefore, that the assembled members of the Senatus had in front of them a printed copy of the work.

But in normal circumstances, merely submitting a treatise, however learned, to a Scottish university would not earn a degree. No earlier music degree from any Scottish university has been uncovered, though in 1706 John Abell was admitted for trial for the doctorate.[23] Why did St. Andrews confer one on Jackson? He had no known connection with the university, and as far as is known, he never visited Scotland, not even to accept the degree. No satisfactory explanation of this surprising award has so far been proposed.

A clue lies in another group of subscribers to the *Treatise* who were medical men: Samuel Rogers, M.D.; William Turnbull, M.D.; "Mr. Furnace, surgeon, Stratford"; "Mr. Church, surgeon, Islington"; and Baron Thomas Dimsdale (1712–1800), the pioneer of inoculation who had been ennobled by Catherine the Great, empress of Russia. Perhaps Mr. Furnace, in nearby Stratford (an eastern suburb of London), provided Jackson's introduction to the others, including Dr. Rogers, who had become his father-in-law in 1787.

It is in this medical connection that we find the likely link with St. Andrews. Turnbull received his doctorate from St. Andrews in 1781, while Rogers signed one of the two testimonials supporting another medical doctorate (Thomas Bradbury's) in the same year. Turnbull, after receiving his own degree, in turn signed testimonials on behalf of others, including one addressed "To Doctor Flint professor of medicine in the University of St Andrews" on March 30, 1790. James Flint was one of the four men on the Senatus who granted Jackson his degree. It seems more than likely that Turnbull, and perhaps Rogers as well (since nepotism was hardly frowned on in the eighteenth century), addressed letters to Dr. Flint proposing a musical doctorate for George Jackson.[24]

Meanwhile, Jackson had resigned his post as organist in 1790. The vestry minutes of St. Alban's Church record a decision on October 7 to announce a vacancy "in the room of Mr. George Jackson who has resigned."[25] There is no sign in the minutes of any troubles or disputes. Since this was his only known salaried post, which he could have retained for life if he had so desired, the resignation suggests some pending change in his life, such as a move away from London. It was just at this time that Jackson was actively building up a body of publications.

LONDON PUBLICATIONS

Table 11 lists all the works that Jackson published in London. They were not given opus numbers until 1791, but for convenience I will refer to them consistently by the numbers they eventually acquired. At that time, Jackson seems to have decided to use the publications to improve his standing as a composer and teacher. Collectively, they are calculated to show the range of his abilities: they cover church music, secular and sacred songs, instrumental music, learned academic composition, and a teaching method.

The various reissues, with altered title pages, show rather clearly the timing of Jackson's planned self-promotion. They are set out in table 12, in six chronological stages that I have labeled A to F.

In stage A, what became his Op. 1 was published. W. Barclay Squire assigned a date of "[c. 1790],"[26] which was followed in *BUC*, but for unknown reasons the catalogue date was later changed to "[1776]," followed in *CPM*. This is certainly wrong for the copy in the British Library, which belongs to a late issue (stage E, deposited 1791) and advertises on its title page the 1791

Table 11. Jackson's London Publications

Opus	Full Title	First Published
1	*Dr. Watts's Divine Songs, set to Music in an Easy and Familiar Stile for one, two, three, & four Voices*	–1789 [1776?]
2	*Ponder my words. An Anthem, For 3 voices taken from the 5 Psalm, with two [3] Canons, For the Use of Country Churches*	–1789
3	*A Favorite Collection of Songs and Duetts for the Voice, Harpsichord, or Piano Forte*	1792–98
[1]ᵃ	L'Adieu	1778–89
[4]	The Grove (duet)	–1789
[6]	Happy Shepherd	–1789
[3]	O'er Desert Plains	1789
[7]	Florella	1790
[9]	L'Amant fidele (duet)	1790
[8]	Daphne	1791
[2]	Sylvia	1791
[5]	The Inconstant	1791
[10]	The Whim	1792–98
4	*A Favorite Sonata for the Harpsichord or Piano Forte*	1791
5	*A Treatise on Practical Thorough Bass with general Rules for its Composition & Modulation Dedicated by Permission to the Earl of Rochford*	–1790

a. The numbers refer to the order of the songs in Op. 3 when it was eventually published as a whole. The order here is that of probable first publication.

Table 12. Chronology of Issues of Jackson's London Publications

Stage	Date Range	Author Designation	Opus Numbers?	Imprint	Stationers' Hall Deposit			Exemplars
					Opus	Date	Depositor	
A	1776–89	George Jackson	No	?	[1]	...	...	[no copy known]
				S. A. & P. Thompson	[3/1]	...	...	GB-Lbl (2), Lcm, LVu, P; US-AA, Wc
B	Up to Aug. 1789	George Jackson	No	For the Author by J. Bland	[3/4]	July 21, 1789	J. Bland	GB-Gu, Lbl
					[2]	Aug. 10, 1789	J. Bland	GB-Cu, Lbl, SA; I-Rsc
					[3/6]	Aug. 10, 1789	J. Bland	GB-Gu, Lbl
C	Nov. 1789–Mar. 1790	George Jackson	No	For the Author	[3/3]	Nov. 29, 1789	Geo. Jackson	GB-Gu, Lbl
					[3/7]	Jan. 9, 1790	G. Jackson	GB-Lbl
					[3/9]	Feb. 22, 1790	G. Jackson	GB-Cu, Gu, Lbl
					[3/1]	Mar. 29, 1790	Geo. Jackson	GB-Cu, Gu, Lbl, Obs
					[5]	...	...	GB-SA
D	Jan. 1791	G. K. Jackson	Yes[a]	For the Author	[3/8]	Jan. 13, 1791	G. K. Jackson	GB-Gu, Lbl, Ob
					[3/2]	Jan. 13, 1791	G. K. Jackson	GB-Gu, Lbl, Ob
					[3/5]	Jan. 13, 1791	G. K. Jackson	GB-Gu, Lbl, Ob
					4	Jan. 13, 1791	G. K. Jackson	GB-Gu, Lbl, Ob, SA
					5	Jan. 13, 1791	G. K. Jackson	GB-Lbl, Ob, SA
E	May 1791–?	Dr. Jackson	Yes	For the Author	1	May 13, 1791	Dr. Jackson	GB-Lbl; US-Bh, NH, NL
					2	...	...	US-Bh
					3(?)	...	...	[no copy known]
					4	...	...	US-Bh
					5	...	...	US-Bh, R
F	1792–98	Dr. Jackson	Yes[a]	Longman & Broderip	3	...	...	US-Bh
					[3/3]	...	...	US-NH
					[3/9]	...	...	US-NH
					4	...	...	GB-Ge
					5	...	...	AUS-CAnl; GB-Ge; US-Cn, NYp (2)

a. Excluding concerto parts of Op. 3

issue of Op. 2. But the cataloguer may have found a 1776 newspaper advertisement for the first issue of the work. In any case the first issue cannot have
been later than August 1789, for the record of Op. 2 entered at Stationers' Hall
on August 10, 1789, describes Jackson on its title page as "Author of Dr. Watt's
Hymns." The plates were reused for the 1791 issue (stage E), with an altered
title page, as can be seen from the fact that the word "Dr." is misaligned on
the latter (fig. 11). The words "Opr. 1st" were also probably added at that time.

No copy of the early issue has been located. Also, Samuel, Ann, and Peter Thompson published what was to be Jackson's most popular song,
"L'Adieu" (see p. 182, fig. 21). "The Grove," the first to be deposited at Stationers' Hall (on July 21, 1789), refers to the composer as "George Jackson,
Author of L'adieu"; S. A. and P. Thompson had opened for business in
about 1779,[27] so they must have published the song between that date and
1789, probably in the earlier part of the date range.

In stage B, Jackson used another established London publisher, John
Bland, to print and sell his works (either Bland or Thompson may have published Op. 1 in stage A as well). Bland published Op. 2 and the first two songs
of what was to become Op. 3, all of which he deposited at Stationers' Hall in
1789.[28]

In stage C Jackson decided to take over his own publishing. The imprint
was now "Printed for the Author N°. 40 Great Prescot Street Goodmans
Fields." He deposited three more songs of Op. 3, probably as soon as they were
composed and printed, and also "L'Adieu" [Op. 3/1], which was revised and
re-engraved for the purpose. The earliest issue of the *Treatise* also appears at
this stage (fig. 12): the only copy, now at St. Andrews, was no doubt in the
hands of the Senatus when it voted on his degree, but it was a prepublica-
tion issue, not yet deposited at Stationers' Hall.

In stage D, he changed the form of his name on the title page of Op. 5
from "George Jackson" to "G. K. Jackson" (fig. 13), and published Op. 4 and
three more songs from the set for which Op. 3 was reserved, using the same
form of his name. (His middle name Knowil had been given to him at baptism, but he had not previously used it publicly.) He also began adding opus
numbers at this stage.[29] These changes were made before January 13, 1791, as
can be inferred from entries at Stationers' Hall where the form "G. K. Jackson" was used. Just five days earlier, he had received his doctorate—presumably too late to incorporate "Dr." on these title pages.

A few months later, in stage E, he changed the plates again to read "Dr.
Jackson" (fig. 14), added a third canon to Op. 2, and added an advertisement
for this version of Op. 2 on the title page of Op. 1 (see fig. 11). He must have

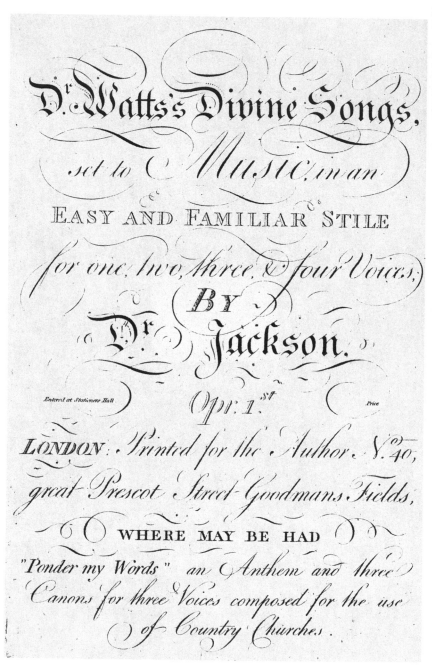

Figure 11. Jackson, *Dr. Watts's Divine Songs* (Courtesy Harvard Musical Association)

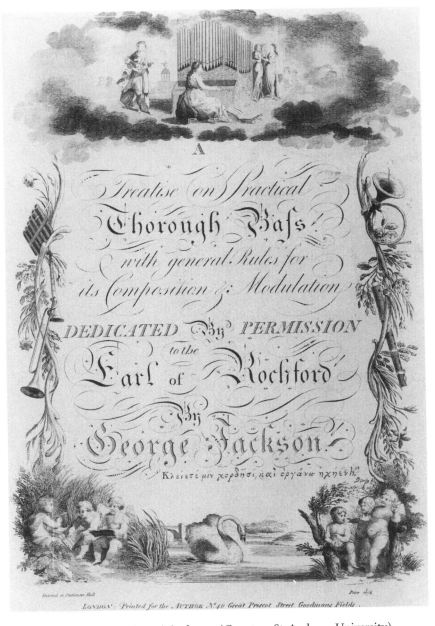

A

Treatise on Practical Thorough Bass with general Rules for its Composition & Modulation

DEDICATED by PERMISSION to the

Earl of Rochford

By *George Jackson*

"Κλειετε μιν χορδησι, και οργανω ηχηενη."

Entered at Stationers Hall   Price 10/6

LONDON: Printed for the AUTHOR N.º 40 Great Prescot Street Goodmans Fields.

Figure 12. Jackson, *Treatise,* original state (Courtesy St. Andrews University)

Figure 13. Jackson, *Treatise,* second state (Courtesy St. Andrews University)

A

Treatise on Practical
Thorough Bass
with general Rules for
its Composition & Modulation

DEDICATED By PERMISSION
to the
Earl of Rochford
By
Dr. Jackson

Κλείετέ μιν χορδῆ βι, καὶ ὀργάνω ἠχηεντι.

Op. 5.

LONDON: Printed for the AUTHOR N.º 40 Great Prescot Street Goodmans Fields.

Figure 14. Jackson, *Treatise,* third state (Courtesy Harvard Musical Association)

purchased from Bland the plates and copyright of Op. 2 and the first two songs. The dating of this stage is based on the deposit entry for Op. 1 (May 13, 1791). Probably he also completed Op. 3 and added its title page at this time, but if so, no such copy has been found.

In stage F, Longman and Broderip took over. All ten songs were issued with a new collective title page as Op. 3; the sole surviving exemplar of this complete set includes the only known copy of Op. 3/10, "The Whim." In this copy, at the Harvard Musical Association, Boston, both the overall title and the half-titles of individual songs, including No. 10, have Jackson's original designation plainly altered to "Dr.," and the imprint altered to "Longman and Broderip." Hence the likelihood that this is a reprint of a complete Op. 3, published by Jackson, and probably first issued in stage E.

Turning now to the surviving exemplars of these issues, all the ones deposited at Stationers' Hall would have been distributed to the British copyright libraries, which accounts for most of those listed in table 12 for stages B, C, and D. These libraries would also have received Op. 1 after it was deposited on May 13, 1791. Many of the other surviving exemplars from stages E and F are in U.S. libraries. The only complete set of all Jackson's London publications is at the Harvard Musical Association, bound in one of his personal teaching volumes. In every case the composer is called "Dr. Jackson" and there is an opus number. This set may have been assembled by Jackson to take with him to America.

At some stage between 1792 and 1798, he sold (or presented) the plates of Op. 3, 4, and 5 to Longman and Broderip, a leading London firm of the time. They altered all the title pages to remove Jackson's name from the imprint. In some cases they printed a page of advertisements on the back of the last page of music, but unfortunately these do not narrow the date range.[30] There is nothing to suggest that Longman and Broderip reissued Op. 1 and 2, and indeed they took the trouble to delete *Ponder my words* (Op. 2) from the list of works advertised below the half-title of "L'Adieu," the first song in Op. 3.

It seems most likely that Jackson sold the plates shortly before he left for America in 1796. The additional copies of the Op. 5 *Treatise* now held in American libraries may have been ordered from London by Jackson or his students after he had arrived in the States.

"L'Adieu" was to be Jackson's lone commercial success. Besides his own reissue of 1790, it was published as "One kind kiss" by Carr (Philadelphia), Aitken (Philadelphia), and, with accompaniment for flute and piano, by the composer (Boston).[31] These versions will be compared in some detail later on.

EMIGRATION

Thus, in the years 1790 and 1791, Jackson took several steps that suggest a new purpose in his life. He gave up his organist's post; he arranged to acquire a doctorate; he produced a solid series of publications. If his purpose was emigration, however, it was delayed for at least five years.

There is a complete hiatus in our knowledge of his activities between May 13, 1791, when he personally deposited his Op. 1 at Stationers' Hall, and May 24, 1797, when he was appointed organist of St. Peter's Church, Philadelphia, "his salary to commence from the 25 March last."[32] Parker's statement that Jackson "migrated to this country, in 1796" is confirmed by the record of his registration as an alien in July 1812, which states that he had been sixteen years in the country,[33] and again by an article "Dr. Jackson" in the *New England Palladium,* March 23, 1813, evidently based on an interview, which states that "Doctor JACKSON has been in this country about *seventeen years.*"

Yet Parker leaves us with no clue as to why he resigned his post in 1790, what he did for the next six years, how he fed his growing family, or why he eventually left for the United States. Perhaps he joined the household of his patron, the Earl of Rochford, at Easton, Suffolk, as a private musician and teacher; if so, there is nothing to prove it. Another possible explanation is that he hoped by means of the degree and publications to build a lucrative teaching practice, tried to do so for five years, and when he could no longer hope for success, decided to emigrate instead. But where did he live? Not, surely, in London, or he would have retained his church position. He is not to be found in London street directories of the time.

At any rate, the publications and the doctorate were well calculated to impress potential American pupils or employers. We know that he brought copies of the publications to America, for in about 1800 he published a song that advertised them for sale.[34]

No doctor of music had ever set foot in America, but the title "Dr." was carefully attached by Americans to the names of those English composers who were entitled to it, such as Alcock, Arnold, Blow, Burney, Croft, Greene, Hayes, Miller, Nares, Randall, and Wainwright.[35] It gained additional prestige when, in 1791 (six months after Jackson received his degree), Oxford conferred an honorary doctorate on Joseph Haydn. Jackson never failed to use his title in his American publications and advertisements. The use of opus numbers also was calculated to place him on the level of such composers as Corelli, Handel, Haydn, and Mozart, and well above any American musician. The *Treatise* had a quotation in Greek alphabetic script engraved on its title page (see figs. 12–14). These outward marks of status may have contributed to his American reputation as a learned man and helped him attract pupils. But he had no easy success. Had there been a sponsor waiting to launch him on his American career, he would not have moved so rapidly from place to place (table 13). His position at St. Peter's lasted less than a year; he was succeeded by Taylor in April 1798. Early mentions in American newspapers suggest that he was not doing very well. He was twice successfully sued for debt in the New Brunswick courts, losing nearly £100 in October 1797 and a smaller amount in June 1799.[36] In the absence of any known vices such as drinking or gambling, these facts suggest that he was simply not earning enough money to pay for his needs and those of his family.

However, in August 1798 he was employed as a music teacher by Miss Hay, an Englishwoman who had opened a new girls' school in New Brunswick, New Jersey. And on September 22, 1799, he gave his first recorded American concert at the court house there, with a long and very miscellaneous program, featuring his wife as a singer and several of his pupils both as singers and as instrumentalists. It included some insignificant compositions of his own. Clarinets and two pianos were played. A review noted that "Mr. Hewitt and his well-chosen band" took part, the earliest known instance of his collaboration with his fellow expatriate James Hewitt (1770–1827). But no orchestral piece appears on the program. A similar concert was given in April 1800.[37]

After a brief stay in Newark, New Jersey, where in November 1800 the Jacksons took a "commodious house and garden" at which they briefly opened a school for girls,[38] they moved to New York, no later than February 1801.

Table 13. Jackson's Residences in the United States, 1796–1801

Area	Dates	Details	Information Sou
Norfolk, Va.	1796	"Arrived . . . remained a short time"	Parker
Alexandria, Va.	1796–97?	"Removed" there soon after arrival	Parker
Baltimore	1796–97?	"Visited"	Parker
Philadelphia	1796–97?	"Visited"	Parker
	May 24, 1797	Appointed organist of St. Peter's church	Church reco
Elizabethtown, N.J.	1796–7?	"Resided"	Parker
New Brunswick, N.J.	Oct. 1797	Named as resident in lawsuit	Court record
	1798–1800	Teacher in Miss Hay's school	Advertiseme
	Sept. 20, 1799	Gave concert at the Court House	Advertiseme
	July 4, 1800	Performed in Independence Day celebrations	Newspaper report
Newark, N.J.	Nov. 1800	Opened school	Advertiseme
New York	Feb. 1801	Published compositions	Advertiseme
	Apr. 9, 1801	Gave concert at Little's Hotel	Advertiseme

NEW YORK

Jackson's activity in New York has been thoroughly investigated and documented by Charles Kaufman, and it will be summarized here. Jackson continued to devote most of his energies to teaching, but he occasionally organized or participated in a public concert. He published and performed quite a few compositions. As Kaufman points out, the city of New York "was to provide by far the most opportunity for the performance of his compositions." Both composing and concertizing may have been primarily intended to keep his name before the public in order to enhance his prestige as a teacher. Most of his New York publications are clearly aimed at amateurs; some are directly pedagogical, others are dedicated to his pupils. He probably began his teaching activities soon after arrival, attending pupils individually in their own houses or having them come to his.[39]

However, there is one clear difference from his London situation. In New York, he quickly became a prominent performer, something he had never achieved in London. Consequently, many of his publications, though necessarily catering to domestic amateurs, were based on public performances that are mentioned in their titles. Jackson's published London songs, unlike Taylor's and countless others, had never claimed to have been "sung by Miss X to universal applause." Several of his New York songs do just that.

Soon after arrival in the city, he advertised a "Grand Concert and Ball" to be given at Little's Hotel, Broad Street, on April 9, 1801; the concert was to include a number of his compositions, but it was twice postponed and we cannot be sure that it took place.[40] In December 1802 he was appointed organist of St. George's Chapel in the Episcopal parish of Trinity, at the relatively high salary of £100. Public concerts involving Jackson occurred in July 1803, January 1805, April 1805, and April 1806. He also directed performances of his own music at the Presbyterian Church, the French Church du Saint Esprit in Pine Street, the New York Musical Society, and the Grand Lodge of Freemasons. In each year from 1801 to 1812 Kaufman has found evidence of Jackson's residence at some address in New York City.[41]

It is surprising, therefore, to discover that in 1805 he attempted to launch a second career in Hartford, Connecticut.[42] On September 11 the following appeared in the *Connecticut Courant:* "Dr. Jackson, just arrived from New-York in the city of Hartford, has opened a School for instruction in every branch of Theoretic and Practical Music, at separate hours and upon separate terms for the Piano Forte or Organ the fingering according to the celebrated Pasqualis method. Solmization (or singing by notes) either French,

English, or Italian including Transposition by cliffs. Thorough Base with the art of modulation. Likewise composition in any number of parts. For particulars enquire at his house in Church street near Miss Pattens Boarding School. September 4." The advertisement ran for three weeks. In October Jackson and his wife gave three concerts "at the great Room over the Bank," Hartford, consisting in the main of Handel selections. It is noticeable, however, that all three were given on Thursdays, and thus were not necessarily incompatible with his duties at St. George's Church in New York. He probably commuted every week to give lessons at Hartford. According to Nathan Hale Allen, Jackson "had first come to Hartford as organist of the Episcopal Church" and took part in the dedication of the new Center Church edifice in 1807,[43] but no confirmation of these statements has been found.

Even if Hartford was his main place of residence in the fall of 1805, it was not for long. An announcement of December 16 "respectfully acquaints his friend[s] and the public that his school is open at his house, No. 91 Greenwich Street [New York], on the usual moderate terms of twelve dollars pr. quarter. Ladies attended at their own houses as usual."[44] Presumably, only "gentlemen" attended the school, and we may assume that, as in England, his teaching of theory and composition was designed for male pupils. This is confirmed in an announcement of April 7, 1806, which provides other insights into Jackson's philosophy: "Dr. Jackson proposes to open an Evening School for the purpose of teaching the science of Music to a select number of gentlemen. The object is to teach the art of composition for voices or instruments, in from two to any number of parts; with the art of modulation. A scholar who has been thus instructed will be able to read any piece of music at sight and test its merits by unerring rules: an acquisition of which it is presumed every gentleman amateur must immediately perceive the value. A knowledge of the above will not more aid the theorist than assist and advance the performer."[45]

Jackson later taught at schools at 85 Maiden Lane (in January 1807) and at 13 or 17 Dey Street (in September 1808); the last was also the address of an academy for young ladies run by Henry Priest, and Kaufman concludes that Jackson was hired there as music teacher. There is evidence of increasing activity and a crowded timetable: in 1809 he taught for thirty hours a week at two institutions, as well as receiving pupils at his home. There was a slight decline during his remaining years in New York.[46]

As Kaufman points out, Jackson's compositions were now less often included in concert programs, with virtually none after 1809. His own concerts were more and more exclusively made up of Handel's music. Those of 1799–

1800 had been decidedly of the modern school: they included sonatas (or "Lessons") by Muzio Clementi, Domenico Corri, and Ignaz Pleyel; songs by James Hook, William Jackson of Exeter, and Stephen Storace; glees by John Wall Callcott; Franz Kotzwara's *The Battle of Prague;* and excerpts from operas by André Grétry and William Shield, as well as several compositions of Jackson's. The only work identifiable as Handel's is "Let the bright seraphim" from *Samson.*[47] By contrast, an "Oratorio" directed by Jackson at the French Church du Saint Esprit, Pine Street, in 1805 consisted entirely of Handel selections.[48] A "Concert of Sacred Music" given for the benefit of Mrs. Moller at the Assembly Room, Broadway, on April 3, 1806, "under the direction of Dr. Jackson and Mr. Weldon," though not in fact made up entirely of sacred music, had twelve excerpts from *Messiah* and the overtures to *Samson* and the *Occasional Oratorio;* these were complemented by four unidentified instrumental works, "Before Jehovah's awful throne" (probably Martin Madan's "Denmark"), an unnamed vocal trio, and one composition of Jackson's (the *Funeral Dirge*).[49]

NEW YORK PUBLICATIONS

Jackson's American publications are numerous, and in some cases difficult to date with assurance. Most lack any place or date of publication; some, published by Jackson himself, are labeled "Printed for the Author," while others do not identify the publisher at all. Those published in New York, presumably during his residence there, are listed in table 14. They are uniformly in upright "sheet music" format, and on close inspection are seen to have been largely the work of two engravers, who are identified (on some of them) as William Pirsson and Edward Riley.

In his early years in New York, Jackson had Pirsson engrave his music and published it himself, in some cases advertising it for sale. In early 1808, however, there is evidence that he had entered an agreement with a commercial publisher, John Butler, of 156 Broadway. On January 18 of that year Butler advertised for sale three *Petits Duos* and a song, *The Fairies to the Sea Nymphs.* Copyright for the *Petits Duos* had been granted to Jackson on December 23, 1807; he either sold them to Butler or agreed to share any profits with him. *The Fairies* is labeled "Publish'd (for the Author) by J. Butler." Both of these works were engraved by Riley, who was, like Jackson, an immigrant from Britain. It seems probable that Riley was Butler's engraver, whereas Pirsson, a composer and publisher but a much less skilled engraver, was closely associated with Jackson, identifying himself on one of his own publications as

Table 14. Jackson's New York Publications

Short Title of Publication[a]	Forces	Publisher	Date	K	References		Engraver	Copies Examined
					Wolfe	Other		
New Miscellaneous Musical Work The Cricket; Waft me; Huzza! for Liberty; Sweet are the banks; American Serenade; Cancherizante; A Winter's Evening; New York Serenade; Ah! Delia; Dirge for Gen. Washington; The Fairies; Gentle Air	1–3v, (pf)	Author	1800?	68	...	...	[W. Pirsson?]	US-Bh, Wc
[b]*I Rudimenti di Musica*	pf	Author?	1800?	95?	...	...	?	None located
A Prey to Tender Anguish	v, pf	Author	1800?	...	4554A	...	?	US-PROu
New Bagatelles The Alphabet; Numeration Table;	v, pf	Author	1801	93	4554	...	W. P[irsson]	US-Cn
Addition Table; Subtraction Table; Multiplication Table; Pence Table				67	4510 4511 4529 4532 4558 4545	...	[W. Pirsson?]	US-Bh
President Jefferson's New March Immortal Jefferson (Mrs. Jackson)	v, pf	Author	1801	92	4553	...	?	None located
Freedom and Our President Immortal Jefferson (Mrs. Jackson)	v, fl/vn, pf	Author	1801	42	4523	...	[W. Pirsson?]	US-Bh
Close Canon for Six Voices Come, lads, your glasses fill	6v	Author	1801–2?	17	...	...	[W. Pirsson?]	US-Bh
The Task. A Whimsical Canon Jack knows his merit	4v	Author	1801–2?	109	...	...	[W. Pirsson?]	US-Bh
[b]*Dr. Jackson's Selection* The Sylph; March & Quick Step	(v), pf	[Author?]	1803?	28	2537	...	[W. Pirsson?]	Various
Verses for the Fourth of July When gen'rous freedom (Mrs. Jackson)	v, chor, pf	[Author?]	1803?	111	4562	...	W. Pirsson	US-Bh

Table 14 (cont.)

Short Title of Publication[a]	Force	Publisher	Date	K	References		Engraver	Copies Examined
					Wolfe	Other		
Ode for the Fourth of July Once more has the morn (Townsend)	v, chor, wn, pf	[Author?]	1803?	77	...	...	W. Pirsson	US-Bh
[b]David's Psalms 35 psalm tunes	4v, org	[Author?]	1804	24	...	C 282	[W. Pirsson?]	US-Wc
Ode for Genl. Hamilton's Funeral Ye midnight shades	4v	[Author?]	1804	78	4536	...	W. Pirsson	US-Bh (2)
A New Musical Score of Easy Canons Praise the Grand Master; Two Masonic Canons; Genius of Masonry; Two Masonic Canons; The Task; May all the Universe be Free; Behold how good and pleasant; O 'twas a joyful sound; Sit lux; O God, the Father of heaven	2–10v	[Author?]	1804–6	69	4514	...	[W. Pirsson?]	US-Bh
[b]Thanksgiving Anthem by Dr. Nares O 'twas a joyful sound	3v, org	Jackson (?)	1806–7?	...	6457	...	?	US-NH
Sacred Music for the Use of Churches 2 chants; Arise, O Lord; Gloria Patri; 3 psalm tunes	v, org	[Author?]	1807?	96	...	...	[W. Pirsson?]	US-Bh, AItet
Pope's Universal Prayer and Celebrated Ode Father of all (Pope)	v, chor, wn, pf	[Author?]	1808?	89	4548	C 283	W. P[irsson], E. Riley	US-Bh
Petits Duos Vital spark of heav'nly flame (Pope)	pf 4 hands	[J. Butler]	1807–8	30 31 32	4518 4519 4517?	...	[E.] Riley [E.] Riley [E. Riley?]	US-Bh, Wc US-Bh, Wc None located
The Fairies to the Sea Nymphs Hasten from your coral caves (Miss Seward)	v, chor, pf	J. Butler	1808	37	4522	...	E. Riley	US-Wc

Table 14 (cont.)

Short Title of Publication[a]	Forces	Publisher	Date	References			Engraver	Copies Examined
				K	Wolfe	Other		
The Entered Apprentices Song When quite a young spark	2v	[J. Butler?]	1808–11	34	4520	…	[E. Riley?]	US-Bh
A Musical Coalition	fl, pf	[J. Butler?]	1808–11	64	4530	…	[E. Riley?]	US-Wc
Content. A favorite Canzone Halcyon nymph with placid smile	3v, bass	[J. Butler?]	1808–11	20	4515	…	[E.] Riley	US-Bh
A favorite Canzone Soft pleasing sighs are love's delight (Mrs. Jackson)	3v, pf	[J. Butler?]	1808–11	38	…	…	E. Riley	US-Bh

a. Jackson compositions included, or text incipit (author of text).

b. Includes works by other composers.

Note: Publications ascribed to Pirsson in the table all use the same letterpress typeface; clefs, braces, and note forms are also strikingly similar. It is always possible, however, that those not signed by Pirsson were in fact engraved by a partner or precursor who used the same set of dies to stamp his plates. The chronological order of this group of publications, where not determined by external evidence, is based on (1) the presence or absence of "Printed for the Author"; (2) the gradual decline in the proportion of upright medial S's; (3) dating estimates in Wolfe.

"his late pupil."[50] I assume therefore that the publications engraved by Pirsson were published by Jackson before 1808, while those engraved by Riley were published by Butler from 1808 onward. This is consistent with all other available evidence of dating. Examples of Pirsson's and Riley's engraving are shown in figures 17 and 18, below.

New Miscellaneous Musical Work For the Voice and Piano Forte, consisting of Songs, Serenades, Cantatas, Canzonetts, Canons, Glees &c. &c. is a twenty-page collection of twelve vocal pieces, each with a half-title and imprint "Printed for the Author. Copy Right Secured," which shows that they were meant also to be sold separately: and indeed three of them are extant in this form.[51] Nine are for voice and piano, two for two voices unaccompanied, one for three (male?) voices and piano. The overall title page has the same imprint, with no publisher, date, or place of publication stated, and is headed "Nº ," with room for a number to be inserted in manuscript, but no number is present on either of the two known copies (at US-Bh and US-Wc, the latter incomplete). Evidently Jackson had plans to make this the first work in a series. Each piece is specifically "Composed by Dr. G. K. Jackson," but none of them is known to have been brought from England. One is a "Dirge for General Washington," who died in December 1799, and another is called "New York Serenade." "Sweet are the banks" had been performed in New Brunswick in 1799, and "The Cricket" in New York in 1800. For all these reasons it seems likely that the work was published in about 1800, perhaps before Jackson moved to New York in early 1801 (there was no significant music publishing in New Jersey). It is possible that some of the individual numbers had already appeared separately.

Jackson's treatise *I Rudimenti di Musica* is not extant in this edition but was advertised on the next piece and so must have preceded that work in print. The Boston edition will be described later.

A Prey to Tender Anguish is a single song with piano accompaniment, printed on two staves, with an extraordinarily gloomy text in five stanzas. It had been performed in New Brunswick in 1799. Uniquely, as already pointed out, its title page includes an advertisement for all five of Jackson's London publications, and also for *New Miscellaneous Musical Work, I Rudimenti,* and what was probably part of the next work under the title "Polyhymnia, or Numerical Songs, No. 1."[52] The engraver is not Pirsson in this case. The song was reengraved by Pirsson and reissued shortly after, with no imprint or advertisements, but with the legend "Composed for, and respectfully Dedicated to Miss Cornelia Le Roy." A three-stave version with a fuller accompaniment now precedes the two-stave version, but the two separate stanzas of the text are omitted.

New Bagatelles for the Voice & Piano Forte Calculated for Juvenile Improvement was advertised for publication by subscription in the *Daily Advertiser* on March 2, 1801. It is in six numbers, which also have separate half-titles and the same imprint as the previous work. They are for voice and piano on two staves, and are evidently intended to help children learn their letters and simple arithmetic. They are called "The ABC or Alphabet," "Numeration Table," "The Addition Table," "The Subtraction Table," "The Multiplication Table," and "The Pence Table."

President Jefferson's New March and Quick Step, for the Voice and Piano Forte has not been located, but it too was advertised in the *Daily Advertiser* on March 2, 1801, two days before Jefferson's inauguration. It had "words written by Mrs Jackson expressly for the occasion" in eight verses, with chorus: "In manly worth and true-born pride / Let no base plot your states divide."

Freedom and Our President for the Voice & Piano Forte has "Words Adapted to a New Composition called Jefferson's March," and is stated to have been "Sung by Mr. Hodgkinson." It was, in fact, sung by Hodgkinson at Jackson's concert at Little's Hotel on April 21, 1801. This is a later edition of the previous item. But it has a printed note: "The Words written Extempore by Clarissa." We have to conclude that "Clarissa" was a nickname for Jane Jackson. (Further details will be given when this is discussed as a composition.)

Close Canon for Six Voices. For the Use of Masonic Lodges is a two-page publication that also contains a "Catch in Canon for 4 Voices." Not mentioned by Richard Wolfe in *Secular Music in America* or by Kaufman, it is assigned an early date here because it is "Printed for the Author," a label that Jackson seems to have stopped using around 1803.

The Task. A Whimsical Canon on the Eight Notes Ascending & Descending is a single-page print, also "Printed for the Author." The US-Bh copy has handwritten annotations about its origin that were printed, in edited form, when it was reused in *A New Musical Score of Easy Canons*. "Engraved by Wood" is also noted, though not in Jackson's hand. Kaufman interprets this to refer to the engraver of this print, but the only American music engraver by that name was Simeon Wood (1784–1822), who worked in Boston from 1818 to 1822. It seems likely, therefore, that the note refers to a new edition of the piece that was proposed in about 1820 by Edwin Jackson.

Dr. Jackson's Selection is dated "ca 1803" by Wolfe. It consisted of eight or more numbers of one to four pages each, of which five are extant; they contain pieces by various composers, mostly reprinted from London editions. Number 3 has two pieces by Jackson, "The Sylph" (song) and a March and Quick Step.

Verses for the Fourth of July is a setting of a poem by Mrs. Jackson, "When gen'rous freedom leaves her downy bed," in three stanzas, which was published in the *American Citizen* on July 6, 1803. The title page states that the piece was "sung at the Presbyterian Church in New York," while a newspaper announced that it was to be sung "by Mr. Shapter and others of the company" after a play, *The Glory of Columbia*, at Mount Vernon Gardens on July 4 of that year.[53] The score, with accompaniment for violin and piano, is clearly a reduction from an orchestral score, with some of the orchestral parts in small notes and a string-like ritornello. The setting is strophic.

Ode for the Fourth of July Written by Mr. Townsend is an extended adaptation of *Freedom for Our President* with new words, "Once more has the morn op'd the portals of light," and followed by the same quickstep. Like the last item, it was "sung at the Presbyterian Church in New York," an event that Kaufman records as taking place in 1803.

David's Psalms consists of thirty-six tunes for voice and organ, with four-part harmonies attached "for the further improvement of psalmody in singing schools." Jackson styled himself "organist of Saint George's Chapel New York" on the title page, and the psalm texts are from versions likely to have been used in Episcopal worship. Fifteen of the tunes had been previously published in Britain; rather surprisingly, only one of these was taken from his own London collection of hymn tunes (Op. 1). Most of the others were favorites in the Church of England but hitherto little known in America.[54] The remaining twenty-one tunes are new: one by Pirsson, who engraved the work; the rest by Jackson. The year 1804 is printed on the title page.

Ode for Gen!. Hamilton's Funeral has a dedication to the New York Musical Society. It is a four-part piece in the style of a glee for men's voices, and is presumed to date from immediately after Alexander Hamilton's death on July 12, 1804, from wounds incurred in his famous duel with Aaron Burr.

A New Musical Score of Easy Canons is the "Unidentified collection of masonic music" listed by Wolfe (No. 4514). The title page survives in a copy at the Harvard Musical Association. It is an elaborately engraved (but unsigned) pictorial design with a central architectural feature, and with puzzle versions of several of the canons that are fully scored in the rest of the book (fig. 15). The title page was printed oblong, although the rest of the book is in upright format (fig. 16). The publication contains ten canons for from two to ten equal voices unaccompanied. Many of them are adaptations, to new Masonic texts, of previously existing compositions, including two of the three canons in Op. 2, the *Close Canon for Six Voices,* and *The Task.* Wolfe estimates the date at "between 1804 and 1806," on unstated grounds. Both known copies

Figure 15. Jackson, *New Musical Score of Easy Canons,* title page (Courtesy Harvard Musical Association)

(one lacking title page) have, attached to the end, *The Entered Apprentices Song* (see below), paginated 12–14 in ink.

Jackson paid tribute to his old teacher by publishing *Thanksgiving Anthem, for three voices . . . Composed by D*ʳ*. Nares, and Canon for 3 voices, Composed by Dr. G. K. Jackson.* The anthem, four pages in length, is engraved in a style distinct from both Pirsson's and Riley's. The canon is reprinted from the *A New Musical Score of Easy Canons,* with the same page number (9) and with an added footnote, so it must have been later in date than that publication.

Sacred Music for the Use of Churches &c. consisting of *Two Chants Sanctus Gloria Patri and Three Psalm Tunes* is a clearly Episcopal offering, scored on two staves for unison voices and organ. It may have been the subject of Dr. William Smith's 1809 tribute to Jackson for revising "a few chants, some years back . . . with a view to publicity."[55]

Pope's Universal Prayer, engraved by Pirsson (fig. 17) and *Pope's Celebrated Ode,* engraved by Riley (fig. 18), were probably first published separately; each has its own half title, imprint, and pagination. But they are now to be found only in a combined edition. The hastily printed joint title page reads

Figure 16. Jackson, *New Musical Score of Easy Canons*, p. 1 (Courtesy Harvard Musical Association)

Figure 17. Jackson, "Pope's Universal Prayer," p. 1 (Courtesy Harvard Musical Association)

Figure 18. Jackson, "The Dying Christian," p. 1 (Courtesy Harvard Musical Association)

Pope's Universal Prayer and his celebrated Ode The Dying Christian to his Soul, without imprint, in type corresponding to Pirsson's, which makes it probable that the combined edition was published by Jackson rather than Butler. Both pieces are ambitious sacred cantatas.

On December 23, 1807, Jackson was granted copyright in the New York district for "Three petit duos, for the piano forte." Two of them have been identified: No. 1, "For Miss C. Clarkson and Miss Crosby," which was advertised as "just published" on January 18, 1808,[56] and an unnumbered one "For Miss H. Hogan and Miss Burrell," both engraved by Riley. The third may have been the one published by G. Willig of Philadelphia, perhaps a reprint of the lost New York edition (Wolfe 4517).

The Fairies to the Sea Nymphs, a song with chorus, was advertised by Butler as "just published and for sale" in the *New York Evening Post* of January 18, 1808.

The Entered Apprentices Song, for two equal voices unaccompanied (though with a note "This Song may be sung by a single Voice if required"), survives in only two copies, both attached to *A New Musical Score of Easy Canons.* But it is not a canon, it is set by a different engraver, it has a separate dedication "to the Lodges of New York," and it is unpaginated. So it is likely to have been separately published and later attached to copies of the Masonic collection already in print.

A Musical Coalition is a whimsical production "Wherein the prevailing Discords between America, France, & England, are Harmoniously adjusted. or a Humorous Combination of their National Airs. N B Adapted to the Piano Forte and Flute, to which is added a Musical Parody." The tunes are "Ça ira," "Yankee Doodle," and "God Save the King." The Musical Parody, for piano, is "on the Rhythmica of Malbrouke."

Content. A Favorite Canzone for 3 voices (The Subject from Hail Columbia) was "Composed for the Apollo Musical Society—New York," and thus probably intended for male voices; two are in treble clef; one, bass.

A Favorite Canzone For 1.2. or 3. Voices, on the other hand, is dedicated to Miss Susan Moore, probably another pupil of Jackson's, and although it has the same vocal scoring, the two upper voices are presumably meant to be in the female register.

MASSACHUSETTS

The year 1812 was one of crisis in Jackson's life and career. He had never become an American citizen. As he later explained to the press, he "knew of no advantage which it would be to an organist, and music master, to be naturalized, and did not subject himself to the cost of it."[57] He was now to regret this oversight. The war with Great Britain, declared on June 18, made him an enemy alien, and in July he registered at the New York federal marshal's office, declaring that he had a wife and five children.[58]

In October 1812 he moved to Boston. He requested a certificate of his registration from the Massachusetts marshal's office but was told that such would not be needed. Possibly his move was partly due to failing finances, for he left unpaid bills behind him, as we shall see. He may also have hoped for a friendlier attitude to British aliens in the New England capital.

But the specific reason was his appointment as organist of Brattle Street Church. The Boston press received him with enthusiasm, especially when he announced a "Grand Sacred Oratorio" at King's Chapel (still often called the Stone Chapel or the Chapel Church at this date) to be presented on October 29. The *Boston Gazette* announced:

> We have heard with sincere pleasure, that the celebrated Organist and Composer, Dr. G. K. Jackson, from New-york, intends to have publickly performed, some select songs, choruses, overtures, &c. from Handel's Oratorios of the Messiah, Sampson and Judas Maccabeas.
>
> As there has not been an Oratorio performed in this town, since the year 1785, it may not be improper to observe, that all the virtuosos, both in Europe and America, look upon Handel as one of the most sublime composers of sacred harmony. . . .
>
> Doctor Jackson has been at considerable expense, and much trouble, in arranging and getting up the above selections: He will be assisted in the performance, by the Theatrical Band, (Mr. Graupner, leader) by Mrs Graupner, and a large number of the first vocal and instrumental amateurs of both sexes in this place. . . . with Dr. Jackson as grand leader on the organ.[59]

The selection from *Messiah* and the two overtures were almost the same as those in the 1806 New York concert described above. To them were added four items from other Handel oratorios. "Another Oratorio under the direction of Doctor Jackson" was projected for Christmas Day, and there were similar performances at First Church, Salem, on December 1 and in Boston on February 3 and 22, 1813.[60]

Following his earlier practice, Jackson also took steps to establish a teaching connection in Boston, this time in collaboration with two other leading musicians, the German Gottlieb Graupner and the Frenchman Francis Mallet:

PYTHIAN HALL

The public are respectfully informed that Dr. G. K. Jackson, Messrs. Graupner and Mallet, have associated for the purpose of instruction in
Vocal and Instrumental Music,
and with this in view, have taken and furnished the large Hall in Pond-street, where they will teach Ladies the Piano Forte, Singing, and the Theory and Practice of Music. They will arrange and teach Psalmody, to assist in the execution of which, a suitable Organ has been procured, to qualify Singing Societies, for places of public Worship. They will also give lessons on the English and Spanish Guitar.

Days of Tuition for young Ladies—Monday and Thursday, from 10 to 2—Terms of Instruction made known on application to G. GRAUPNER, no. 6, Franklin-street, or at the Hall, where Subscription Books will be kept open.[61]

The announcement differs from all earlier enterprises of Jackson's in its emphasis on psalmody, a form of music that probably counted for much more in Boston than in New York. The committee of Brattle Street Church, in appointing Jackson organist, had stressed the need for improvement in the performance of psalmody and noted that it was "extremely difficult to maintain a musical choir in consequence of the present organist [Dolliver] whose improvement has not kept up with the society in taste and science."[62] Jackson's salary was raised by forty-two dollars in November 1812, perhaps in recognition of his activities at Pythian Hall, and a few months later he was publicly commended for having "almost banished that spiritless method of performance, which is too common in Sacred Music."[63] The Pythian Hall collaboration did not last long, for next March Jackson was proposing to open yet another music school for girls, which would begin operations "as soon as a sufficient number of Pupils make it an object."[64]

Jackson's promising start in Boston was soon curtailed by the law. On February 24, 1813, the U.S. marshal of the District of Massachusetts published warnings that all enemy aliens must report to him without delay or face arrest.[65] Jackson called twice at the marshal's office, presumably showing his certificate of registration from New York, and was again told by the clerk that he need take no further action. Nevertheless, on March 19 he was "ordered to Northampton, Hampshire Co.,"[66] where it was thought he was less likely to assist the British forces.

On that very day, before he could comply, an attorney from New York, who had been attempting to collect Jackson's debts, issued a writ for his arrest. "There was immediately a hue and cry set up, that this was a trick to prevent his compliance with the Marshal's notice." But two members of the Brattle Street Church put up bail for his release, and he then complied with the order, leaving on March 22. The *Boston Centinel* suspected the government action of being "directed possibly in this case by the malice of party feelings."[67]

This shows that Jackson, or at any rate his chief supporters, belonged to the Federalist party. We can see, therefore, that his expulsion from Boston was largely a matter of domestic politics. The Federalists, who opposed the war and the Madison administration, were spoken for by the *Palladium* account, which stressed Jackson's innocence and his value to the community: hence it strongly praised his musical accomplishments. By the same token, the Republican, anti-British *Independent Chronicle* did not mention his musical significance: "We know of no reason why any particular favor should be shewn to this man, more than to any other. . . . One thing is certain, that a more violent British partizan than the above mentioned person, is nowhere to be found."[68] No evidence supporting this claim emerges from his professional practices, unless the production of music by English composers amounted to partisanship. At most one can say that the explicitly (American) patriotic songs and marches often played in his New York concerts are not mentioned in the extant programs of his Boston concerts of 1812–13.

So Jackson left Boston for Northampton, where his disgrace must have hindered public activity. One concert was announced there on November 3, 1813, but may not have taken place, and an attempt to found a musical society led nowhere. He again relied on private teaching for his livelihood. Kaufman suggests plausibly that it was he who advertised a large pianoforte for sale in the *Hampshire Gazette* on March 29, 1815.[69]

When the war ended in April 1815, he was welcomed back to Boston by some of his former admirers. He may or may not have served briefly as organist at his old church (Brattle Street) or at King's Chapel;[70] he was certainly organist of Trinity Church from April 4, 1816, to March 30, 1820, at the reasonable salary of two hundred dollars per annum,[71] which he augmented by keeping a music store at 38 Hanover Street (1815–17). Several pieces of sheet music were "printed and sold at Dr. G. K. Jackson's Music Store" at that address. Once again he advertised for voice and piano pupils.

But his earlier, short-lived domination of Boston's concert life was not to be recovered. His prime opportunity lay in the foundation in 1815 of the Handel and Haydn Society. Its purpose was essentially to resume the type of oratorio concert that Jackson and his colleagues had introduced in 1812, but his name does not appear in the announcements of any of the society's concerts. He was invited to be its organist, but, according to a newspaper account, "demanded such an enormous sum for his services, as amounted to a refusal to perform."[72] The records state that he "positively refused to have anything to do with the society unless he could have the sole direction of its concerns, or in other words be President etc. etc. etc."[73] This suggests that wounded pride was the reason for his refusal, perhaps coupled with resentment over his treatment at the hands of the government. But it must have cost him a struggle, for as usual he was dangerously short of money.

For the rest of his life, church music was almost his only professional activity, and his achievements in that department will be considered below. In 1820 he gave up his position at Trinity Church but was chosen as first organist of the new Episcopal church of St. Paul (now the cathedral). He was commissioned to appraise the organ at Christ Church in February 1821,[74] and later in the same year the Handel and Haydn Society "request[ed] leave to dedicate to him the Handel and Haydn Society Collection of Church Music about to be published and confer with him upon other subjects relative to its publication."[75] The dedication, when it appeared, made it clear that Jackson had revised the work of the young editor, Lowell Mason. It added a tribute to Jackson, noting "the High Estimation in which he is held for his Exquisite Taste, Profound Knowledge, and Unrivalled Skill in the Art and Science of Music." This final reconciliation and recognition must have sweetened the last months of his life.

Jackson played piano and carillon in three more concerts that winter.[76] On March 27, 1822, his wife died of cancer at the stated age of fifty-six (in fact, probably fifty-eight). He appeared no more in public, and he followed her in death on November 18, 1822, at the age of sixty-five. The cause of his death was registered as "Bilious Cholic."[77]

Efforts to find records of the birth or baptism of Jackson's children, either in Britain or the United States, have failed so far. At his death he had three sons: Charles, Edwin Washington, and Samuel. Charles Jackson was the only one registered as an alien in 1812, when his age was given as seventeen, so he must have been the eldest (surviving) son, thus born in England around 1795. Charles married Jane Jones at Trinity Church, Boston, on January 14, 1823, and was buried there at age thirty on November 11, 1826.[78] The other sons were presumably born after Jackson's arrival in the United States in 1796 and so were not classified as aliens. A Mrs. S. L. Pesley was probably his married daughter.[79]

The 1820 census returns yield the following statistics for Jackson's household in Bowdoin Square, Boston. Free white males: 45 and over, one; 16–25, two; free white females: 26–45, one; 16–25, one; 10–15, one; foreigners not naturalized, three.[80] The most probable interpretation of these entries is that Jackson, his wife, and his son Charles were the three aliens; Edwin and Samuel were the two white males aged 16–25 (hence born in the United States between 1796 and 1804); and there were two daughters, one born 1796–1804, the other 1805–10. The remaining adults may have been lodgers or servants. If indeed Jackson and his wife had eleven children, only five of them were living with them in 1820.

Kaufman has uncovered some interesting details of lawsuits among Jackson's heirs, which need not be recounted here. He considers that Jackson advanced a loan of several thousand dollars to his son Charles to enable him to open his music-selling business in 1821. How the father could have found the money is not explained, but in any event, he left a pitiably small estate, officially valued at $98.86.[81] Apart from twenty volumes of Handel's oratorios, valued at two dollars each, which ended up in the library of the Handel and Haydn Society, his other 129 "old music books" were given derisory values varying from six to twenty-five cents each. But he had probably tried to sell some of his teaching books himself at a slightly better price. Several of them have flyleaf inscriptions in Jackson's hand, telling how he used them for teaching, and one (volume 9) has the added words "$2.50 per Volume."

BOSTON PUBLICATIONS

Jackson's newly published collections of music in Boston are limited to three, largely made up of preexisting music. One is *A New Selection for the Flute or Violin*, which is known in only one copy, at Illinois State University. It has a Boston imprint but no date or publisher's name.

The other two are church collections, probably representing the music at Trinity Church. *A Choice Collection of Chants for Four Voices with a Gloria Patri & Sanctus . . . as used in Cathedrals, Churches and Chapels* was copyrighted in March 1816. It contains thirty-seven Anglican chants, twelve of which are claimed as Jackson's; no Gloria Patri (despite the title page); and a revised version of the so-called Sanctus (actually a short introductory sentence, "Arise, O Lord, into thy rest") that had appeared in Jackson's

Sacred Music published in New York. There is also a short introduction about chanting.

The Choral Companion, and Elucidation of Dr. G. K. Jackson's Chants; The Whole Composed, Arranged and Published by Him was printed by E. Lincoln, Boston. Copies carry a copyright notice from the District of Massachusetts dated March 1, 1817, and an undated certificate from Bishop Alexander Griswold recommending it for Episcopal churches of the Eastern Diocese. It provides chants, some composed, others selected, for all the canticles and alternates of Morning Prayer and the sung portions of the Communion Office, as printed in the Book of Common Prayer of the Protestant Episcopal Church. They are more conveniently laid out than in the previous publication.[82]

Charles and Edwin Jackson's music-publishing business, opened in 1821 at 64 Market Street, Boston, was moved (or renumbered) to 44 Market Street later the same year, and it continued until 1826; a second address at 325 Broadway, New York, was in existence in 1825–26. Wolfe lists twenty-one publications issued under the joint name and a further 102 under the name of Edwin Jackson alone. The dispute between the two sons has already been mentioned.

Among their publications are a few reprints of their father's works. These include the songs "A prey to tender anguish," "The Sylph," and "Sweet are the banks" (Wolfe 4555, 4560, 4559); the cantata *A Winter's Evening* (4565); and the *Verses for the Fourth of July* under the title *A Favourite Ode in Celebration of the Fourth of July*. The treatise *I Rudimenti di Musica*, which has not survived in its original New York edition, now reappeared as *I-Rudementi-da-Musica or Complete Instructor for the Piano Forte including most of the Favourite Airs Songs & Dances Arranged & Fingered in Progressive Order also for the Flute & Violin* (Wolfe 4525; K 58, 95).

Many of Jackson's more popular pieces were reprinted in New York, Boston, Philadelphia, and elsewhere—as separate pieces, in anthologies, and in periodicals. Most notably, five of his sacred works were reprinted in *The Boston Handel and Haydn Society Collection of Sacred Music*, which was edited anonymously by Lowell Mason and published in 1821. But they were removed from all later editions of the collection.

APPEARANCE AND PERSONALITY

Our impression of Dr. Jackson's appearance has been strongly colored by H. Earle Johnson's 1943 article, which calls him "this Falstaffian colossus of three hundred pounds." This is based, in turn, on the rather pompous remarks of Gen. Henry K. Oliver (1800–1885), who can have known his subject only in

late-middle or old age: "Dr. Jackson was somewhat tardigrade and undemonstrative; of a measurably lethargic nature, yet without mental obtuseness.
. . . Dr. Jackson was of vast ponderosity, and like Falstaff, 'larded the lean earth as he walked along.' He was a very incarnation of obesity." A more neutral report, noted by the New York registrar of aliens in 1812, reads: "5 ft. 4¹/₂ in., florid complex[ion], dark hair, blue eyes."[83] Beyond that, there is a single surviving portrait of the man, a sketch made from life by Gilbert Stuart Newton (1794–1835) (fig. 19).

Johnson was unable to resist the pleasure of ridiculing Jackson on the sole basis of his size, which he did at several points in his short essay; for instance, referring to his arrival in Boston: "Imagination would like to fancy the populace turning out *en masse* to view the mighty man, come like a ship under full sail, with many children, bound volumes of Handel's celebrated oratorios, a grand pianoforte, and other paraphernalia incidental to a private musical establishment, the procession finally arriving at 18 Pinkney Street, where the great man descended and took up residence at the foot of Beacon Hill."[84]

This may be an unfair caricature. But it does seem that Jackson, at least in his later years, had an inflated view of his own importance and was consequently difficult to deal with. His refusal to join the Handel and Haydn Society unless he was paid an "enormous sum" and given sole direction of the musical events may be an example, though it can be interpreted in other ways. He was certainly in dire need of money, and may have tried to hold out for a larger salary in the hope of paying off some of his debts. And he may have been correct in thinking that nobody in Boston but he had the necessary knowledge and experience to direct oratorio performances in the proper fashion.

But there is little doubt that he could be obnoxious:

Whenever opposition was offered to his will the doctor sent in his resignation, as at Brattle Street Church, when complaint was made that he made too great a display of his accomplishments, and at Trinity [Boston] when Dr. Gardiner requested him to shorten his voluntaries, and he replied by advising the reverend gentleman to curtail his sermons. On the following Sunday, he gave vent to his ill-humour by picking out the psalm tunes with one finger, and on Easter Sunday, in assertion of his dignity as sufficient to exempt him from interference, appeared in the choir attired in the dress of an English Doctor of Music, with plum-colored coat, yellow breeches, and a square cap. This filled the measure of his offences and brought about the acceptance of his resignation.[85]

DR. G. K. JACKSON.

Fac Simile of a Pencil Sketch

by G. S. NEWTON.

Figure 19. Sketch of Jackson by Gilbert Stuart Newton (1794–1835) (Courtesy Boston Athenaeum)

These attributes may have been the reason, also, for his earlier downfall in London. The subscription list in his *Treatise* contains many influential names from several circles of English society. The fact that he failed to build a flourishing career on such patronage, despite his undoubted abilities, hints at the possibility that he was a proud and obstinate man, unwilling to offer the deference that the upper classes expected in those times. Far greater men than he, including Mozart and Beethoven, complained of the low standing of musicians in this period.

To take an example closer to home, Jackson may have shared the fate of his famous English contemporary, Samuel Wesley (1766–1837). Wesley's biographer, reflecting on a relatively unsuccessful career despite outstanding gifts, has written: "Musicians laboured under the disadvantage of the low status that had traditionally been the lot of the profession. Although many were no doubt untroubled by this, for others their low status and the condescending attitudes to be encountered in some employers and patrons and members of the public were a continual source of dissatisfaction. . . . Wesley's caustic wit and his habit of speaking his mind—widely commented on by contemporary observers and in his obituaries—cannot have helped his advancement with his fellow musicians or his potential patrons."[86]

This type of frustration may have been a factor in Jackson's life story also. First he tried to enhance his status in England by means of a series of publications culminating in a doctoral degree. If the result was not what he had hoped, he may have decided to move to the United States, in the belief that musicians would be treated more respectfully in that egalitarian society. Even there, however, he apparently did not receive what he thought was his due. His mode of showing resentment, as we have seen, cost him his job at Trinity Church. It may have hindered his success in other arenas as well.

A more attractive side of Jackson's character emerges in his publications for children, for example the *New Bagatelles for the Voice & Piano Forte* (New York, 1801). The title page says it is "Calculated for Juvenile Improvement," and the contents show a vein of kindly humor. The work consists of amusing settings of the alphabet and various arithmetical tables (ex. 40). Judiciously used, these could help a child in the tedious business of memorizing letters and numbers, while imparting musical skill and knowledge at the same time. Jackson took the opportunity to introduce the student to various keys, meters, and styles ("Pomposo," "Siciliana," and so on). These tuneful and innocuous little pieces suggest that the learned and perhaps self-important doctor was willing to descend to a child's level and to combine fun with instruction—surely the mark of a good teacher.

Example 40. Jackson, *New Bagatelles,* "Subtraction Table," No. 3, "2 for 3," mm. 1–4

TEACHING METHODS

We know that teaching was Jackson's principal activity, especially in his New York period, and that he taught piano, singing, and thorough-bass. His surviving piano tutor, carelessly named (in the Boston edition) *I-Rudementi-da-Musica,* gives few indications of how he taught the piano.[87] After an introductory section explaining music notation, and some scales with conventional fingering, it consists of a well-designed sequence of pieces in progressive order, some based on popular tunes of the day, others specially composed and attributed to "Dr. Jackson." These are modest enough, but they benefit from Jackson's happy ability to write a pleasing tune when he wanted to. There are other published teaching pieces as well, such as the *Petits Duos* for four hands, dedicated to female pupils. There is a similar *Selection for the Flute or Violin,* published in Boston.

Though there is no published singing tutor, several of his song anthologies were doubtless meant as teaching pieces. He also used music as an aid to other branches of education, for instance in the *New Bagatelles for the Voice & Piano Forte* just described.

For more advanced teaching, the volumes of his library, preserved at Illinois State University, show what musical repertories he used. Several of them have flyleaf inscriptions in Jackson's hand, telling how he used them for teaching. However, as these notes were probably connected with an attempt to sell the volumes, it is possible to doubt whether they are strictly accurate. Volume 5, for instance, is inscribed "G. K. Jackson his book, containing MSS. songs for publication and used in his Singing School &c &c and Concerts," from which one might infer that it contained songs composed by him; but in fact almost all the songs are by his father, Joseph Jackson, who died in 1759; some bear mid-eighteenth-century dates. None of George's own published songs are among them. They could, of course, have been used by his voice students, but it seems unlikely he would have chosen so many songs in an outmoded idiom.

Volume 6, in a similarly old binding titled "M.S.S. Vol. 1. ITALIAN SONGS, &c.," was also probably his father's, but with later additions. It is inscribed "G. K. Jackson, his Book. Containing Italian Songs, Concertos for the piano, and Haydn's Sinfonies in score, and used in his singing school and his school for the piano, and for his public Concerts." Volume 8 is inscribed "Manuscript Italian music for the voice and instruments used in instructing his Scholars in the Italian Mode of Blending Voices and Instruments together, and for singing the soprano &c." Volume 10, comprising the second volume of Domenico Scarlatti's "Essercizi" published at London in 1740, is stated to have been "used for the Improvement of his Schoolars [*sic*] in Playing on the Organ, Harpsichord or Piano Forte in his School, &c." This one also has an earlier inscription, "Geo. Jackson, 1780." Evidently the Italian school prevailed, not only, as one might expect, in the singing lessons he gave but in the keyboard lessons as well. By contrast, the volume of English theater songs (volume 9) lacks any inscription stating that it was used for teaching.

Volume 3 relates to his thorough-bass teaching. It is inscribed "G. K. Jackson his Book & used in his Music School for the Theoretic Part of Instruction." It contains a twenty-four-page treatise on notation and harmony entitled "Examples of Composition," which was evidently a draft of *A Treatise on Practical Thorough Bass*, printed about 1790. Like many such works, the *Treatise* combines some traditional academic concepts with the results of practical experience. Thus Jackson feels it necessary to explain the Gamut and the three modes of ancient Greece, but he also makes an honest effort to teach his readers how to realize a figured bass. There is a useful section, which appears to be original, on different ways of filling out chords defined by bass figures, and another on ways to resolve discords. But much space (and production expense) is wasted by pedantically printing out the same progressions in every known key. This is taken to absurd lengths in a manuscript "Toccamento," which reaches to keys with up to twenty-four sharps or flats.[88]

JACKSON AS PERFORMER

Jackson's performing career blossomed only after he arrived in New York; it seems that his talents were not sufficient to overcome the more severe competition that existed in London. His instruments were organ, harpsichord, piano, and bells. There is nothing to suggest that he continued to sing after his voice changed.

As an organist he was clearly considered competent to hold church positions, and in the United States he was regarded as "deservedly celebrated."[89]

Parker called him "pre-eminent" in this role: "Any one acquainted with the true style of Organ playing must acknowledge his unrivalled talents, his voluntaries were elaborate and replete with chromatic harmonies, embracing the most scientific and classic modulations. His interludes to psalmody were particularly appropriate to the sentiments expressed in the subject."[90] This wording is strikingly similar to Carr's description of Taylor's organ playing, cited in chapter 3, which Parker had edited and printed in *Euterpeiad*. Equally high praise comes from William Bentley, pastor of First Church, Salem, who wrote in his diary after the oratorio concert of December 1, 1812: "The celebrated Dr. Jackson, an Englishman, performed on the Organ with great power and pure touch. . . . The instrumental music transcended the vocal. . . . Dr. Jackson's voluntaries were beyond anything I ever heard and the best music was before the Chorus when the Organ was accompanied only with the violins."[91] The *Columbia Centinel,* not always friendly to Jackson, took a more moderate position: "Although Dr. Jackson is entitled to great praise and was perhaps the first [i.e., foremost] organist in the Republic, yet I presume there are more than one in Europe who were his rivals at least."[92]

It appears then that Jackson's organ-playing, like Taylor's, was unusually brilliant by American standards of the time, and it probably displayed "learned" techniques that few others in the States had mastered, such as modulations, suspension chains, and contrapuntal imitation, as well as rapid scales and figures. Of course, American organs, like English ones, lacked pedals. We cannot form much idea of his technical prowess, since no organ voluntary composed by him survives in print or manuscript. A few examples of his interludes were printed, but they are rudimentary and hardly display the virtues praised by Parker.[93]

He may have been at least equally skilled at the harpsichord. He played harpsichord concertos in London in the early 1780s. His Op. 4 sonata "for the Harpsichord or Piano Forte," though not a virtuoso piece, testifies to a good command of the instrument's capabilities. As time went on, of course, the piano was becoming the principal keyboard instrument, and it was used for accompaniment and an occasional solo in Jackson's New York concerts, but there is nothing to suggest that his piano-playing was anything out of the ordinary.

Jackson was also interested in bells, probably a carillon played on a keyboard and representing the diatonic scale. He composed several pieces that incorporated bells, and he played the carillon in the "Celebrated Bell Chorus" from Handel's *Saul* ("Welcome, welcome, mighty king") at the oratorio concert at King's Chapel, Boston, in 1812.

It is notable that Jackson never ventured into the world of theater music, either in London or New York. This cannot have been due to lack of opportunity, for, as we know, the Chapel Royal choirboys often performed in the Italian opera, and Samuel Arnold, also a chapel boy, became a leading composer of opera and had no apparent problem combining that with a career in church music. Nevertheless many churchmen of the time, including Anglicans, disapproved of the theater, and although Jackson is not known to have held any such scruples, some of his patrons may have done so. In New York he could not claim either experience or connections in the theater.

THE JACKSON CANON

Jackson, throughout his career, devoted much attention to canons and related devices, to a degree that was unusual in the classic period. One of the manuscript volumes of his library shows some of the working sketches of his canons.[94] The genre seems to have satisfied two almost opposite traits in his character. One was his boyish liking for tricks and jokes, which never quite deserted him in adulthood, and which he hoped would appeal to the children he taught. The other was a desire to maintain his reputation as a learned composer, worthy of the title of Doctor of Music, which was essential for his teaching career, especially in America.

Not all canons are arcane; not all are difficult to compose. If the pitch interval is unison (that is, all voices sing the melody at the same pitch) and the time interval between the successive entries is two measures or more, the composer needs only to write a short self-contained musical phrase in several equal parts and then repeat it with each voice switching to another part. This is called a round, of course. It was an ancient popular form, going back in English tradition at least to the thirteenth-century Reading Rota ("Sumer is icumen in") and including such perennials as "Three blind mice," "Scotland's burning" (or "London's burning"), and "Great Tom is cast." The shorter the time interval, the more difficult it is to escape harmonic monotony. The only other difficulty faced by the composer is to avoid consecutive fifths, unisons, or octaves among the parts.

Jackson wrote many canons of this type and often reused and improved on them in later publications. The most extensive collection was *A New Musical Score of Easy Canons . . . Sacred to Masonry,* partly based on earlier publications. The Freemasons in New York no doubt revered the art of canon writing as a "mystery" comparable to their own, and this aspect is emphasized in the elaborate engraved titled page, noted earlier.

The first canon in the book, "Praise the Grand Master of the Universal Lodge" (see fig. 16, p. 149), is an elaboration of "Three blind mice," made more learned by combining the tune with its retrograde. Another (ex. 41) is based on the old English song "One evening having lost my way." This tune was better known by the text set to it by John Gay in *The Beggar's Opera* (1728), Lucy's song in act 3, "I'm like a skiff on the ocean tossed." It was the basis of the overture to *The Beggar's Opera*, composed by John Christopher Pepusch. Jackson had already used it as a jolly drinking song, "Come, lads, your glasses fill with glee," in the *New Miscellaneous Work*, adding "huzzas" on repeated tonic and dominant notes to the four-bar melody. Now he changed the words to a Masonic text and added a two-measure rest during which each singer is invited to "Drink a Bumper." In this humorous fashion he was able to string the tune out to ten measures and, by having the voices enter at one-measure intervals, to set it out in score over two tall pages as a "Convivial MASONIC CANON for 10 Voices."

He had enough command of the canonic art to be able to write a free-flowing and natural-sounding melody that would work well as a canon. One of his best in this respect, also from the Masonic collection, is "On the Level we meet" (ex. 42), with a punning text that may or may not be Jackson's own. Not the least attractive feature is that the melody repeats after nine measures

Example 41. Jackson, *New Musical Score*, "May all the Universe"

Example 42. Jackson, *New Musical Score*, "On the Level"

rather than the expected eight, mitigating the inevitable repetitiveness of the harmony by shifting the metric stress.

Jackson seems never to have attempted the more demanding task of writing a canon at an interval other than the unison or octave. But at times he set himself the challenge of overcoming the harmonic repetition characteristic of unison canons. In the three canons published with the anthem "Ponder my words" as Op. 2, he was perhaps thinking of pleasing an audience (not to mention critics) as well as the singers themselves, and therefore he needed to vary the harmonic progression to make a satisfying whole. The first, "O God, the Father of heaven" (ex. 43), is for three voices at the octave, with

Example 43. Jackson, Op. 2, "O God, the Father of heaven" (canon 3 in 1 at the octave), mm. 1–14

a one-measure time interval between entries that would tend to force har-monic repetition. But by using rests between the successive phrases Jackson was able to progress through differing harmonic patterns: the first phrase has I–V in each measure, the second V–I, the third IV–V, and by the fourth we find we have reached the dominant key, where the opening phrase is repeat-ed in modified form (m. 11); eventually Jackson negotiates a return to the tonic. Successful modulation in a strict canon at the unison is a genuine in-tellectual feat. Although there is some sense of strain here, there is also an intensity lacking in his more convivial canons.

The second canon, "Hear my prayer, O Lord" (ex. 44), is for three voices at the unison. It never departs from the I–V pattern of its opening measure, but maintains interest by a delightfully unexpected leap to a high A, and lat-er by momentarily touching on the parallel minor. The third canon, "There in incessant songs of praise," is more monotonous, but redeemed by a shapely melodic line. All three of these canons found a place in the Masonic collec-tion, with minor adjustments and, in two cases, new words.

Jackson achieved harmonic variety in an attractive two-voiced unison can-on, "Waft me some soft and cooling breeze," published in the *New Miscella-neous Musical Work*. The same publication contains an ingenious song, "The groves, the plains," that is sung first forward and then backward, together with its instrumental bass.[95] He heads it *Cancherizante*, a reference to the crab can-on—that coveted symbol of musical learning—though strictly speaking it is not a specimen of the genre. Jackson did write at least one real crab canon, "Praise the Grand Master" (already described). He also published an amusing but not very learned quodlibet, entitled "A Musical Coalition: Wherein the prevailing Discords between America, France, & England, are Harmoniously adjusted. or a Humorous Combination of their National Airs." It ingeniously

Example 44. Jackson, Op. 2, "Hear my prayer, O Lord" (canon 3 in 1 at the unison)

combines "Ça ira" in G, then C (set for "French Zauber Flote or Enchanted Flute"), with "Yankee Doodle" in C (set for "American Martial Band," but only a melodic line). They are accompanied by "God Save the King," rhythm only, for "English Man of War: Drum Beating," in 3/4 meter against the duple meter of the other two tunes.

SACRED COMPOSITIONS

Jackson published twenty-eight original hymn tunes proper, and seven moral songs, in *Dr. Watts's Divine Songs,* Op. 1 (London, [c. 1785]); twenty original hymn tunes in *David's Psalms* (New York, 1804); and three more in *Sacred Music* (New York, [c. 1807?]).[96] A few were reprinted in one or two other collections, but none became as widely popular as, for instance, Taylor's "Stepney."

The strongest point in Jackson's early tunes is their flowing melody, making much use of appoggiaturas (ex. 45). A curious defect is their tendency to spend too much of their short length in the dominant key, throwing their tonality off-center. No less than seven of the twenty-eight tunes in Op. 1, including the one shown here, have a middle half-cadence on V/V, a most unusual feature in four-line tunes (and oddly reminiscent of Selby's first song: see ex. 7). In example 45 the music persists in the same direction in measures 10–11 and seems well on the way to a full cadence in B flat, when it is wrenched back to E flat in the concluding phrase.

As already pointed out, this collection would not have been used in Anglican churches at the time, and we know nothing of the music of St. Alban, Wood Street, where Jackson was organist. He published only one anthem, "Ponder my words," Op. 2 (unless the three canons in the same publication are counted as such). It is a very modest, treble-dominated piece in ternary form, for three voices and organ, which might possibly have been sung by the children's choir at St. Alban's with the help of a volunteer bass singer.

Jackson was also active in Episcopal churches in America, holding several organists' positions, as we have seen. Like Taylor, he was pressed into service by the Reverend William Smith, who acknowledged his help. He took considerable pains to assist the Episcopal Church's efforts to develop a choral tradition, including chanting. Ruth Wilson considers that Jackson, rather than Taylor, was "generally recognized as the leading authority on English cathedral music," and she adduces the remarks of the Reverend Jonathan Wainwright in *A Set of Chants* (Boston, 1819): "With respect to the music, the Compiler . . . has been able to avail himself of the important assistance of Dr.

Example 45. Jackson, *Dr. Watts's Divine Songs*, Op. 1: Song XVII (bass figures omitted)

G. K. Jackson, whose profound knowledge of the science of harmony, and long acquaintance with Cathedral music, render him in every way competent to the task."[97]

In view of this encouragement from church leaders, it is surprising that Jackson did not compose and publish any anthems or canticle settings for Episcopal use in either New York or Boston. An undated *Te Deum* setting in E flat, for four-part choir and organ with verses for soloists, remained unfinished.[98] He did, however, contribute more than a dozen single and double psalm chants, mostly in the ornate style that was admired at the time. Though their reciting notes often seem too high for a parish choir, they are effectively harmonized in four parts (ex. 46; notation standardized).

Jackson's most significant religious works were nonliturgical, and could be called "sacred cantatas." They were published separately, then together, at New York in about 1808, under the combined title *Pope's Universal Prayer and Sacred Ode*. Alexander Pope (1688–1744), the Roman Catholic turned deist and satirist, might seem an odd choice of poet at this stage of Jackson's career. But

Example 46. Jackson, *A Choice Collection of Chants,* Double Chant No. 32 (bass figures omitted)

the two poems concerned are hardly typical of their author. Both were well known in America and had been set by other composers. They may have appealed to the Unitarian sentiment that now prevailed in Boston. Neither refers directly to Christ. As lyrics they are somewhat abstract, but they have the advantage of evoking an abundance of images and emotions that invite musical setting.

The *Universal Prayer* (see fig. 17, p. 150) has an ecumenical or even pantheistic text, beginning:

> Father of all, in ev'ry Age,
> In ev'ry Clime ador'd,
> By Saint, by Savage, or by Sage,
> Jehovah, Jove, or Lord.

Jackson set it as a long and elaborate cantata for solo voice and piano (but still with figured bass), with a final "Cho[ru]s" for two high voice parts only. The entire work is set on two staves and extends to 418 measures, in nine sections (with some tempo and meter changes within sections as well), and it has a well-planned tonal structure. It might prove tediously long in performance, but there are some sections that are undeniably expressive (ex. 47). The style is basically Mozartian, aiming at tender sensibility, with many expression marks, but it reverts to a Handelian idiom for the "Fuga" (for solo voice and instrumental bass) and for the final chorus.

The ode entitled "The Dying Christian to His Soul" (see fig. 18, p. 151) was a well-known text that had attracted several British and American composers. The earliest known setting, by Edward Harwood (1707–87), was immensely popular in both Britain and the United States; there was also a setting by William Billings.[99] In spite of the word "Christian" in the title, and the adaptation of a famous text from 1 Corinthians 15:55 ("O death, where is thy sting? O grave, where is thy victory?"), the ode is short on doctrine, dwelling instead on the imagined feelings of a soul in the process of dying. Jackson's

Example 47. Jackson, *Pope's Universal Prayer*, mm. 34–62

setting is for solo voice, three-part chorus or possibly trio (SSB), violin, and piano. There is a figured bass, and the piano accompaniment would be self-sufficient in the absence of a violin. Again, the right hand shares a stave with the voice part.

This is a work of considerable interest, and it is on a more compact scale than the *Universal Prayer* (191 measures in six principal sections). It begins in robust fashion (see fig. 18), but its momentum is interrupted to express the sentiment "Oh, the pain, the bliss of dying." Another energetic section (3/8 *agitato*) is slowed at "Let me languish into life" (that is, death and eternal life). Now a genuinely original choral effect illustrates the whispering of the angels (ex. 48). After further exchanges, the solo has her last utterance in a pathetically descending phrase ("The world recedes, it disappears"). The tempo and mood of the opening are brought back in the last chorus, which makes effective use of unisons (ex. 49).

Jackson presumably published both these works for domestic use, and no public performance of either is on record. They have none of the coloratura writing found in some of Taylor's "public" songs arranged for the domestic market. But they make considerable demands on amateur singers, especially in regard to range—the *Prayer* takes the soprano to b" flat, the *Ode* to c'''—and they both have a grand, symphonic-style ending. They are, by a long way, the most ambitious compositions attempted by Jackson after his arrival in the United States. Perhaps, though this is mere speculation, they were prompted by the death of one of his children: of the eleven he is said to have had, only five were recorded in the 1820 census.

On the borderline between the sacred and the patriotic are his funeral pieces for American statesmen. The "Dirge for General Washington" is a simple lament without religious overtones. The music, for voice and piano, was published, along with a short programmatic Dead March, in *New Miscellaneous Musical Work*. It is classical in idiom, in a slow 3/4 meter and in binary form with repeats; the diction is restrained and dignified, with a few rhetorical pauses; the harmony is largely diatonic.[100] In Sterling Murray's view of the Dirge, "the composer has blended the naiveté of a Vauxhall song with the nobility of a Handelian aria, matching the union perfectly to the occasion." It is scorned by Wilfred Mellers, whose agenda for American music rejected most European influences.[101]

Far different in character is the *Ode for Gen!. Hamilton's Funeral* (1804), issued as a separate publication. It is a glee for unaccompanied men's voices (AATB) in the authentic English manner, scored (unusually for an American print) in C clefs for the three upper voices. I conclude that the New York Musical

Example 48. Jackson, *The Dying Christian to his Soul,* mm. 68–72 (bass figures omitted)

Example 49. Jackson, *The Dying Christian to his Soul*, mm. 150–54 (bass figures omitted)

Society, to which it is dedicated, was a men's glee club along English lines. We have already observed the scarcity of countertenors in America, so it is quite possible that the parts were taken by British expatriates, including possibly Jackson himself, when it was sung at a gathering of the society. The music shows, like no other surviving piece of Jackson's, his experience and skill in writing for men's solo voices in rich close harmony, surmounted by the melancholy wail of the countertenors (exx. 50, 51). The many dynamic marks and carefully timed rests show his concern for exquisitely sensitive expression. The tragic circumstances of Hamilton's death became the pretext for an orgy of grief. If Jackson learned to write like this in England, there is no surviving example to show it. At the same time I know of no other American composition of the period that resembles this glee. Since the words are general in their references to death, he may have composed it in England, brought it with him in manuscript, and later published it for this suitable occasion.

SECULAR VOCAL MUSIC

There are two patriotic effusions by Jackson of a more public character; they have been mentioned among the New York publications. One, "Jefferson's March," seems to have enjoyed a good deal of popularity in the first decade of the nineteenth century. It began as an instrumental march in C, followed by a simple quickstep. An untitled autograph manuscript survives, originally scored for clarinets, horns, bassoons, timpani, and strings (fig. 20).[102] Later annotations add flutes, and an untexted voice part below the score.

On March 2, 1801, the *Daily Advertiser* announced the sale of *President Jefferson's New March and Quick Step, for the Voice and Piano Forte* with "words written by Mrs Jackson expressly for the occasion in eight verses with chorus: 'In manly worth and true-born pride / Let no base plot your states divide.'" These words reflect the hotly contested election that had recently taken place between Adams and Jefferson, with the House of Representatives deciding the outcome. Two days later Jefferson was inaugurated. Subsequent events suggest that Jackson is likely to have been a supporter of the defeated Adams, but that was not the point. The name "Jefferson's New March" shows a desire to compete with a popular anonymous piece called "Jefferson's March" that was used in the inauguration procession.[103]

No copy of this advertised edition has been found. But not long afterward, Jackson published *Freedom and Our President for the Voice & Piano Forte.* It is evidently a different edition, for it has a new title and an added part for violin or flute. It is followed by the same quickstep, and the words answer

Example 50. Jackson, *Ode for Genl. Hamilton's Funeral*, mm. 1–17

Example 51. Jackson, *Ode for Genl. Hamilton's Funeral*, mm. 75–83

the advertised description of the earlier edition: there are eight verses, beginning "Immortal Jefferson, in tuneful lays" followed by the chorus "In
manly worth" as above.

The music is essentially that of figure 20 but is now transposed into D
major, probably to accommodate trumpets. It is a martial song in binary
form. The chorus is a strenuous shout of patriotism, now taking the voice
to a high b".

Two years later, a third version of the same music was adapted to new
words by a Mr. Townsend, performed at the Presbyterian Church, and published as *Ode for the Fourth of July*. As the new lines were four-foot anapests
instead of five-foot iambics, some revision was needed (ex. 52b). Jackson also
brought the music closer to a formal aria, adding an eleven-bar opening ritornello and a middle symphony. In the chorus the high B's are replaced and
the huzzas removed. Perhaps a more moderate tone was thought appropriate for a church performance.

Figure 20. Jackson, March in C Major, autograph manuscript (Courtesy Milner Library Special Collections, Illinois State University)

Finally, there must have been a revival of the original published version (ex. 52a). The only known exemplar of the 1801 print *Freedom and Our President* has corrections in ink in Jackson's hand: "Jefferson's March" is altered to "Washington's March" in the heading, and "Immortal Jefferson" to "Immortal Washington" in the text. And a copyist manuscript of a viola part of this version, under the title "Washington's March" (with the quickstep following), survives.[104] It must have been used on an occasion where a specific reference to the current president was not appropriate.

(a) *Freedom and our President*, opening

(b) *Ode on the Fourth of July*, opening

Example 52. Two versions of a song by Jackson

A different work celebrating Independence Day was published about 1803 as *Verses for the Fourth of July*. It too had words by Jane Jackson and was sung at the Presbyterian Church, but, as already noted, it was also sung at Mount Vernon Gardens on July 4, 1803, following a play called *The Glory of Columbia*. It is quite similar in style, though not in musical content, to the last version of "Immortal Jefferson," and it is even more clearly in the form of a concert aria, often bringing to mind the name of a close contemporary of Jackson's, Mozart.

Two other public songs later issued with reduced accompaniments are "The Cricket, . . . Sung by Miss Brett with Applause," in which the main feature is a chirpy imitation of the insect on an "Octave Flute" (piccolo), and "Ah! Delia, . . . Sung by Mrs. Hodgkinson with Applause," published on three staves with an accompaniment for harp, with a tune not unlike that of "L'Adieu."

In the realm of domestic songs—probably the easiest kind of music to sell in Jackson's time—he produced a fairly constant flow through most of his active career, though he was not as prolific as Taylor. His first published song was probably "L'Adieu" (fig. 21), known in America as "The Kiss" or "One kind kiss." As Jackson's most successful publication, it has attracted the notice of writers on American popular song, but it has been misunderstood. Tawa chose it as a typical example of "Saying good-bye to home and dear one, . . . an often heard theme in pre-1840 American songs."[105] Hamm, also believing it to be an "American" song, developed the same idea, calling it "a minor masterpiece. . . . It is a simple song of parting," and later suggesting that "there is a difference in temper of songs written here in the decades surrounding the turn of the century and those written in England at the same time. America had only recently experienced a difficult and divisive struggle for independence. . . . Americans had experienced separation from loved ones." It is not surprising, Hamm continued, that "many of the most popular songs written in America . . . deal with the pain of separation from a loved one."[106]

In reality the theme of "L'Adieu"/"One kind kiss" has nothing to do with leaving home or the pains of war. It is a simple lovers' parting—not forever, but "'till we meet." The words are by the English poet Robert Dodsley (1703–64). Its bittersweet pathos of love frustrated by external forces, surely one of the oldest topics of song, was particularly popular in the eighteenth-century Italian *canzonetta* and its English imitations, including Haydn's. The two earliest settings of this text were published in London about 1743, on the same page, both titled "The Parting Kiss."[107] One was anonymous, the other "Set by Mr [James] Oswald." The former (ex. 53a) was already popular in America when Jackson arrived, as "One kind kiss." Indeed, some of the publications that have been cited as evidence of the popularity of Jackson's song are actually of the anonymous earlier setting.[108]

When it became part of the Op. 3 *Collection,* Jackson's "L'Adieu" gained an eight-measure introduction similar to the conclusion. Its arrival in America preceded its composer's; it was probably brought over by Mrs. Hodgkinson, an English soprano who made her American debut in New York in 1793. In American editions, it lost its delicate violin *obbligato* and its original title. The first, published as "One kind kiss" by Carr and dated 1796 by Evans,[109] has a twelve-measure introduction and many minor revisions. It was copied, misprints and all, in an edition by John Aitken (Philadelphia, [1808–11]). By changing the title Jackson was clearly hoping that his setting would replace the anonymous one in the popular mind. The left-hand accompaniment of

Figure 21. Jackson, "L'Adieu," London edition (Courtesy British Library)

meet shall pant for you   One kind Kifs be-fore we part Drop!drop!a

Tear Drop!drop!a   Tear   Drop   a Tear and bid a — dieu

2
Yet, yet weep not fo my Love,
    Let me Kifs that falling Tear,
Tho' my Body muft remove,
    All my Soul muft ftill be here
Yet, yet weep not fo my Love,
    Let me Kifs that falling Tear.

3
One kind Kifs before we part
    Drop a Tear and bid adieu
All my Soul and all my Heart,
    Ev'ry wifh fhall pant for you,
One kind Kifs then e'er we part
    Drop a Tear and bid adieu.

Figure 21 (cont.)

Example 53(a). Anonymous, "The Parting Kiss" (London, c. 1743), mm. 1–6

Example 53(b). Jackson, "L'Adieu" / "One kind kiss," edition of 1808–11, mm. 13–18

Example 53(c). Jackson, "L'Adieu" / "One kind kiss," edition of 1815–22, mm. 13–18

figure 21 is changed to an Alberti pattern (ex. 53b) and is more frequently interrupted by rests, plain chords, and fermatas; there are additional ornaments in the voice part. This is evidently the form that Hamm had in mind when he perceptively noted that it is "the work of an accomplished and sensitive musician. With its arpeggiated accompaniment, a graceful melodic line with effective use of appoggiaturas, and text repetition reflecting the unfolding melodic ideas, it is more reminiscent of Italian music than of English stage and concert songs."[110]

But Jackson was not yet finished with the song. He republished it himself between 1815 and 1822 (ex. 53c). It was now transposed down to E flat and provided with a full piano accompaniment on its own pair of staves.

The long-lost violin *obbligato* was restored in revised form, now for flute. Changes in the opening measure and in the texture of the accompaniment make it look and sound more like the rival anonymous setting (compare [c] to [a] in ex. 53), perhaps a final attempt to "bury" the older song. This edition was reissued by the composer's sons, C. and E. W. Jackson (Boston, 1825).

To return to the other songs of Op. 3, all but one deal with romantic love, thus catering primarily to feminine tastes of the time—no drinking, hunting, or indelicacy.[111] Many seem earlier in style than "L'Adieu," more in the voice-and-bass tradition of Arne (for example, Jackson's "The Inconstant," ex. 54), though there are no actual bass figures. Jackson's melodic facility seldom deserted him. Two of the ten pieces are duets, the voices moving mainly in parallel thirds in the *canzonetta a due* manner.[112]

Jackson published about a dozen new songs during his early years in New York. Several appeared in the *New Miscellaneous Musical Work,* with texts more varied in character than those of Op. 3. Two with a specifically American slant have already been discussed: the "Dirge for General Washington" and "Huzza! for Liberty" ("Come, lads, your glasses fill with glee"), the latter to be later turned into a canon. Another is called "American Serenade," but its words invoke Cupid and Venus and its music is purely lyrical. "The

Example 54. Jackson, "The Inconstant," mm. 9–19

Cricket" and "The Fairies" are simple melodies in 6/8, with broken-chord accompaniments. This is also true of the separately published songs "A Prey to Tender Anguish," "The Sylph" (words by Thomas Moore), and "The Fairies to the Sea Nymphs." All five bear a marked general similarity, even though "A Prey to Tender Anguish" has a text of suicidal gloom while the others are relatively cheerful.

One of the best songs from the *New Miscellaneous Musical Work* is "Sweet are the banks: A favorite Canzonet," which takes the form of a duet for two equal voices with instrumental bass. There is a two-part opening symphony that "may be played or omitted at pleasure," then a binary movement with repeats, without any additional stanzas. The words are of love in a natural setting. The first half discourses on the beauties of nature; the second half confesses "But oh! how sweeter far than these are the Kisses of her I love." The music is modeled on the *canzonetta a due,* and although the basic texture is one of parallel thirds, Jackson follows the best Italian models by using occasional contrapuntal entries and playing with dissonance (ex. 55).

A more ambitious effort from the same publication, but one of doubtful merit, is "A Winter's Evening. A Favorite Cantata, sung by Mr. Hodgkinson. Describing a forlorn Mother & Infant Perishing in the Snow." The anony-

Example 55. Jackson, "Sweet are the banks," mm. 23–26

mous text is excessively melodramatic, and to modern tastes approaches "high camp." Jackson labels and extravagantly illustrates such features as "Shivering," "Fall of Snow," and "Blast of Wind" in the accompaniment to the opening recitative, but the following "Air" (ex. 56) is a varied strophic song, providing little beyond pauses, expression marks, and one excursion into the parallel minor to reflect the turbulent emotions of the protagonist in the tragic scene.

It is interesting to compare this essentially classical rendering of a very unclassical text with a romantic setting of the same words, a few years later, by the short-lived Anglo-Italian genius George Frederick Pinto (1785–1806).[113] Pinto declines to illustrate the natural elements, but embodies the girl's crisis of despair in chromatic harmony and an increasingly agitated accompaniment, making full use of the powers of the piano (ex. 57). The horrific conclusion would take a Schubert to provide adequate musical treatment (one thinks of the end of *Erlkönig*). Pinto comes close (ex. 58), but Jackson is clearly out of his depth (ex. 59).

We know that Jackson was capable of a more intense and even romantic idiom from the already discussed *Ode for Genl. Hamilton's Funeral,* which for some reason stirred him to unusual creative effort. But it was rare for him to venture on texts of strong emotional content. His other compositions of the glee or part-song type are elegantly written and safely classical. *Content, A Favorite Canzone for 3 voices Composed for the Apollo Musical Society,* has a text "Halcyon nymph with placid smile" and is set as a simple rondo (ABABA) in strict four-bar phrases, accompanied by a figured bass. The Apollo Musical Society is likely to have been another glee club. *A Favorite Canzone For 1.2. or*

Example 56. Jackson, *A Winter's Evening,* second section, mm. 1–5

Example 57. George Frederick Pinto, *The Distress'd Mother,* mm. 25–35

3. *Voices* also has a harmlessly amorous text in a pastoral vein ("Soft pleasing sighs are love's delight"), written by Mrs. Jackson, and is dedicated to a Miss Susan Moore. It is set out for two (presumably women's) voices, a bass voice, and a piano part supplying a mostly Alberti-type accompaniment. This time the form is ternary.

If one can generalize about Jackson's vocal music, it seems that he usually relied on his melodic facility and competent technique to provide easily written, elegant products that reliably appealed to his female pupils and their friends, or to the choirs and congregations of churches. Occasionally, he could rise to greater efforts, to express the national pride or grief of his new American compatriots, or, in the case of the two Pope cantatas, to embody a philosophy of life and death that struck a chord in his own breast.

Example 58. Pinto, *The Distress'd Mother,* conclusion

Example 59. Jackson, *A Winter's Evening,* conclusion

INSTRUMENTAL MUSIC

Like his colleagues, such as Carr, Taylor, and Reinagle, Jackson soon found that there was no steady demand in America for original orchestral music going beyond marches, quicksteps, and dances, which gave little scope for originality. Some of these made their way into print in piano arrangements, along with teaching pieces for two and four hands. The manuscripts preserved at Illinois State University contain several such compositions, including the march later known as "Jefferson's New March," which turned into the songs that have already been discussed. It is a rare surviving example of Jackson's writing for orchestra. There is also a March and Troop for clarinet and posthorns that presumably was used at some military function. More interesting compositions are known from newspaper advertisements to have been publicly performed in New York, such as an "Overture with Double Fugue and Grand March," performed in 1801, and a Viola Concerto, performed in 1805, but unfortunately these have not survived.[114]

The only extant nonfunctional instrumental works date from his time in England. The three manuscript sonatas for violin and bass, already described, are immature student works in an antiquated style. More important is *A Favorite Sonata for the Harpsichord or Pianoforte*, in D major, published as Op. 4 in 1791, when Jackson was thirty-three years old.[115] It is quite evidently a serious effort in sonata writing, intended not so much to delight amateurs (and there is no dedicatee) as to claim significant standing for its composer. The writing is vigorous, mostly in two parts, and seems inspired by the harpsichord rather than the piano, despite occasional *crescendo* and *diminuendo* markings. (Most published keyboard works of that time catered to both instruments.) All three movements make much use of dotted rhythms and the "Scotch snap," which, being well past the peak of its appeal by 1791, contributes to the slightly old-fashioned character of this sonata.

Although Jackson is likely to have been familiar with sonatas of Haydn, Mozart, Clementi, and Dussek, he adopted an earlier style, with strong suggestions of C. P. E. Bach. For instance, the form of his first movement is not the classical sonata-allegro with a recapitulation in the tonic, well established by 1791, but the older type that Newman calls "binary sonata form."[116] Its exposition is a procession of idiomatic melodies: the first in D (ex. 60, mm. 1–8), the next modulatory (mm. 9–18), and at least three forming the second group, in A. After the double bar, the first theme is stated in A, then the second theme also begins in that key but leads on into extensive development. Some of the second-group material is recapitulated in G, the rest in D, making an extended but nicely balanced movement.

The second movement is marked *Andante: Affettuoso*. The first word describes its character better than the second. It is a stately minuet rather than a tender expression of feeling. Its texture throughout is that of a well-pointed melody over a walking bass. There are strong reminders of the angular chromaticisms of C. P. E. Bach, especially in a modulating sequence during the second half of the movement (ex. 61). The finale is a rollicking galop (ex. 62), in the form of a rondo. The two episodes are identical, as are the three statements of the rondo tune, suggesting a slight flagging of inventive power.

This admirable sonata bears little resemblance to anything else in Jack-

Example 60. Jackson, Piano Sonata, Op. 4, 1st movement, mm. 1–13

Example 61. Jackson, Piano Sonata, Op. 4, 2d movement, mm. 25–34

son's output. Here he is tough and wiry; elsewhere he is soft and melting. This can be interpreted as a sign of self-discipline. He had set himself the task as part of his plan to acquire *gravitas*. In this he succeeded, especially in the first movement, which would have done credit to any English composer of his generation. That the task was not altogether congenial is confirmed by the fact that he never wrote another sonata.

Example 62. Jackson, Piano Sonata, Op. 4, 3d movement, mm. 1–9

THE SIGNIFICANCE OF GEORGE JACKSON

More than Selby or Taylor, Jackson placed his faith in musical learning (and teaching), and to that extent he achieved success. The fact that he tacked one of his canons onto his New York edition of James Nares's *Thanksgiving Anthem* suggests that he was profoundly influenced by what he had learned from Dr. Nares when he was a Chapel Royal boy, and aspired to equal his master's achievement, not to mention his title. He persisted with the discipline of canons and other learned devices even after arriving in America, where it may be guessed that few people were equipped to appreciate them. He also took musical education seriously enough to publish several purely pedagogical works.

In Britain, though he acquired good connections and a doctorate and produced a quite impressive series of published compositions, he does not seem to have made any significant impression on either the musical establishment or the wider public, perhaps in part because of defects in his personality. But in America, he did succeed in overawing the public with his degree, his learned canons, and his undoubted knowledge of English church music and oratorio. There are signs that he reached a position of eminence, based on respect rather than affection, and was looked up to by musicians and clergy as the ultimate resident authority on musical correctness and propriety.

Like some other composers of the day, in both Britain and America, Jackson did not need to deploy his technical skills to their limits in order to write publishable compositions. He contributed his share of trivial popular music, including some apparently learned canons that were in fact quite easy to write. His melodic gifts often give considerable charm to his music for domestic amateurs, especially in songs like "L'Adieu"/"One kind kiss." And like Taylor, in a few cases he challenged himself to his best efforts—not only to maintain his reputation as a master composer, and hence preserve or enhance his income from teaching, but partly also, we may suppose, for his own satisfaction. My personal list of these "serious" works would include the canon "O God, the Father of heaven," Op. 2; the keyboard sonata, Op. 4; the *Ode for Genl. Hamilton's Funeral;* the setting of *Pope's Universal Prayer;* and the ode *The Dying Christian to His Soul.* By these works Jackson earned the right to be treated as a serious composer.

Conclusions

To migrate to America in the eighteenth century was not a step that any musician would take lightly. One who had a secure niche in the Old World would not be inclined to give it up for the unknown risks of the New, where earning a living was hard and unpredictable, and permanent appointments were virtually unknown. Why did William Selby, Rayner Taylor, and George K. Jackson decide to leave Britain?

Their musical reputations in London were good enough to give the lie to the harsh judgment of Maurer, who claimed that the professional musician "came to America because his second- or third-rate talent was no match for that of the brilliant virtuosi who abounded in the cities and courts of Europe."[1] All three of our subjects had done quite well in Britain, and, considered simply as musicians, they could have expected at least as bright a future there as in the United States. Why, then, did they emigrate?

WHY THEY LEFT BRITAIN

Selby gave up two secure jobs on the eve of his departure. He must have had a strong incentive to do so. He surely did not see great opportunities in New England, though he did at least have an offer of a church job there, and his brother was in a position to give him some informed advice and perhaps help him to get established. The important thing was that he had to leave London. His (inferred) scandalous dismissal from the Magdalen Chapel would have ruined the prospect of a successful career. True, he could not legally be deprived of his other two jobs. But his main source of income was probably private teaching, and this may well have collapsed along with his moral reputation, since most of those who would pay to study music were young ladies. Without influence in high places, nobody in Georgian England was going to achieve eminence. And Selby's own behavior may well have shut him out of such patronage.

Taylor seems to have been somewhat at a loose end after he left Sadler's Wells in 1791. He had failed to secure a London church job, and his only reliable income was from work at the Apollo Gardens, presumably augmented by teaching. On the other hand he was well known as an organist, director, and composer. It is hard to see how he can have expected that America, where he was unknown, would offer any immediate improvement in his professional standing. He had no kinsman there to get him started, nor had he been recruited or invited by any potential patron or colleague, or by his former pupil Reinagle. As with Jackson, the obvious explanation for his move is a personal one—a love affair with the young ingénue, Miss Huntley. Whether or not his wife was still living, he may have thought it easier to start a new life in a place where his personal history would not be well known.

Jackson's motive is the most difficult to guess. His behavior in 1789–91 looks like a determined effort to raise his standing. He was not a prominent public performer like Taylor, and apart from one song his compositions had not been much acclaimed. But the list of subscribers to his *Treatise,* headed by a wealthy nobleman, suggests that he had some influential support as well as a flourishing teaching practice. And he used some of this support to secure an impressive-sounding title. He published a substantial series of compositions. Were these efforts planned as the prelude to a new career in America? He resigned his organist position in 1790. But unlike Selby he did not first secure a corresponding position in America. And, inexplicably, he waited six years before crossing the ocean. No personal reason for him to leave Britain has been found, nor was there any known reason to think he would receive a warm welcome in the States. My best guess, based on what is known of his personality, is that his status-building efforts were at first designed to enhance his career and income in Britain; that he then "gave himself airs" in a way that made him too many enemies; and that he eventually concluded that he needed a fresh start in a place where he was not previously known, and where his paper credentials might open the way to a successful second career. But it was a gamble.

There remains the possibility that politics played a part in these musicians' migration. Did they feel sympathy for the ideals of the American revolution, or did they at least wish to escape the hierarchical society they had known in Great Britain, and to benefit from the freedoms promised by the U.S. Constitution? All three men produced patriotic odes, marches, and the like, soon after they had arrived in America. But no amount of analysis of these scores can reveal whether they express sincere feelings on the part of the composers. It was clearly in their interests to support the fervent American patriotism of the time, even if it meant renouncing the land of their birth. This was particularly true for Selby, who found himself in Boston at a dangerous moment—the conclusion of the Revolutionary War, when his brother had left with the British Empire Loyalists. He went so far as to advertise publicly his support for the new nation. Jackson was in similar trouble during the War of 1812, but his patriotic compositions are all of earlier date, and he seems to have made no move to escape internment by professing loyalty. On the contrary, a hostile reporter called him a "violent British partizan." Perhaps that is one reason why he was rebuffed in his last years by the Boston Handel and Haydn Society.

The intriguing case in this respect is Taylor. In the world of the London theater there were many who looked with sympathy on radical causes. The most famous was Richard Brinsley Sheridan, statesman, playwright, and manager of Drury Lane Theatre, whose active support of the American, French, and Irish republican movements at one point brought him close to arrest for treason.[2] Sheridan's version of Kotzebue's *Pizarro* (1799) introduced revolutionary ideas that were obvious enough to be detected by George III.[3] Perhaps Taylor, too, had motives beyond professional ones when he wrote some of the new music for *Pizarro* for the Philadelphia production of 1800.

Taylor's Huguenot background on his mother's side may have predisposed him toward challenges to royal authority. The Huguenots had come to England to escape persecution by Louis XIV; is it a coincidence that Taylor's greatest theatrical triumph depicted a popular celebration in France, in which Louis XVI was compelled to bow to a revolutionary settlement? Could he have been attracted to a similar idealism that he discerned in the American republic?

It is certain, at any rate, that he was the only one of our little sample of three who chose to become a naturalized American citizen. Being half French, he may have felt that much less patriotically British. He could have learned to speak French fluently from his mother and her relatives. In addition to the songs from *The Champs de Mars*, he published a surprisingly large number with French or half-French texts: "La petite Savoyarde" from *The Gates of Calais* (1786, reprinted in Paris about 1790), "De tout mon coeur" (1791–92), "En verité" (1791–92), "Ma chère et mon cher" (c. 1800), and "Ma jolie petite fille" (1801). He used "Ça ira" in at least three separate compositions. The strong ties between France and the United States that persisted after the War of Independence tended to arouse envy and alarm in most British people. In Taylor's mind they may have been a positive factor.

HOW THEY FARED IN AMERICA

Whatever our musicians may have expected to find on arrival in the States, all three had an uphill struggle there and had to wait for at least a year before establishing themselves in a major city. Selby at least had a salaried position awaiting him, one of very few available to musicians in New England at that time. But he again fell out of favor, first at Trinity, Newport, then at Trinity, Boston. This may have been due to a weakness for adolescent girls. It may have been because he was suspected of Toryism. Whatever the reason, he was once more in a precarious position, with little support from the society in which he was living.

He dealt with the situation by publicly asserting his support of the Revolution in the 1782 advertisement, backing it up with patriotic odes. Having declared that the young republic should be "In Song unequall'd as unmatch'd in war," he set about showing how this was to be achieved. First, summoning up the experience of his youth, he gave Bostonians a model for choral festivals that they could compare with travelers' descriptions of the great Handel commemorations in Westminster Abbey, or of the Oratorio Concerts at Covent Garden Theatre. Then, in 1791, he began to publish a series that would offer models for American composers, including in it, among established classics, some of his own best efforts at "scientific" composition. The publication failed, but it may have given him the satisfaction of showing what he could do at his best. The congregations of the Stone Chapel supported him generously. At last, in his fifties, he had achieved a degree of success that could give him self-respect and a measure of economic security.

Taylor also set his sights on getting an organist's post. Like Selby, he soon lost his first and second jobs, and presumably had to support himself and Miss Huntley on the proceeds of occasional entertainments and by his teaching and the sale of his compositions. He won a lasting post as organist only in 1798. Work for Philadelphia theaters, circuses, public gardens, societies, the Masonic Lodge, and the University of Pennsylvania was sporadic at best. He never achieved a permanent position in the theater, and probably was chronically short of money. In his last years he lived on charity. On the other hand, he gained professional esteem that must have exceeded what he had attained in Britain. His reputation as an organist was second to none, he was a recognized authority on musical matters, many of his songs were published and performed, and he achieved one more great success in the theater, The Æthiop.

Jackson's American story was similar, however much he differed from Taylor as man and musician and perhaps in political views. A permanent church job eluded him for several years; he earned his living chiefly through teaching, but it was insufficient for his large family. He barely kept his head above water financially, was several times caught by his creditors, and died almost penniless. But his authority as a learned musician remained high, bolstered in part by his doctorate; he too was famous for his organ playing; and he brought out a long series of publications. He seems to have taken teaching more seriously than either Selby or Taylor did, perhaps regarding it as his principal vocation; but he also continued to produce significant compositions.

We may conclude that despite the undoubted demand in America for musicians trained in Britain, earning a living was not easy in the decades around 1800, and it was probably more difficult in Boston, New York, or Philadelphia than in London. The United States was not yet a land of opportunity for professional musicians. They had to rely chiefly on what Carr called "the drudgery of teaching and a scanty organ salary," and it was not enough for a family man. An interesting question is whether they knew that this would be the case when they made the decision to move. Communications were slow, but there was surely a constant flow of information between expatriate musicians and their friends and colleagues who were still in Britain. Typically, immigrants wrote home to inform their family and friends about conditions in America. Carr wrote back soon after his arrival to urge his father and brother to follow him. But Carr had a reliable source of income denied to most musicians: a successful publishing business.

If Selby, Taylor, and Jackson did know about the hardships that awaited them, it reinforces the conclusion that they must each have had a strong personal reason for changing the scene of their activity.

WHAT THEY ACHIEVED AS COMPOSERS

Most of the musical institutions found in England, and the forms that went with them, existed also in America. (The principal exceptions were the Chapel Royal and the endowed cathedral choirs.) Immigrant composers could therefore, for the most part, continue to write the kinds of music they had written before, but they often had to lower their expectations.

Of course, the great advantage that composers like Selby, Taylor, and Jackson had over American-born composers lay in their training. Self-taught composers like William Billings, Lewis Edson, and Oliver Shaw could achieve much by combining reading with practical experience and imagination. But they could not fully master the idioms of European art music, and increasingly, this was the kind of music that most middle-class Americans wanted to hear and practice.

A second undoubted advantage was that they came from the place that was, for the time being, the fountainhead for American ideas of public music-making. "London's domination was complete," as D. W. Krummel put it;[4] he was speaking of Philadelphia's musical life in the two decades after 1800, but the same could just as well be said of Boston, New York, or any other large city in the former British colonies.

However, the prestige that London-trained musicians enjoyed in the young republic has been reversed by history. In the revival of early American music that took place in the later twentieth century, they were seen by some scholars as symbols of a snobbish anti-American prejudice. The native composers whom they had displaced in their lifetimes were now unearthed and held up for admiration, while they themselves were devalued as an undesired foreign import. This reaction may have reached the point of inverted prejudice. At any rate I have tried to form a fresh evaluation of each man in his whole life and output.

All three composers recognized that their strength lay in their mastery of the British or European idiom. It was as much sought after in America, and as easy to recognize, as American popular music is in Europe today. By doing what came naturally to them, they would almost automatically be accepted as first-rate musicians by the leaders of American opinion. On the other hand, they soon learned that if they were to please the larger public as well, their music must be simple, and must avoid anything too challenging, "scientific," or unfamiliar.

The clearest contemporary statement of this dichotomy comes in a 1796 review of one of Alexander Reinagle's theater pieces: "With respect to the music between the acts, it was more than commonly dull and heavy. . . . It is strange and most culpable conduct, after so many expressions of the public will on the subject, that attention is not paid to gratify that part of the audience who are not *amateurs* [that is, connoisseurs]. If Mr. Reinagle will persist in giving pieces of music occasionally to please the cognoscenti, let him, in compassion to the ears of the unlearned, introduce in turn those favorite Scotch and Irish airs, which light up pleasure in the countenances of nineteen twentieths of those who fill the house. The will of the majority ought to prevail in a place of amusement as well as in a Senate."[5] Reinagle complied in his public music-making, and he was commended by the same newspaper on June 11, 1797. If he also occasionally wrote music like the "Philadelphia Sonatas" to please the "cognoscenti," or just to please himself, he had been made painfully aware that it would not bring him financial reward or even much credit with the general public.

Financial need and the pressure of publishers, theater managers, and clergy often induced composers to lower their ideals and write "democratic" music in which popularity displaced art as the main goal. This was in no way a shameful act. Haydn, Mozart, and Beethoven did the same thing from time to time. But in German-speaking Europe, composers made most of their living from the cultivated aristocracy, where fine art-music was most appreciated and composers were encouraged to develop their highest talents. Britain was more democratic than Germany and Austria; it had a wealthy middle class, largely independent of the nobility, which encouraged simpler and more obvious musical effects. Those "favorite Scottish and Irish airs" were hugely popular in London.

The United States was even more democratic than Britain, and thus generated still more pressure on composers to lower their standards. The absence of royal, ecclesiastical, or aristocratic patronage left composers with only one paymaster: the public. They had no choice but to cater to it. (Of course, it was the wealthier portion that mattered. Those who were too poor to spend any money on music were outside the equation altogether.)

It was in the theater that there was the least difference between British and American musical tastes. In London, the aristocracy patronized the Italian opera at the King's Theatre, Haymarket, and tended to disdain the English operas performed at Covent Garden and Drury Lane, let alone the burlettas and pantomimes of Sadler's Wells or the melodramas and farces of the other "minor" theaters. In these places the managers depended directly on audience approval to balance their books. Audiences made it very clear if they were bored or offended by what was going on. Thus the control of music in the theater was almost as "democratic" in London as it was in Philadelphia. But the audiences in Britain had much broader experience of European art music.

What remains of Taylor's theater music consists primarily of the few songs that were successful enough to be taken on by publishers. Not surprisingly, these are much the same in character and artistic level, whether published in London or Philadelphia. But the two complete vocal scores and the published music from *The Champs de Mars* suggest that a somewhat higher level of sophistication was expected in London, especially in his younger days. And Carr remembered that "eminent professors of music" who visited Sadler's Wells under Taylor's regime "were delighted with the pleasing yet scientific style of the music."

Other forms of public music-making included the symphony and concerto; we have no surviving examples of these from the selected composers, other than Taylor's opera overtures in piano reduction. These suggest that he was an accomplished writer of orchestral music. The concert song also survives only in reduced arrangements, often designed to simulate the effect of orchestral instruments. A subset of these is the patriotic song. The only British example from our composers is Jackson's orchestration of "God Save the King"; but there was, for obvious reasons, a much greater demand on the American side, which all three strove to meet, partly no doubt to demonstrate their loyalty. A loud, slightly hollow kind of militancy pervades the odes, songs, and marches they wrote. Convention seemed to demand that patriotic harmonies should be limited to the three major diatonic chords. Other public odes and cantatas appeared, but they are rarely among their composers' most interesting works. In a class of its own is Jackson's glee in memory of Alexander Hamilton, a distinct throwback to an English genre that does not seem to have been widely adopted in America.

In the realm of church music, where all three composers were active, there was a similar need to cater to the public. Their hymn tunes and chants achieved some circulation in publications for church use. Though a "high" form of church music existed in the Chapel Royal and some cathedrals, none of the three was ever called on to provide music for use there: Taylor's three cathedral-type anthems were written for a magazine, not a cathedral choir. Their best efforts were in the form of domestic sacred music. Devout family gatherings were the probable destination of Selby's "Magdalen" hymn settings, Jackson's *Dr. Watts's Divine Songs,* and even Taylor's "cathedral" anthems. In all three cases, but especially Taylor's, the composer aimed at a higher artistic level than was practical in functional church music.

A further question concerns the three musicians' relationship to country psalmody, which was flourishing in both Britain and America throughout the period covered by this book. The parochial anthem and the fuging tune, however popular with voluntary choirs, were generally avoided by ambitious professional composers in England, except when they set out to "reform" parish-church music—as Arnold did, with the assistance of John Callcott, in *The Psalms of David* (London, 1791). Taylor's "Try me, O God" and Jackson's "Ponder my words" are simple anthems probably written for the urban choirs they directed, dominated by children's voices. So were the psalm or hymn tunes by all three composers that appeared in sundry collections.

In America, however, the music analogous to English country psalmody carried no stigma in the 1770s, and it was particularly popular with New

England singing schools. Selby, who is not known to have written for English country choirs, contributed four anthems and a doxology to the American repertory. In the first three anthems he followed the Billings model, sometimes trying to improve it by organ accompaniment and by using more advanced harmonies including modulation, sometimes deliberately imitating its bareness in order to gain acceptance in democratic circles. In his last anthem, "The heavens declare," he allowed himself to attempt something in the cathedral manner, with organ accompaniment, and included it at his own risk in a serial publication. It was a quixotic effort, and when the publication failed, the anthem disappeared without trace. By that time (1791), American tastes were changing. There was no longer any advantage for a professional composer to imitate the country church style, and neither Taylor nor Jackson attempted to do so. Instead, they lent their knowledge and energies to the goal of establishing the Anglican art-music traditions they knew in the Protestant Episcopal Church of the United States.

All three composers wrote a substantial amount of domestic music, partly for the use of their pupils, partly to win a little fame and a very little profit from the sale of sheet music. Selby and Jackson wrote some attractive songs. Taylor had larger ambitions, and although he found unexpected limits in the art of accompaniment when he reached America, he persisted in his goal, and in a few cases succeeded in writing and publishing a true art-song.

The contrast between British and American reception was most acute for chamber and keyboard music. Works in fugue or sonata form were little appreciated in America. Selby's "Lesson" was very modest in scope and appeared only in his doomed series *Apollo and the Muses,* as did his "Fuge or Voluntary" in D. Taylor reprinted one of his Op. 2 sonatas in Philadelphia, but then abandoned the attempt and published only simple marches and dances, plus one set of variations. It was much the same with Jackson. Yet all three composers were highly regarded keyboard performers and improvisers and had published substantial keyboard works in London. This is probably the part of their work that suffered most from their migration.

Each composer, when the opportunity arose, aspired to high art in the idiom of the best English or European models. As I have repeatedly suggested, their motives for this may have been mixed: besides purely intellectual satisfaction, they may also have sought to raise their standing in order to promote their teaching careers. This is particularly clear in Jackson's case. It in no way detracts from the value of the serious music he and the others left behind them. No doubt much of their best was unpublished and is now lost. But even among what remains there is much to enjoy. Some of Selby's music is capable of giving pleasure today. Taylor and Jackson, whose gifts were of a higher order than Selby's, each left a handful of masterly works that deserve occasional revival.

The United States was destined to join the European mainstream in its cultivation of classical music, and eventually to produce its own composers and performers who would rival those of European countries. By the mid-nineteenth century, America had become—as Britain had been for centuries—a magnet that attracted German, Italian, and Central European musicians to better prospects than they could hope to find at home.

But this was not yet true in the period covered by this book. Then, in some cases at least, musicians came not for perceived professional opportunity, but to resolve a personal dilemma. Americans were fortunate, in this early phase, to have in their midst a handful of talented and trained composers, from both Britain and the European Continent, to lead and guide their endeavors. The composers were able and willing to adapt their musical training and abilities to meet the new situation, and soon found themselves in positions of leadership. Americans appreciated their presence, their knowledge, and their efforts, though they could not yet provide adequate financial reward. The three composers enjoyed greater esteem in America than they could have attained in Britain. But this did not translate into a higher standard of living. Nor did it create frequent opportunities to exercise their composing skills in full.

Notes

Preface

1. The best modern studies of Reinagle's life and career are Hopkins, "Preface" (including a chronological list of compositions), and Krauss, "Alexander Reinagle."
2. See Sprenkle, "Life and Works of Benjamin Carr"; R. Smith, "Church Music"; Meyer, "Preface."

Chapter 1: Emigrants and Immigrants

1. I expounded this theory in greater detail at a conference, Nineteenth-Century Theater Music in English, held at the Pierpont Morgan Library, New York, in June 1985. This was subsequently published in Temperley, "Musical Nationalism," and further developed in Temperley, "Nationalism."
2. Strasser, "Société Nationale," 240.
3. Britton et al., *American Sacred Music Imprints,* 9–11.
4. Temperley, *Music of the English Parish Church,* 1:202, 227–28.
5. Law, *The Art of Singing* (1800), 9, quoted in Britton et al., *American Sacred Music Imprints,* 401.
6. Hubbard, *Essay,* 9.
7. Ibid., 15 n.
8. Ibid., 16–17.
9. *First Church Collection,* preface.
10. Daniel Read, letter of May 7, 1829, quoted in Lowens, *Music and Musicians,* 175.
11. These terms were coined and defined in Crawford, *American Musical Landscape,* 7.
12. See Johnstone and Fiske, *Eighteenth Century,* 344.
13. See their treatment in Chase, *America's Music,* and Hitchcock, *Music in the United States.*
14. Berthoff, *British Immigrants,* 15.
15. Hansen, *Atlantic Migration,* 52.
16. Ibid., 53.
17. See Redway, "The Carrs," for a detailed account of the family's publishing business.
18. See Krummel, "The Displaced Prima Donna."
19. Hansen, *Atlantic Migration,* 60–65.
20. See Crawford, *American Musical Landscape,* part 1: "Histories."
21. Howard, *Our American Music,* 72.
22. Britton, "Theoretical Introductions," 366.

23. Lowens, *Music and Musicians,* 173.

24. See Britton et al., *American Sacred Music Imprints.*

25. Chase, *America's Music,* xvii, xix. As Crawford points out (*American Musical Landscape,* 249 n. 99), "These fighting words do not appear in the revised third edition [Urbana, Ill., 1987] of Chase's book."

26. Chase, *America's Music,* 130–31.

Chapter 2: William Selby

1. Sonneck, *Early Concert-Life,* 270.

2. See McKay, "William Selby."

3. See, for instance, Howard, "Selby"; Crawford, "Selby"; Lambert, "Music Masters," 1112–13.

4. Dawe, *Organists,* 142.

5. Owen, "The Other Mr. Selby"; idem, *Organs and Organ Music,* 38–44.

6. *Boston Evening Post,* November 14, 21, 28, 1774.

7. Ibid., September 13, 1773.

8. Dawe, *Organists,* 41, 55.

9. These notices, and similar ones cited below, are summarized in McKay, "William Selby," and set out in full in Lambert, "Music Masters."

10. Owen, *Organs and Organ Music,* 39.

11. Announced in the *Massachusetts Gazette,* May 12, 1775.

12. Owen, *Organs and Organ Music,* 44.

13. Sonneck, *Early Concert-Life,* 271 n. 2.

14. Owen, *Organs and Organ Music,* 44.

15. Dawe, *Organists,* 42.

16. The church was also known as All Saints, Bread Street.

17. London, Guildhall Library, MS. 3149/6, March 30, 1760, quoted in Dawe, *Organists,* 65. The church was also known as St. Sepulchre, Newgate, or St. Sepulchre, Snow Hill.

18. Brown and Hopkins, "Seven Centuries," 205.

19. *Public Advertiser,* February 21, 1760, located from *CLC.* The reference is to "Mr. Selby"; of course, it could have been John Selby.

20. See Ehrlich, *Music Profession,* 27–29.

21. Dawe, *Organists,* 11.

22. Ehrlich, *Music Profession,* 26–27; Dawe, *Organists,* 7–9.

23. Pohl, *Mozart und Haydn in London,* 212–13.

24. Dawe, *Organists,* 8.

25. McGuinness and Johnstone, "Concert Life," 38.

26. The location of the records is unknown to the present Magdalen Hospital trustees. But they were available in 1917 to H. F. B. Compston when he wrote the history of the institution, which includes a table of organists (Compston, *Magdalen Hospital,* vi, 169 n. 2).

27. Compston, *Magdalen Hospital,* 169; Temperley, "Hymn Books," 20.

28. Temperley, *Hymn Tune Index,* 1:113, source *MCC B2 a.

29. See Temperley, "Hymn Books," 24–25.

30. For details see Temperley, *Hymn Tune Index,* 3:603, tune 3335.

31. London, Guildhall Library, MS 3149/6, p. 106.

32. Mason, *Annals of Trinity Church, Newport*, 157.

33. McKay, "William Selby," 613.

34. *Newport Mercury*, January 3, 1774, transcribed in Lambert, "Music Masters," 1116.

35. Owen, *Organs and Organ Music*, 41.

36. Oliver and Peabody, *Records of Trinity Church, Boston*, 173–90 (quote, 173).

37. Ibid., 181–90 (first quote, 181; second quote, 183; third quote, 190). See also Hitchings, "Musical Pursuits," 647.

38. *Continental Journal*, January 6, 1780.

39. *Boston Gazette*, April 22, 1782.

40. *Boston Evening Post*, February 2, 1782.

41. McKay, "William Selby," 621–23. This is the source of information for subsequently mentioned concerts unless otherwise noted.

42. *Boston Gazette*, April 15, 22, 1782.

43. McKay ("William Selby," 614) reproduces a print entitled "William Selby conducting a concert in King's Chapel in the year 1786." However, Barbara Owen has pointed out to the author that the print cannot be contemporary, since it shows additions to the chapel organ that were made in the later nineteenth century.

44. See Sonneck, *Early Concert-Life*, 275–76; Lambert, "Music Masters," 1125–26 (with facsimile, p. 826); Owen, *Organs and Organ Music*, 77–78.

45. W. Shaw, *Three Choirs Festival*, 3–13 (Shaw notes the *Messiah* performance on p. 12); Husk, *Account*; Birmingham Triennial Festivals, programs for 1820 and 1823 (British Library, 7894.s.1).

46. See *A Liturgy . . . for the Use of the First Episcopal Church in Boston*.

47. Ibid., fol. A2v (first quote); *Worcester Collection*, 165 (second quote).

48. See Temperley, *Music of the English Parish Church*, 1:135.

49. See Felsted, *Jonah*.

50. *Philadelphia Herald*, January 28, 1786.

51. The *Philadelphia Herald* review and the one in the *Massachusetts Centinel* (January 17, 1787) are set out in full in Sonneck, *Early Concert-Life*, 275–80, and Lambert, "Music Masters," 1127, 1130–31.

52. Stone Chapel, October 4, 1787; Christ Church, May 21, 1788; Stone Chapel, October 27, 1789, and December 2, 1789; St. Peter, Salem, November 25, 1790. The programs are reproduced in McKay, "William Selby," and Lambert, "Music Masters."

53. McKay, "William Selby," 619 n. 19, 622.

54. Lambert, "Music Masters," 1112–13.

55. The announcement is reproduced in Lambert, "Music Masters," 1133–34.

56. Sonneck, *Early Concert-Life*, 275.

57. Lambert, "Music Masters," 1141.

58. The advertisement in the *Columbian Centinel* (June 15) is transcribed by Lambert ("Music Masters," 1142) and reproduced in facsimile in the same volume (p. 826).

59. I am indebted to J. Bunker Clark for this suggestion. It was a popular piece, frequently known as "Martini's Grand Battle Overture."

60. *Columbian Centinel*, July 19, 1794.

61. Sonneck, *Early Concert-Life*, 270.

62. *Boston Evening Post*, February 2, 1782.

63. Britton et al., *American Sacred Music Imprints*, no. 455.

64. *Boston Gazette*, August 19, 26, September 2, 1782.

65. The announcement (*Columbian Centinel*, June 16, 1790, transcribed in Lambert, "Music Masters," 1138–39) gives a more detailed prospectus.

66. Partially transcribed in McKay, "William Selby," 623. McKay does not state the source of this 1791 announcement, which is not mentioned by Lambert in "Music Masters."

67. For the 1790 proposal see Evans 22881. On the two issues see McKay, "William Selby," 623–24. The two issues are of fourteen and six pages in length, respectively, so it seems probable that the second is incomplete in this, the only known copy. Three dollars would have been an exorbitant price for six pages of music.

68. For details see Temperley, *Hymn Tune Index*, tunes 2831, 2860, 3327–28, 3330–34, 3336–37.

69. See *The Hymns Anthems and Tunes with the Ode Used at the Magdalen Chapel* (London, [c. 1766]).

70. *Pennsylvania Herald*, January 28, 1786.

71. *Boston Gazette*, January 15, 1787.

72. *Massachusetts Gazette*, January 2, 1786.

73. For a modern edition see Daniel, *Anthem in New England*, 210–16.

74. *Boston Gazette*, August 19, 1782, transcribed in Lambert, "Music Masters," 1124.

75. Daniel, *Anthem in New England*, 210–16. For examples in Handel's *Messiah*, see "But who may abide," mm. 5–11; "Behold, and see if there be any sorrow," m. 3; "The trumpet shall sound," mm. 159–61.

76. For a modern edition (based, however, on a derivative source) see Kroeger, *Early American Anthems*, 2:18–26.

77. This is stated at the head of the anthem in the *Worcester Collection*, 159.

78. Hill, *History of the Old South Church*, 2:215 n.2.

79. McKay, "William Selby," 618.

80. Daniel, *Anthem in New England*, 88; see the full discussion of the three anthems on pages 85–89.

81. McKay, "William Selby," 624.

82. Newman, *Sonata in the Classic Era*, 19–20. Newman points out, for example, that each of the *Eight Lessons*, Op. 7, by Samuel Arnold (London, [c. 1770]) is individually called "Sonata" in the publication.

83. One of these is reproduced in Temperley, *London Pianoforte School*, 7:1.

84. Both are available in a modern edition: Owen, *Century of American Organ Music*, 1:10, 2:8.

85. See Clark, *Dawning of American Keyboard Music*, 257–58.

Chapter 3: Rayner Taylor

1. See Cuthbert, "Taylor"; Yellin, "Taylor"; McLucas, "Taylor"; Hamm, *Yesterdays*, 39–41.

2. See "Musical Reminiscences"; also, "G. J. Jackson" [*sic*], in Parker, *Musical Biography*, 129–31.

3. The letter of December 7, 1821, is one of a series of letters from Carr to Parker

from 1818 to 1822 held by the Annenberg Rare Book and Manuscript Library of the University of Pennsylvania, which kindly supplied me with complete copies. Unless noted otherwise, all Carr letters quoted in this chapter are from this collection.

4. The baptism and marriage registers of St. Anne's Church are in *IGI*.

5. Cuthbert, "Taylor," 11.

6. *London Encyclopædia*, 792.

7. Colyer-Fergusson, *Registers*, 4:101. Jacob's baptism is recorded thus: "Petit, Jacob, fils de Samuel P., ———, et Ester, sa femme, in Fleet Street, Stepney parish . . . Nov. 12 [1704]." Ibid., 3:256. The dash following Samuel's name is in the space generally used to show a man's occupation.

8. Highfill et al., *Biographical Dictionary*, 12:273–76; Cuthbert, "Taylor," 142 n. 10.

9. Highfill et al., *Biographical Dictionary*, 14:372.

10. *The Meretriciad* (1761), quoted in Highfill et al., *Biographical Dictionary*, 11:274.

11. All quotes from Carr's sketch of Taylor's life in this chapter come from the same source: "Musical Reminiscences."

12. Chamberlayne, *Magnae Britanniae Notitia*, 12–13

13. A brief biographical sketch in the *European Magazine* 7 (1782): 352 says Taylor was "a chorister in the King's Chapel under the tuition of Mr. Gates and Dr. Nares." Gates resigned in October 1757.

14. London, Public Record Office, Lord Chamberlain's Accounts, LC 5/28, p. 226. I am grateful to Robert Bucholz for making his database of Chapel Royal appointments available to me in advance of its publication.

15. Reginald Spofforth, *Musical Reminiscences* (1785), quoted in Baldwin, *Chapel Royal*, 329. See also W. Shaw, "Nares."

16. Stevens's diary, quoted in Cuthbert, "Taylor," 41.

17. Baldwin, *Chapel Royal*, 328.

18. Unidentified newspaper clipping in the Marybone Gardens Collection, St. Marylebone Public Library, described by Cuthbert, "Taylor," 9.

19. *Public Advertiser*, August 6, 1765.

20. Ibid., May 5, 1767.

21. Information about these performances, gleaned from the *Public Advertiser*, is assembled in *CLC* and is also discussed in Cuthbert, "Taylor," 48–69. The identities of the singers are based on entries in Highfill et al., *Biographical Dictionary*, and on Cuthbert.

22. D. Johnson, "Music and Society," 142.

23. *Edinburgh Evening Courant*, April 9, 1770, quoted in Cuthbert, "Taylor," 12.

24. Although no score has survived, a detailed scenario was printed when Taylor revived the work in Philadelphia. See *Maryland Gazette*, January 14, 1793, quoted in Cuthbert, "Taylor," 425.

25. Krauss, "Alexander Reinagle," 428.

26. According to Humphries and Smith (*Music Publishing*, 217) the partnership of Longman, Lukey and Company existed only from about 1769 to 1775.

27. Pearce, *Notes on English Organs*, 133; Grieve, *The Sleepers and the Shadows*, 171–72.

28. *Chelmsford Chronicle*, July 9, 1773, quoted in Cuthbert, "Taylor," 15.

29. Cuthbert, "Taylor," 115.

30. Grieve, *The Sleepers and the Shadows*, 172–73.

31. See, for instance, the description in the notice soliciting subscribers for *Six Sonates* in the *Chelmsford Chronicle* of November 3, 1780, and on the title page of the same sonatas published the following year.

32. See Cuthbert, "Taylor," 88.

33. For the general background see Temperley, *Music of the English Parish Church*, 1:124–34.

34. Grieve, *The Sleepers and the Shadows*, 115–16.

35. Ibid., 220.

36. *Chelmsford Chronicle*, September 4, 1772, quoted in Grieve, *The Sleepers and the Shadows*, 172.

37. *Chelmsford Chronicle*, September 3, 1773, quoted in Grieve, *The Sleepers and the Shadows*, 173.

38. See Temperley, "Croft and the Charity Hymn."

39. *Chelmsford Chronicle*, August 26, 1774, quoted in Cuthbert, "Taylor," 96.

40. Grieve, *The Sleepers and the Shadows*, 173.

41. See Temperley, *Music of the English Parish Church*, 1:367–81.

42. It appeared in vol. 1 [1774], pp. 33–37.

43. York, Minster Library, M87s, fols. 139r–140r. Dr. Wilson kindly lent me her notes on this manuscript.

44. Cuthbert, "Taylor," 108.

45. *Chelmsford Chronicle*, March 4, 1775.

46. Cuthbert, "Taylor," 118.

47. Ibid., 153–55.

48. See the list in Cuthbert, "Taylor," 448–50.

49. *European Magazine* 7 (1785): 352.

50. Dawe, *Organists*, 29, 44.

51. Yellin, "Taylor," 54–55.

52. Wagner, "Hewitt," 40–43; Cuthbert, "Taylor," 230, 239.

53. *Virginia Argus*, September 12, 1792, quoted in Cuthbert, "Taylor," 249. The term "Professor" carried no academic implication, of course. It was roughly equivalent to the modern noun "professional."

54. Hogan, *London Stage, Part 5*, 3:1311; *Universal Magazine* 87 (1790): 321–23.

55. *Times* (London), March 1, 1791.

56. Yellin, "Taylor," 59.

57. Buried at St. Peter's Church, Philadelphia; see Yellin, "Taylor," 58.

58. Yellin points out that the census taker originally wrote a "2" in the column headed "Free White Female of twenty-six and under forty-five," then crossed it out and replaced it with a zero. He comments: "Unexplained is why two women who were originally counted were removed from the enumeration" (Yellin, "Taylor," 57–58). But a corrected entry is more likely to be accurate than an ordinary one, since it indicates careful checking. Most likely the numeral 2 was first entered in the wrong column, then transferred to the right column, the one for women between sixteen and twenty-six.

59. *Maryland Journal and Baltimore Advertiser*, October 9, 1792 (first quote); *Baltimore Daily Repository*, October 18, 1792 (second quote).

60. *Maryland Gazette,* October 18, 1792, fully transcribed Cuthbert, "Taylor," 257.

61. Keefer, *Baltimore's Music,* 39.

62. Cuthbert, "Taylor," 259–60.

63. *Philadelphia Gazette,* June 10, 28, August 14, 1793.

64. Ibid., October 23, 1793. Cuthbert ("Taylor," 267) also presents a facsimile of a letter from Taylor soliciting a subscription for the anthem.

65. A "Mr. Carr," probably Benjamin, disembarked from the ship *George Barclay,* according to the *Philadelphia Gazette,* April 10, 1793.

66. *Philadelphia Gazette,* May 12, 1795, quoted in Cuthbert, "Taylor," 281.

67. *American Daily Advertiser,* October 21, 1800.

68. Cuthbert, "Taylor," 292–94.

69. *Poulson's American Daily Advertiser,* February 28, 1805.

70. Gerson, *Music in Philadelphia,* 42.

71. Cuthbert, "Taylor," 303–13.

72. *Philadelphia Gazette,* June 26, 1797.

73. *Poulson's American Daily Advertiser,* July 10, 1811, quoted in Cuthbert, "Taylor," 355.

74. Yellin, "Taylor," 62–65; Yellin based his findings on church records held by the Historical Society of Pennsylvania.

75. Transcripts of Taylor's letter of remonstrance and of his letter informing the St. Peter's vestry of his decision to resign are provided by Yellin, "Taylor," 63–65.

76. *Gazette of the United States,* November 11, 1800. The whole advertisement is transcribed in Yellin, "Taylor," 60.

77. Cuthbert, "Taylor," 475.

78. I am indebted for this information to Raoul F. Camus, who kindly forwarded to me an abstract of a paper entitled "Camp Dupont and Its Music," which was delivered by Clyde S. Shive Jr. at the Sonneck Society meeting in Tallahassee, Florida, March 1986.

79. *The Æthiop* has been edited, orchestrated, and "realized" by Victor Fell Yellin. In this form it was staged by the Federal Music Society Opera (John Baldwin, conductor) in 1978 and has also been recorded (New World Records 80232-2).

80. Yellin, "Taylor," 67. Keefer, *Baltimore's Music,* 69 n. 23, states that Taylor earned fourteen dollars as an organist playing under Henry Gilles in Philadelphia in 1819, but he gives no exact date or reference.

81. Swenson-Eldridge, "Musical Fund Society," 25 (first quote), 27 (second quote), 38 (third quote).

82. The inscription was recorded in Hildeborn, *Inscriptions,* and from there transcribed in Yellin, "Taylor," 69.

83. Gerson (*Music in Philadelphia,* 328) says Taylor was still performing at Vauxhall Gardens in 1819, but he cites no evidence.

84. No musical materials from the Edinburgh performance are known to have survived.

85. Burney, *Account,* [part 2], "Commemoration of Handel," 19–21.

86. For instance, see ex. 50, p. 177.

87. See Fiske, *English Theatre Music,* 270–72.

88. Haydn, *Correspondence,* 273–74.

89. Carr wrote in 1821: "it is very difficult to find Counter Tenors in all the Choirs I have anything to do with—the only way is to take the highest voices of the tenors." Letter to Parker, June 30, 1821.

90. *Poulson's American Daily Advertiser*, March 2, 1815.

91. *Euterpeiad*, January 19, 1822, 170.

92. Cuthbert, "Taylor," 420–66.

93. *Daily Universal Register*, April 19, 1786.

94. See Yellin, "Taylor," 54–55. Cuthbert ("Taylor," 466, no. 484) treats this as an arrangement of a song by Shield.

95. "A sailors life at sea" was the song titled "Jack the Guinea Pig" (this meaning of "guinea pig," now obsolete, was "A midshipman in an East Indiaman," according to *The Shorter Oxford Dictionary*). It was also praised in the *Times* (London, May 12, 1790) as the "excellent sea song" performed "in the first stile" by Mrs. Harlowe as a gallant young midshipman. Its success is illustrated by the fact that it was issued by two London publishers and was later popular in America.

96. It was apparently unknown to Cuthbert or Yellin, but *RISM* records a copy at the Bibliothèque Nationale, Paris, attributed to "Taylor, Richard." I am grateful to Kenneth Smith for helping me to procure a copy of this print.

97. *Times* (London), August 2, 1790.

98. Ibid., August 21, 1790. The print survives in only one copy, at the Bibliothèque Nationale, Paris (reproduced in fig. 7). A note in Taylor's hand at the top of the title page, severely cropped, reads in part: "This with R. Taylor's comp[limen]ts begs [?]."

99. The piece in this adapted form was added to the second edition of Carr's *Sacred Harmony* ([Baltimore], c. 1805)—a publication not listed in Britton et al., *American Sacred Music Imprints*—between pp. 33 and 34. See Wolfe, no. 7722b; Temperley, *Hymn Tune Index*, #SHSA b.

100. Hoskins, "Theatre Music II," 261.

101. Fiske, *English Theatre Music*, 297–98.

102. Ibid., 436.

103. In fact the rhyme itself may have evolved from the ballad in Congreve's 1695 play. Iona and Peter Opie, in *The Oxford Dictionary of Nursery Rhymes*, 405, cite no earlier source for this particular combination of trades.

104. Bruce Carr, "Theatre Music," 292.

105. Root, *Nineteenth-Century American Musical Theater*, 2:157–272. A facsimile of the original vocal score is in Schleifer, *American Opera*, 25–47.

106. Planché, *Recollections and Reflections*, 1:80.

107. Most of these have half-titles and imprints, indicating that the publisher, G. E. Blake, intended to sell them separately, though only one separate edition has come to light, "The Camel's Bell," registered for copyright on March 16, 1814 (Krummel, "Philadelphia Music Engraving and Publishing," item B 295).

108. Root, *Nineteenth-Century American Musical Theater*, 2:xxi–xxv.

109. Although Taylor could not have seen this opera, the vocal score was published in 1785.

110. For further discussion see Temperley, *Haydn: The Creation*, 84.

111. Two songs ascribed to him in *BUC* and *CPM* are not, in fact, his. "The Advice" [c. 1765], "set by Mr Taylor," is musically illiterate in a way that is not believable in a

work by Rayner Taylor. "The British Soldier," an ultra-patriotic song, also by "Mr Taylor," was entered at Stationers' Hall on November 27, 1800, eight years after Rayner Taylor had left Britain for good.

112. Sadie, "Music in the Home II," 341, 344.

113. See Tawa, *Sweet Songs*, chap. 7.

114. Ibid., 126.

115. Sadie, "Music in the Home II," 353.

116. Tawa, *Sweet Songs*, 78.

117. Ibid., 178.

118. Chiron, "Remarks on the Use and Abuse of Music," *Euterpeiad* 3 (1822): 36, 44, quoted in Tawa, *Sweet Songs*, 79.

119. "Hunting Song" ("Hark, hark, the joy-inspiring horn"), printed first in the London *Collection* of c. 1772, then by G. Willig, Philadelphia, 1805–9 (Shaw-Shoemaker 9451).

120. A facsimile appears in Tawa, *American Solo Songs*, 176–77.

121. *Encyclopædia Britannica*, 11th ed. (Cambridge, 1911), 18:811.

122. It was also the subject of an opera by Charles Horn, premiered at the Theatre Royal, Dublin, in 1818, and later of works by Gasparo Spontini and Anton Rubinstein (*Feramorz*, 1863). A section of the poem, "Paradise and the Peri," was to be the basis of Robert Schumann's only opera.

123. Hamm, *Yesterdays*, 40.

124. A rough count from Wolfe's *Secular Music in America* shows that Taylor's output of songs published between 1801 and 1825 was exceeded only by those of his countrymen Benjamin Carr and James Hewitt and the native-born American Oliver Shaw (1779–1848).

125. For details, see Cuthbert, "Taylor," 420–57, nos. 4, 18, 22, 23, 39, 40, 103, 105, 132, 192, 219, 262, 328, 360, 361. Another, not listed, is a "Military Glee," "Merry is the trade that soldiers lead" (published by Preston, London, about 1775).

126. Circumstantial details are supplied in Murray, "Weeping and Mourning," 289–92.

127. The advertisement for the concert in the Philadelphia *Aurora* (March 15, 1815) is fully transcribed in Cuthbert, "Taylor," 350–52.

128. For details see Temperley, *Hymn Tune Index*, tunes 5255, 5290, 5319, 5325. Tune 5319 ("Sheffield") may have been by Richard Taylor of Chester.

129. Its first American appearance was in *Sacred Harmony* (Philadelphia: Carr and Schetky, [1803–4]), 14–15.

130. White, *Thoughts on the Singing of Psalms*, 9.

131. See Wilson, *Anglican Chant*, chap. 8, "Early Episcopal Music in America."

132. Ibid., 229.

133. For a detailed list see Wilson, *Anglican Chant*, 256–58.

134. Crotch's chant is printed in Wilson, *Anglican Chant*, 123.

135. Benjamin Carr, *Masses, Vespers*, 37–54.

136. This uses the Vulgate numbering. It is Psalm 112 in the English Bible.

137. See, for instance, Wilson, *Anglican Chant*, 247–49 (ex. 8.8).

138. This point is particularly well documented in Shapiro, "Drama."

139. Evans 27783. It was advertised for sale on December 26, 1793.

140. Cuthbert, "Taylor," 371. The only known copy of this work, held at the Library of Congress, was missing at the time of writing.

141. This ungrammatical text incipit was added, presumably by Taylor, to the biblical passage that follows.

142. *Poulson's American Daily Advertiser,* March 31, 1814. For a modern edition see Kroeger, *Early American Anthems,* 2:153–54.

143. Owen, *Century of American Organ Music,* 1:22–25.

144. Clark, *Dawning of American Keyboard Music,* 262.

145. For a discussion of the origins of this march see Davis, *History of Music in American Life,* 80.

146. See *An Easy and Familiar Lesson for Two Performers* (Evans 45796).

147. Op. 1/2 has been edited by J. Bunker Clark, *Anthology,* 1:6. For a modern edition of the Op. 2 sonatas see Taylor, *Chamber Music.*

148. Sadie, "Music in the Home II," 326.

149. Newman, *Sonata in the Classic Era,* 808. For a modern edition of these sonatas by John Metz and Barbara Bailey-Metz, see Taylor, *Chamber Music.*

150. See Krummel, "Philadelphia Music Engraving and Publishing," 361–62.

151. I follow Newman in using this term to mean a sonata movement in roughly equal halves, in the form ||: A B :||: A'B' :||, the second half beginning with the main theme in the dominant key and later recapitulating the second theme and cadential materials in the tonic. This form is discussed in detail in Newman, *Sonata in the Classic Era,* 143–44.

152. "Cetra" was one of many names for the English guitar. See Spencer and Harwood, "English Guitar," 244.

153. See Cole, *Pianoforte in the Classical Era,* 250–53; Boalch and Williams, "Claviorgan" (with illustration).

154. The two tunes are compared in Cuthbert, "Taylor," 301.

Chapter 4: George K. Jackson

1. Kaufman, "Jackson."

2. H. Johnson, "George K. Jackson."

3. See "G. J. Jackson" [*sic*], in Parker, *Musical Biography,* 129–31. All quotations from Parker in this chapter refer to this source.

4. "Musical Reminiscences."

5. *Jackson's Oxford Journal,* March 24, 1759, quoted in Wollenberg, *Music at Oxford,* 57.

6. Sutherland and Mitchell, "The Eighteenth Century," 206.

7. Kaufman, "Jackson," 3, 5. I am grateful to Simon Bailey, Oxford University archivist, for ascertaining that no degree was awarded and for explaining the meaning of *privilegiatus,* found under Jackson's name in Foster, *Alumni.* The privileges, which had declined in practical value by the eighteenth century, included exemption from the city's jurisdiction.

8. Normal (Illinois), Illinois State University, M1.A1 J3, v.5. The volume is one of twelve, some printed, some manuscript, that formed part of George K. Jackson's musical library; they were acquired by Illinois State University in 1973.

9. *Jackson's Oxford Journal,* November 24, 1759, quoted in Wollenberg, *Music at Oxford,* 57.

10. London, Public Record Office, Lord Chamberlain's Accounts, LC 5/30, October 22, 1773.

11. Dawe, *Organists,* 22, 27, 115.

12. London, Guildhall, MS. 1265/1, various entries from 1770 to 1790. Information kindly supplied by Ruth Mack Wilson.

13. Matthews, *Royal Society of Musicians,* 80.

14. A Boston reissue of Jackson's *Ode for the Fourth of July,* published by E. W. Jackson in 1821–23, has "Words by Mrs. J. Jackson," although the "J." is not recorded by Wolfe (no. 4563).

15. The occasions were Daniel Arrowsmith's benefit concert at Paul's Head Tavern, Cateaton Street, February 7, 1782; and a concert for the benefit of "a young lady who has sustained a considerable loss by robbery," at the Crown and Rolls Tavern, Chancery Lane, February 21, 1783. *Public Advertiser* and *Morning Herald,* respectively, located from CLU. The only musical source that may represent this concerto is the viola part of a work in D major titled "Concerto by G. K. Jackson," written out by a copyist (US-NL, M1.A1 J3, v.7, item 33).

16. US-NL, M1.A1 J3, v.5, items 68–70.

17. Autograph score: ibid., v.4, item 6; copied viola part: ibid., v.7, item 39a.

18. See W. Shaw, *Succession of Organists,* 19, 320–21, 335.

19. *Dictionary of National Biography,* s.v. "Nares, Robert."

20. G. E. C[ockburn], *Complete Peerage,* 11:55.

21. Venn and Venn, *Alumni Cantabrigienses,* s.v. "Lindsey, James."

22. St. Andrews University, Muniments, UY452/8.1.1791, reproduced in facsimile in Kaufman, "Jackson," 8.

23. Information kindly supplied by Christopher Field.

24. These details are entirely due to the research of Christopher Field and Elizabeth Frame.

25. London, Guildhall Library, MS. 1264/2, p. 320. I am indebted to Ruth Mack Wilson for this citation.

26. Squire, *Catalogue of Printed Music,* 1:127.

27. Humphries and Smith, *Music Publishing,* 309.

28. Very few musical publications of any kind were deposited at Stationers' Hall before 1789. In that year there was a sudden rush to deposit among London music publishers, probably due to a legal opinion (not yet discovered) that music copyright was enforceable by law. Thus, any works entered in 1789 may well have been printed and sold earlier.

29. The title page of Op. 4 in this state is reproduced in Temperley, *London Pianoforte School,* 7:7.

30. I am grateful to Claire Nelson for comparing these pages with Longman and Broderip catalogues in the British Library, and to James Randall for studying the firm's advertisements in *The Times.* It turns out that these plates were from old catalogues, and the pieces advertised on them date from the 1780s. Nelson found the same plates on the following publications: Thomas Attwood, *The Prison* [1792]; Muzio

Clementi, *Three Sonatas,* Op. 21 [1795]; Adalbert Gyrowetz, *Three Sonatas,* Op. 23 (Longman and Clementi, [1799]). These cover the full range of years from 1792, the earliest year that Longman and Broderip could have acquired the plates, through 1798, when their partnership was dissolved.

31. See *RISM* J 44, JJ 44a, and Wolfe, nos. 4541–44.

32. Philadelphia, Historical Society of Pennsylvania, St. Peter's Church Account Book, p. 109.

33. Scott, *British Aliens,* 137.

34. See *A Prey to Tender Anguish Composed by Dr. G. K. Jackson. Printed for the Author of whom may be had his Practical Treatise on Thorough Bass . . . An Anthem with Canons for the use of Country Choirs Dr Watts's Hymns, A Sonata, a Collection of Songs and Duetts . . .* [New York: 1800?]. See also table 14 in the present book.

35. See, for instance, Britton et al., *American Sacred Music Imprints,* 663–82.

36. Details in State of New Jersey, Middlesex County Common Pleas, Execution 4 (1795–99), pp. 194, 335, discovered by Kaufman, who quotes it in "Jackson," 10–11.

37. Details of the program, with conjectural identifications of some of the works played, are given by Kaufman, "Jackson," 12, 14, taken from the *Guardian; or, New-Brunswick Advertiser,* September 3, 1799, and April 11, 1800. The great majority of the identifiable pieces are English, but the patriotic choruses "Adams and Liberty" (adapted to music composed by John Stafford Smith) and "Hail Columbia" were featured.

38. Kaufman ("Jackson," 16) quotes an advertisement to this effect from the *New York Commercial Advertiser.*

39. Kaufman, "Jackson," 16–23 (quote, 16), 81.

40. Ibid., 17–18.

41. Ibid., 81.

42. All the information in this paragraph was provided by Ruth Mack Wilson, who also kindly let me see photocopies of the newspaper advertisements mentioned, from which I quote.

43. Watkinson Library, Hartford, Conn., Nathan Hale Allen, MS. essay, "Music in a New England State: From Psalmody to Symphony in Connecticut 1636–1900," 333.

44. *New York Evening Post,* quoted in Kaufman, "Jackson," 20.

45. Ibid., 21.

46. Kaufman, "Jackson," 22.

47. The programs are transcribed in detail by Kaufman ("Jackson," 12, 14) with tentative composer attributions; they are derived from advertisements in the *Guardian; or New-Brunswick Advertiser,* September 3, 1799, and April 11, 1800.

48. See the printed wordbook, *Oratorios, Selection the First* (SS 8686).

49. Harvard, Houghton Library, Early American Playbills, Pl.CO2.07.18.

50. Pirrson, *Twelve Anthems.*

51. "The Cricket," "Cancherizante," and "Ah, Delia" (*RISM* JJ 36b, 36a, 35a, respectively).

52. The US-Bh copy of "Numeration Table" has its heading deleted in ink and replaced by "Polyhymnia / or / Songs of Various Numbers / No. 1 The Numeration Table"; it also has an added imprint "Printed & Sold by E. W. Jackson No. 44 Market Street" and was evidently an engraver's copy for a planned Boston edition in the early 1820s.

53. *Daily Advertiser,* July 2, 1803, quoted in Wolfe, no. 4562. This song was reprinted about 1823 by E. W. Jackson (Boston) under the title *A Favourite Ode in Celebration of the Fourth of July* (Wolfe, no. 4563).

54. For details see Temperley, *Hymn Tune Index,* 1:263 (source JackGDP).

55. W. Smith, *Churchman's Choral Companion,* preface. *Sacred Music* was omitted from Temperley, *Hymn Tune Index,* but has been added to the Web version (source JackGSM).

56. *New York Evening Post,* quoted in Wolfe, no. 4518.

57. "Dr. Jackson," *New England Palladium,* March 23, 1813.

58. Scott, *British Aliens,* 137; Suffolk County (Massachusetts) Index of Deaths, 1810–48, quoted in Kaufman, "Jackson," 38.

59. *Boston Gazette,* October 29, 1812, quoted in H. Johnson, "George K. Jackson," 116–17.

60. Details provided by Kaufman, "Jackson," 27, derived from Bentley, *Diary,* 4:135; *Columbia Centinel,* January 30, 1813; and *New England Palladium,* March 2, 1813.

61. *Boston Gazette,* November 12, 1812.

62. Boston, City Hall, MS. "Proceedings of the Standing Committee of the Society in Brattle Street from September 1805," quoted in Kaufman, "Jackson," 25.

63. "Dr. Jackson," *New England Palladium,* March 23, 1813, article reproduced in facsimile in Kaufman, "Jackson," 83.

64. *Independent Chronicle,* March 4, 1813, quoted in Kaufman, "Jackson," 28.

65. *Columbia Centinel,* February 24, 1813, quoted in Kaufman, "Jackson," 27.

66. Scott, *British Aliens,* 27. The date is given as March 19, 1812, and Jackson's age as thirty-four, but these are errors for 1813 and fifty-four, respectively. There is no question that the doctor is the subject of this entry, as he is identified both as "George K. Jackson" and "prof. of music, Boston."

67. See "Dr. Jackson," *New England Palladium,* March 23, 1813, article reproduced in facsimile, Kaufman, "Jackson," 83; *Hampshire Gazette,* April 14, 1813, quoted in Kaufman, "Jackson," 31.

68. *Independent Chronicle,* March 25, 1813, quoted in full in Kaufman, "Jackson," 82.

69. Kaufman, "Jackson," 31–32.

70. Ibid., 32–33; Owen, *Organs and Organ Music,* 48.

71. Oliver and Peabody, *Records of Trinity Church, Boston,* 308–16.

72. *Columbia Centinel,* April 16, 1817, quoted in Kaufman, "Jackson," 34.

73. Boston Handel and Haydn Society, Minutes, May 14, 1817, quoted in Kaufman, "Jackson," 34.

74. Babcock, *Christ Church Salem Street Boston,* 87.

75. Boston Handel and Haydn Society, Minutes, October 4, 1821.

76. Kaufman, "Jackson," 37–38.

77. Suffolk County (Massachusetts) Index of Deaths, 1810–48, quoted in Kaufman, "Jackson," 38.

78. Oliver and Peabody, *Records of Trinity Church, Boston,* 762, 829. Their son Charles Erwin was baptized in the same church on September 11, 1825, at age sixteen months (hence born around May 1824); their daughter Jane Louisa was baptized May 1, 1828, aged two years, hence born around May 1826 (Oliver and Peabody, *Records of Trinity Church, Boston,* 705, 708).

79. Kaufman, "Jackson," 39.

80. Census Returns, Massachusetts, Suffolk County, Boston, Ward 5, p. 116, showing "George K. Jackson" living in Bowdoin Square.

81. Kaufman, "Jackson," 40.

82. For more detailed descriptions of these two publications see Wilson, *Anglican Chant*, 239–41.

83. H. Johnson, "George K. Jackson," 114 (first quote); Metcalf, *American Writers and Compilers*, 50–51 (second quote); Scott, *British Aliens*, 27 (third quote).

84. H. Johnson, "George K. Jackson," 115–16.

85. Perkins and Dwight, *Handel and Haydn Society*, 1:49.

86. Olleson, "Samuel Wesley," 36.

87. For a discussion of this work see Clark, *Dawning of American Keyboard Music*, 296–97.

88. US-NL, M1.A1 J3, v.4, item 11.

89. *Columbia Centinel*, April 16, 1817.

90. Parker, "G. J. Jackson" [*sic*], 130.

91. Bentley, *Diary*, 4:135.

92. *Columbia Centinel*, October 22, 1823, quoted in H. Johnson, "George K. Jackson," 120.

93. See W. Smith, *Churchman's Choral Companion*. See also Wilson, *Anglican Chant*, 238.

94. See US-NL, M1.A1 J3, v.4.

95. For a modern edition see Hitchcock, *Music in the United States*, 40 (ex. 2-5).

96. For details see Temperley, *Hymn Tune Index*, tunes 5823–57, 10614–32, 10634, 18167–69 (the last are included only in the Web version of the *Index*, released in 2002; see <http://hti.music.uiuc.edu>).

97. See Wilson, *Anglican Chant*, 238–41.

98. See US-NL, M1.A1 J3, v.4, p. 10.

99. See Bruce Carr, "Vital Spark"; Temperley, *Music of the English Parish Church*, 1:213–14.

100. The Dirge and the March are transcribed in full in Murray, "Weeping and Mourning," 290–92.

101. Murray, "Weeping and Mourning," 289; Mellers, *Music in a New Found Land*, 19.

102. See US-NL, M1.A1 J3, v.4, item 33. A different, unfinished piece headed "Mr. Jeffersons March" is sketched in two versions on the previous two pages.

103. Wolfe, nos. 4608–11.

104. See US-NL, M1.A1 J3, v.7, item 35.

105. Tawa, *Sweet Songs*, 131.

106. Hamm, *Yesterdays*, 38 (first quote), 41 (second and third quotes).

107. British Library, G. 796.(44, 45). Incidentally, the second (Oswald) setting is the only one that makes sense of the third and fourth lines of text: "Tho' we sever, my fond heart 'Till we meet shall pant for you."

108. The anonymous setting was reprinted as "One Kind Kiss" by P. A. von Hagen, at Boston around 1800 (*RISM*, A/I Anhang 2, AN 2052); by G. Graupner, Boston, 1803–6; and for voice only as "The Kiss" in *The Songster's Museum* (Northampton, Mass., 1803), 174, and *The Nightingale*, Samuel Larkin, ed. (Portsmouth, N.H., 1804), 265.

These have been misidentified as editions of Jackson's song in *RISM* (JJ 44b, 44c), Wolfe (nos. 4539, 4540), Kaufman ("Jackson," 90), Hamm (*Yesterdays*, 38), and some library catalogs.

109. Evans 30931.

110. Hamm, *Yesterdays*, 39.

111. The exception is No. 10, "The Whim" (the last to be published). It is a setting of the alphabet forward and backward, the first of his many joke publications for children.

112. Besides solo canzonets, many sets of Italian duets for high voices by Felice Giardini, Johann Christian Bach, Gaetano Quilici, and others had been published in London, followed by some equally popular English-language imitations, most notably William Jackson of Exeter's two sets of *Twelve Canzonets for Two Voices*, Op. 9 [c. 1770] and Op. 13 [c. 1782].

113. See "The Distressed Mother," No. 1 of Pinto's *Six Canzonets* (Birmingham: Woodward, [1803?]). For a discussion of this composer see Temperley, "George Frederick Pinto," or the *New Grove* article. Both Jackson and Pinto may have taken the text from an anonymous cantata, *The Distressed Mother*, published by Longman and Broderip, London, about 1795.

114. See Kaufman, "Jackson," appendix 5, nos. 85 and 19, respectively.

115. This sonata is reproduced in edited facsimile in Temperley, *London Pianoforte School*, 7:7–19.

116. See chapter 3, n. 151.

Conclusions

1. Maurer, "'Professor of Musick,'" 513.

2. O'Toole, *Traitor's Kiss*, 100–106, 258–64.

3. Ibid., 351.

4. Krummel, "Philadelphia Music Engraving and Publishing," 17.

5. *Philadelphia Gazette*, February 27, 1796, transcribed in full in Cuthbert, "Taylor," 242–43.

Bibliography

Archives

Boston, Mass., City Hall Annex. Proceedings of the Standing Committee of the Society in Brattle Street from September 1805.

Boston, Mass., City Hall Annex. Records of King's College Chapel, Boston.

Cambridge, University Library. Archives of the Society for Promoting Christian Knowledge.

Cambridge, Mass., Harvard University, Houghton Library. Early American Playbills.

London, City of London, Chamberlain's Office. Freedom Certificates of the City of London.

London, Guildhall Library. MS. 1265. Churchwardens' Accounts of St. Alban, Wood Street.

London, Guildhall Library. MS. 3149/6. Vestry Minutes of the Parish of St. Sepulchre.

London, Public Record Office. Lord Chamberlain's Accounts.

Philadelphia, Historical Society of Pennsylvania. St. Peter's Church Account Book.

St. Andrews, Scotland, University of St. Andrews. Minutes of the Senatus.

Worcester, Mass., Massachusetts Historical Society. Records of King's Chapel, Boston.

Manuscripts

Hartford, Conn., Watkinson Library. MS. essay by Nathan Hale Allan, "Music in a New England State: From Psalmody to Symphony in Connecticut 1636–1900."

Normal, Ill., Illinois State University, Special Collections Library. M1.A1 J3, v. 3–9. Volumes from G. K. Jackson's library.

Philadelphia, University of Pennsylvania, Annenberg Rare Book and Manuscript Library. MS. Coll. 186, folder 51. John Rowe Parker Papers.

York, Minster Library. MS. M87s. Volume of parochial church music.

Printed Sources and Dissertations

Babcock, Mary Kent Davey. *Christ Church Salem Street Boston: The Old North Church of Paul Revere Fame. Historical Sketches: Colonial Period.* Boston, 1947.

Baldwin, David. *The Chapel Royal Ancient and Modern.* London, 1990.

Bentley, William. *The Diary of William Bentley.* 4 vols. Salem, Mass., 1914.

Berthoff, Rowland Tappan. *British Immigrants in Industrial America, 1790–1850.* Cambridge, Mass., 1953.

Boalch, Donald Howard, and Peter Williams. "Claviorgan." In *The New Grove Dictionary of Music and Musicians,* edited by Stanley Sadie, 6:21–22. Rev. ed. London, 2001.

The British Union-Catalogue of Early Music Printed before the Year 1801 [*BUC*]. Edited by Edith B. Schnapper. 2 vols. London, 1957.

Britton, Allen Perdue. "Theoretical Introductions in American Tune-Books to 1800." Ph.D diss., University of Michigan, 1949.

Britton, Allen Perdue, and Irving Lowens, completed by Richard Crawford. *American Sacred Music Imprints, 1698–1810: A Bibliography.* Worcester, Mass., 1990.

Brown, E. H. Phelps, and S. V. Hopkins. "Seven Centuries of Building Wages." *Economica* 22, n.s. (1955): 195–206.

Burney, Charles. *An Account of the Musical Performances in Westminster-Abbey, and the Pantheon, . . . 1784. In Commemoration of Handel.* London, 1785.

Carr, Benjamin. *Masses, Vespers, Litanies, Hymns, . . . for the use of the Catholic churches in the United States of America.* [Baltimore], 1805.

Carr, Bruce. "Theatre Music: 1800–1834." In *The Romantic Age 1800–1915,* ed. Nicholas Temperley, 288–306. The Blackwell History of Music in Britain, vol. 5. Oxford, 1988.

———. "Vital Spark, or the Dying Christian: A Study of the Musical Settings of Pope's Ode as They Appeared in Selected Early American Tunebooks." M.A. thesis, State University of New York at Buffalo, 1967.

The Catalogue of Printed Music in the British Library to 1980 [*CPM*]. Edited by Laureen Baillie and Roger Balchin. 62 vols. London, 1981–87.

Chamberlayne, John. *Magnae Britanniae Notitia.* 38th ed. London, 1755.

Chase, Gilbert. *America's Music from the Pilgrims to the Present.* 3d ed. Urbana, Ill., 1987.

Clark, J. Bunker. *The Dawning of American Keyboard Music.* New York, 1988.

———, ed. *An Anthology of Early American Keyboard Music, 1787–1830.* Recent Researches in American Music, vols. 1–2. Madison, Wisc., 1977.

C[ockburn], G. E. *The Complete Peerage.* Revised by G. H. White. 13 vols. London, 1949.

Cole, Michael. *The Pianoforte in the Classical Era.* Oxford, 1998.

Colyer-Fergusson, T. C., ed. *The Registers of the French Church, Threadneedle Street, London.* Vols. 3, 4. Huguenot Society of London, Publications 12 (Aberdeen, 1906), 23 (London, 1916).

Compston, H. F. B. *The Magdalen Hospital: The Story of a Great Charity.* London, 1917.

Crawford, Richard. *The American Musical Landscape.* Berkeley, Calif., 1993.

———. "Selby, William." In *The New Grove Dictionary of American Music,* edited by H. Wiley Hitchcock and Stanley Sadie, 4:184. London, 1984.

Cuthbert, John A. "Rayner Taylor and American Musical Life." Ph.D. diss., West Virginia University, 1980.

Daniel, Ralph. *The Anthem in New England before 1800.* Evanston, Ill., 1966.

Davis, Ronald L. *A History of Music in American Life. Vol. 1: The Formative Years, 1620–1865.* Malabar, Fla., 1982.

Dawe, Donovan. *Organists of the City of London, 1666–1850: A Record of One Thousand Organists, with an Annotated Index.* Padstow, Cornwall, Eng., 1983.

Ehrlich, Cyril. *The Music Profession in Britain since the Eighteenth Century: A Social History.* Oxford, 1985.

Evans, Charles. *American Bibliography: A Chronological Dictionary of All Books,*

Pamphlets, and Periodical Publications Printed in the United States of America from the Genesis of Printing in 1639 Down to and Including the Year 1820. Vols. 1–12, Chicago, 1903–34. Vol. 13, completed by Clifford K. Shipton, Worcester, Mass., 1955.

Felsted, Samuel. *Jonah.* Edited by David P. McKay. Miami, [1988].

Filby, P. William, comp. *Passenger and Immigration Lists: Index.* Detroit, 1981, and supplements to 1995.

The First Church Collection of Sacred Musick. 2d ed. Boston, 1806.

Fiske, Roger. *English Theatre Music in the Eighteenth Century.* London, 1973.

Foster, Joseph. *Alumni Oxonienses: The Members of the University of Oxford, 1715–1886.* 4 vols. Oxford, 1891.

Gerson, Robert A. *Music in Philadelphia.* Philadelphia, 1940.

Graziano, John, ed. *American Chamber Music.* Three Centuries of American Music, vol. 8. [Boston], 1991.

Grieve, Hilda. *The Sleepers and the Shadows: Chelmsford: A Town, Its People and Its Past, Vol. 2, From Market Town to Chartered Borough, 1608–1888.* Chelmsford, Eng., 1994.

Hamm, Charles. *Yesterdays.* New York, 1979.

Hansen, Marcus Lee. *The Atlantic Migration, 1607–1860: A History of the Continuing Settlement of the United States.* Cambridge, Mass., 1940.

Haydn, Joseph. *The Collected Correspondence and London Notebooks.* Translated by H. C. Robbins Landon. Fair Lawn, N.J., 1959.

Highfill, Philip H., Jr., Kalman A. Burnim, and Edward A. Langhans. *A Biographical Dictionary of Actors, Actresses, Musicians, Dancers, Managers and Other Stage Personnel in London, 1660–1800.* 16 vols. Carbondale, Ill., 1973–93.

Hildeborn, Charles B., ed. *Inscriptions in St. Peter's Churchyard.* Philadelphia, n.d.

Hill, Hamilton A. *History of the Old South Church (Third Church) Boston, 1669–1884.* 2 vols. Boston and New York, 1890.

Hitchcock, H. Wiley. *Music in the United States of America: A Historical Introduction.* 3d ed. Englewood Cliffs, N.J., 1988.

Hitchings, Sinclair. "The Musical Pursuits of William Price and Thomas Johnston." In *Music in Colonial Massachusetts, 1630–1820,* vol. 2, 631–44. Publications of the Colonial Society of Massachusetts, vol. 54. [Boston, 1985].

Hogan, Charles B., ed. *The London Stage, 1660–1800. Part 5: 1776–1800.* 3 vols. Carbondale, Ill., 1968.

Hopkins, Robert. "Preface." In *Alexander Reinagle: The Philadelphia Sonatas,* vii–xxiv. Recent Researches in American Music 5. Madison, Wisc., 1978.

Hoskins, Robert. "Theatre Music II." In *The Eighteenth Century,* edited by H. Diack Johnstone and Roger Fiske, 261–312. The Blackwell History of Music in Britain, vol. 4. Oxford, 1990.

Howard, John Tasker. *Our American Music: Three Hundred Years of It.* New York, 1931.

———. "Selby, William." *Dictionary of American Biography,* 16:566–67. New York, 1935.

Hubbard, John. *An Essay on Music.* Boston, 1808.

Humphries, Charles, and William C. Smith. *Music Publishing in the British Isles from the Beginning until the Middle of the Nineteenth Century.* 2d ed. Oxford, 1970.

Husk, William Henry. *An Account of the Musical Festivals on St. Cecilia's Day.* London, 1857.

Johnson, David. *Music and Society in Lowland Scotland in the Eighteenth Century.* London, 1972.

Johnson, H. Earle. "George K. Jackson, Doctor of Music (1745–1822)." *Musical Quarterly* 29 (1943): 113–21.

———. *Hallelujah, Amen! The Story of the Handel and Haydn Society of Boston.* Boston, 1965.

———. *Musical Interludes in Boston, 1795–1830.* New York, 1943.

Johnstone, H. Diack, and Roger Fiske, eds. *The Eighteenth Century.* The Blackwell History of Music in Britain, vol. 4. Oxford, 1990.

Kaufman, Charles H. "Doctor George K. Jackson, American Musician of the Federal Period." M.A. thesis, New York University, 1968.

Keefer, Lubov. *Baltimore's Music: The Haven of the American Composer.* Baltimore, 1962.

Krauss, Anne McClenny. "Alexander Reinagle, His Family Background and Early Professional Career." *American Music* 4 (1986): 425–56.

Kroeger, Karl, ed. *Early American Anthems.* 2 vols. Recent Researches in American Music, vols. 36–37. Madison, Wisc., 2000.

Krummel, Donald W. "The Displaced Prima Donna: Mrs. Oldmixon in America." *Musical Times* 108 (1967): 25–28.

———. "Philadelphia Music Engraving and Publishing." Ph.D. diss., University of Michigan, 1958.

Lambert, Barbara. "Music Masters in Colonial Boston." In *Music in Colonial Massachusetts 1630–1820,* vol. 2, 935–1157. Publications of the Colonial Society of Massachusetts, vol. 54. Boston, 1985.

Law, Andrew, ed. *The Art of Singing; in Three Parts.* Part 1. Cheshire, Conn., 1800.

A Liturgy, Collected Principally from the Book of Common Prayer, for the Use of the First Episcopal Church in Boston; Together with the Psalter, or Psalms of David. Boston, 1785. (Evans 18938.)

The London Encyclopædia. Edited by Ben Weinreb and Christopher Hibbert. London, 1983.

Lowens, Irving. *Music and Musicians in Early America.* New York, 1964.

Mason, George C. *Annals of Trinity Church, Newport, Rhode Island, 1629–1821.* Newport, R.I., 1890.

Matthews, Betty, comp. *The Royal Society of Musicians of Great Britain: List of Members, 1738–1984.* London, 1985.

Maurer, Maurer. "The 'Professor of Musick' in Colonial America." *Musical Quarterly* 36 (1950): 511–24.

McGuinness, Rosamond, and H. Diack Johnstone. "Concert Life in England I." In *The Eighteenth Century,* edited by H. Diack Johnstone and Roger Fiske, 31–95. The Blackwell History of Music in Britain, vol. 4. Oxford, 1990.

McKay, David. "William Selby, Musical Émigré in Colonial Boston." *Musical Quarterly* 57 (1971): 609–27.

McLucas, Anne Dhu. "Taylor, Raynor." In *The New Grove Dictionary of Music and Musicians,* edited by Stanley Sadie, 25:140–41. Rev. ed. London, 2001.

Mellers, Wilfrid. *Music in a New Found Land.* New York, 1987.

Metcalf, Frank J. *American Writers and Compilers of Sacred Music.* New York, 1925.

Meyer, Eve R. "Preface." In *Benjamin Carr: Selected Secular and Sacred Songs,* edited by Eve R. Meyer, vii–xxiii. Recent Researches in American Music, vol. 15. Madison, Wisc., 1986.

Murray, Sterling E. "Weeping and Mourning: Funeral Dirges in Honor of General Washington." *Journal of the American Musicological Society* 31 (1978): 282–308.

"Musical Reminiscences. Or Biographical Notices. No. 3." *Euterpeiad* 2 (1821–22): 162.

Newman, William S. *The Sonata in the Classic Era.* Chapel Hill, N.C., 1963.

Oliver, Andrew, and James Bishop Peabody, eds. *Records of Trinity Church, Boston, 1728–1830.* Vol. 1. Publications of the Colonial Society of Massachusetts, vol. 55. Boston, 1980.

Olleson, Philip. "Samuel Wesley and the Music Profession." In *Music and British Culture, 1785–1914: Essays in Honour of Cyril Ehrlich,* edited by Christina Bashford and Leanne Langley, 23–38. Oxford, 2000.

Opie, Iona and Peter, eds. *The Oxford Dictionary of Nursery Rhymes.* Oxford, 1951.

Oratorios, Selection the First. [New York], 1805.

O'Toole, Fintan. *A Traitor's Kiss: The Life of Richard Brinsley Sheridan.* New York, 1998.

Owen, Barbara. *The Organs and Music of King's Chapel, Boston, 1713–1991.* 2d ed. Boston, 1993.

———. "The Other Mr. Selby." *American Music* 8 (1990): 477–82.

———, ed. *A Century of American Organ Music.* 4 vols. Dayton, Ohio, 1975–76; Miami, Fla., 1983–91.

Parker, John Rowe, comp. *Musical Biography.* Boston, 1824.

Pearce, Charles W. *Notes on English Organs.* London, 1911.

Pemberton, Carol A. *Lowell Mason: A Bio-Bibliography.* Bio-Bibliographies in Music, vol. 11. Donald L. Hixon, series editor. New York, 1988.

Perkins, Charles C., and John Sullivan Dwight. *History of the Handel and Haydn Society, of Boston, Massachusetts.* 2 vols. New York, 1977–79.

Phelps Brown, E. H., and Sheila V. Hopkins. "Seven Centuries of Building Wages." *Economica* 22, n.s. [1955]: 195–206.

Pirsson, William, comp. *Twelve Anthems Selected, Composed, & Respectfully Dedicated to Dr. G. K. Jackson by his Late Pupil Wm. Pirsson.* New York, [1801–5] (C 407).

Planché, J. R. *The Recollections and Reflections of J. R. Planché.* 2 vols. London, 1872.

Pohl, Carl Ferdinand. *Mozart und Haydn in London.* Vol. 2. Vienna, 1867.

Porter, Susan L. *With an Air Debonair: Musical Theater in America, 1785–1815.* Washington, D.C., 1991.

Redway, Virginia Larkin. "The Carrs, American Music Publishers." *Musical Quarterly* 18 (1932): 150–77.

Répertoire international des sources musicales [RISM]. Series A/I: *Einzeldrucke vor 1800,* edited by Karlheinz Schlager and Otto E. Albrecht. 9 vols. Kassel, 1971–81.

Root, Deane L., ed. *Nineteenth-Century American Musical Theater.* 16 vols. New York, 1994.

Sadie, Stanley. "Music in the Home II." In *The Eighteenth Century,* edited by H. Diack Johnstone and Roger Fiske, 313–52. The Blackwell History of Music in Britain, vol. 4. Oxford, 1990.

Salloch, William, comp. "Special Collection: Dr. George K. Jackson (1745–1823)." In *The World of Music. Part I: Early American Music*, Catalogue 301, 16–22. Ossining, N.Y., [1973].

Schleifer, Martha Furman. *American Opera and Music for the Stage: Eighteenth and Nineteenth Centuries*. Three Centuries of American Music, vol. 5. [Boston], 1990.

Scott, Kenneth, comp. *British Aliens in the United States during the War of 1812*. Baltimore, 1979.

Shapiro, Alexander H. "'Drama of an Infinitely Superior Nature': Handel's Early English Oratorios and the Religious Sublime." *Music and Letters* 74 (1993): 215–45.

Shaw, Ralph R., and Richard H. Shoemaker [Shaw-Shoemaker]. *American Bibliography: A Preliminary Checklist for 1801–1819*. 19 vols. New York, 1958–63.

Shaw, Watkins. "Nares, James." In *The New Grove Dictionary of Music and Musicians*, edited by Stanley Sadie, 17:639–41. Rev. ed. London, 2001.

———. *The Succession of Organists of the Chapel Royal and the Cathedrals of England and Wales from c. 1538*. Oxford, 1991.

———. *The Three Choirs Festival: The Official History of the Meetings of the Three Choirs of Gloucester, Hereford and Worcester, c. 1713–1953*. Worcester, 1954.

Shive, Clyde S., Jr. "Camp Dupont and Its Music." Paper delivered at the meeting of the Sonneck Society, Tallahassee, Florida, March 1985.

Smith, Ronnie L. "The Church Music of Benjamin Carr." D.M.A. diss., Southwestern Baptist Theological Seminary, 1969.

Smith, William. *The Churchman's Choral Companion to His Prayer Book*. New York, 1809.

Sonneck, Oscar. *A Bibliography of Early Secular American Music*. Revised by William Treat Upton. Washington, D.C., 1945.

———. *Early Concert-Life in America*. Leipzig, 1907.

Spencer, Robert, and Ian Harwood. "English Guitar." In *The New Grove Dictionary of Music and Musicians*, edited by Stanley Sadie, 8:244–46. Rev. ed. London, 2001.

Sprenkle, Charles A. "The Life and Works of Benjamin Carr." 2 vols. Ph.D. diss., Peabody Institute, 1970.

Squire, W. Barclay. *Catalogue of Printed Music Published between 1487 and 1800 Now in the British Museum*. 2 vols. London, 1912.

Strasser, Michael. "The Société Nationale and Its Adversaries: The Musical Politics of *L'Invasion germanique* in the 1870s." *Nineteenth-Century Music* 24 (2001): 225–51.

Sutherland, Lucy S., and Leslie G. Mitchell, eds. *The Eighteenth Century*. The History of the University of Oxford, vol. 5. Trevor H. Aston, general editor. Oxford, 1986.

Swenson-Eldridge, Joanne Eggert. "The Musical Fund Society of Philadelphia and the Emergence of String Chamber Music Genres Composed in the United States." M.A. thesis, University of Iowa, 1969.

Tawa, Nicholas. *Sweet Songs for Gentle Americans: The Parlor Song in America, 1790–1860*. Bowling Green, Ohio, 1980.

———, ed. *American Solo Songs through 1865*. Three Centuries of American Music, vol. 1. [Boston], 1989.

Taylor, Rayner. *The AEthiop*. Edited by Victor Fell Yellin. Nineteenth-Century American Musical Theater, vol. 2. Deane L. Root, general editor. New York, 1994.

————. *Chamber Music*. Edited by John Metz and Barbara Bailey-Metz. Recent Researches in American Music 43. Middleton, Wisc., 2001.

Temperley, Nicholas. "Croft and the Charity Hymn." *Musical Times* 119 (1978): 539–41.

————. "George Frederick Pinto, 1785–1806." *Musical Times* 106 (1965): 265–70.

————. *Haydn: The Creation*. Cambridge, 1991.

————. "The Hymn Books of the Foundling and Magdalen Hospital Chapels." In *Music Publishing and Collecting: Essays in Honor of Donald W. Krummel*, edited by David Hunter, 1–37. Urbana, Ill., 1994.

————. "Musical Nationalism in English Romantic Opera." In *The Lost Chord: Essays on Victorian Music*, edited by Nicholas Temperley, 143–57. Bloomington, Ind., 1989.

————. *The Music of the English Parish Church*. 2 vols. Cambridge, 1979.

————. "Nationalism." In *The Oxford Companion to Music*, edited by Alison Latham, 826–29. Oxford, 2002.

————, ed. *The London Pianoforte School, 1766–1860*. 20 vols. New York, 1982–85.

Temperley, Nicholas, assisted by Charles G. Manns and Joseph Herl. *The Hymn Tune Index*. 4 vols. Oxford, 1998.

Venn, John, and J. A. Venn, comps. *Alumni Cantabrigienses*. Part 1: *From the Earliest Times to 1751*. 4 vols. Cambridge, 1922. Part 2: *From 1752 to 1900*. 6 vols. Cambridge, 1940.

A Volume of Records relating to the Early History of Boston, containing Boston Marriages from 1752 to 1809. Boston, 1903.

Wagner, John. "James Hewitt: His Life and Works." Ph.D. diss., Indiana University, 1969.

White, Rev. William. *Thoughts on the Singing of Psalms and Anthems in Churches*. Philadelphia, 1808.

Wilson, Ruth Mack. *Anglican Chant and Chanting in England, Scotland, and America*. Oxford Studies in British Church Music. Oxford, 1996.

Wolfe, Richard J. *Secular Music in America, 1801–1825: A Bibliography*. 3 vols. New York, 1964.

Wollenberg, Susan. *Music at Oxford in the Eighteenth and Nineteenth Centuries*. Oxford, 2001.

The Worcester Collection. Worcester, Mass., 1786.

Yellin, Victor Fell. "Rayner Taylor." *American Music* 1, no. 3 (1983): 49–73.

————. "Rayner Taylor's Music for *The AEthiop*." *American Music* 4 (1986): 249–67; 5 (1987): 20–47.

Databases

Calendar of London Concerts 1750–1800 Advertised in the London Daily Press [*CLC*]. Compiled by Simon McVeigh.

Church of Jesus Christ of Latter-Day Saints. *International Genealogical Index* [*IGI*].

The Hymn Tune Index [*HTI*]. Compiled by Nicholas Temperley.

Officials of the Royal Household, 1660–1837. Compiled by Robert O. Bucholz.

Index

NICHOLAS TEMPERLEY is the author of *The Hymn Tune Index: A Census of English-Language Hymn Tunes in Printed Sources from 1535 to 1820; The Music of the English Parish Church;* and *Haydn: The Creation.* He is also the editor of *The Lost Chord: Essays on Victorian Music; The Romantic Age, 1800–1914;* and *The London Pianoforte School, 1766–1860* (20 vols.). He was a founding member of the Sonneck Society for American Music and was editor-in-chief of the *Journal of the American Musicological Society* (1980–82).

Music in American Life

"Happy in the Service of the Lord": Afro-American Gospel Quartets in Memphis
  Kip Lornell
Paul Hindemith in the United States   *Luther Noss*
"My Song Is My Weapon": People's Songs, American Communism, and the Politics of
  Culture, 1930–50   *Robbie Lieberman*
Chosen Voices: The Story of the American Cantorate   *Mark Slobin*
Theodore Thomas: America's Conductor and Builder of Orchestras, 1835–1905
  Ezra Schabas
"The Whorehouse Bells Were Ringing" and Other Songs Cowboys Sing   *Guy Logsdon*
Crazeology: The Autobiography of a Chicago Jazzman   *Bud Freeman, as Told to
  Robert Wolf*
Discoursing Sweet Music: Brass Bands and Community Life in Turn-of-the-Century
  Pennsylvania   *Kenneth Kreitner*
Mormonism and Music: A History   *Michael Hicks*
Voices of the Jazz Age: Profiles of Eight Vintage Jazzmen   *Chip Deffaa*
Pickin' on Peachtree: A History of Country Music in Atlanta, Georgia
  Wayne W. Daniel
Bitter Music: Collected Journals, Essays, Introductions, and Librettos   *Harry Partch;
  edited by Thomas McGeary*
Ethnic Music on Records: A Discography of Ethnic Recordings Produced in the United
  States, 1893 to 1942   *Richard K. Spottswood*
Downhome Blues Lyrics: An Anthology from the Post-World War II Era
  Jeff Todd Titon
Ellington: The Early Years   *Mark Tucker*
Chicago Soul   *Robert Pruter*
That Half-Barbaric Twang: The Banjo in American Popular Culture   *Karen Linn*
Hot Man: The Life of Art Hodes   *Art Hodes and Chadwick Hansen*
The Erotic Muse: American Bawdy Songs (2d ed.)   *Ed Cray*
Barrio Rhythm: Mexican American Music in Los Angeles   *Steven Loza*
The Creation of Jazz: Music, Race, and Culture in Urban America   *Burton W. Peretti*
Charles Martin Loeffler: A Life Apart in Music   *Ellen Knight*
Club Date Musicians: Playing the New York Party Circuit   *Bruce A. MacLeod*
Opera on the Road: Traveling Opera Troupes in the United States, 1825–60
  Katherine K. Preston
The Stonemans: An Appalachian Family and the Music That Shaped Their Lives
  Ivan M. Tribe
Transforming Tradition: Folk Music Revivals Examined   *Edited by Neil V. Rosenberg*
The Crooked Stovepipe: Athapaskan Fiddle Music and Square Dancing in Northeast
  Alaska and Northwest Canada   *Craig Mishler*
Traveling the High Way Home: Ralph Stanley and the World of Traditional Bluegrass
  Music   *John Wright*
Carl Ruggles: Composer, Painter, and Storyteller   *Marilyn Ziffrin*
Never without a Song: The Years and Songs of Jennie Devlin, 1865–1952
  Katharine D. Newman
The Hank Snow Story   *Hank Snow, with Jack Ownbey and Bob Burris*

The University of Illinois Press
is a founding member of the
Association of American University Presses.

Composed in 10.5/13 Minion
with Americana display
by Celia Shapland
for the University of Illinois Press
Designed by Paula Newcomb
Manufactured by Thomson-Shore, Inc.

University of Illinois Press
1325 South Oak Street
Champaign, IL 61820-6903
www.press.uillinois.edu